English Poetry
of the
Seventeenth Century

George Parfitt

Longman

London and New York

LONGMAN GROUP LIMITED
Longman House, Burnt Mill, Harlow
Essex CM20 2JE, England
Associated companies throughout the world

Published in the United States of America by
Longman Inc., New York

First published 1985

BRITISH LIBRARY CATALOGUING IN PUBLICATION DATA
Parfitt, George
    English poetry of the seventeenth century.
    — (Longman literature in English series)
    1. English poetry—Early modern, 1500–1700
    — History and criticism
    I. Title
    821'.409   PR541

ISBN 0-582-49233-5 csd
ISBN 0-582-49232-7 ppr

LIBRARY OF CONGRESS CATALOGING IN PUBLICATION DATA
Parfitt, George A. E.
    English poetry of the seventeenth century.

    (Longman literature in English series)
    Bibliography: p.
    Includes index.
    1. English poetry—Early modern, 1500–1700
    —History and criticism. I. Title. II. Series.
    PR541.P3   1985   821'.7'09   84–15481
    ISBN 0–582–49233–5
    ISBN 0–582–49232–7 (pbk.)

Set in 9/10 pt Bembo (Linotron 202)
Produced by Longman Singapore Publishers (Pte) Ltd.
Printed in Singapore.

1135190X

Contents

Editors' Preface

The multi-volume Longman Literature in English Series provides students of literature with a critical introduction to the major genres in their historical and cultural context. Each volume gives a coherent account of a clearly defined area, and the series, when complete, will offer a practical and comprehensive guide to literature written in English from Anglo-Saxon times to the present. The aim of the series as a whole is to show that the most valuable and stimulating approach to literature is that based upon an awareness of the relations between literary forms and their historical context. Thus the areas covered by most of the separate volumes are defined by period and genre. Each volume offers new and informed ways of reading literary works, and provides guidance to further reading in an extensive reference section.

As well as studies on all periods of English and American literature, the series includes books on criticism and literary theory, and on the intellectual and cultural context. A comprehensive series of this kind must of course include other literatures written in English, and therefore a group of volumes deals with Irish and Scottish literature, and the literatures of India, Africa, the Caribbean, Australia and Canada. The forty-six volumes of the series cover the following areas: Pre-Renaissance English Literature, English Poetry, English Drama, English Fiction, English Prose, Criticism and Literary Theory, Intellectual and Cultural Context, American Literature, Other Literatures in English.

David Carroll
Michael Wheeler

Longman Literature in English Series

General Editors: David Carroll and Michael Wheeler
University of Lancaster

Pre-Renaissance English Literature

English Literature before Chaucer
English Literature in the Age of Chaucer
English Medieval Romance

English Poetry

English Poetry of the Sixteenth Century
*English Poetry of the Seventeenth Century *George Parfitt*
English Poetry of the Eighteenth Century, 1700–1789
English Poetry of the Romantic Period, 1789–1830
English Poetry of the Victorian Period, 1830–1890
English Poetry of the Early Modern Period, 1890–1940
English Poetry since 1940

English Drama

English Drama before Shakespeare
English Drama: Shakespeare to the Restoration, 1590–1660
English Drama: Restoration and Eighteenth Century, 1660–1789
English Drama: Romantic and Victorian, 1789–1890
English Drama of the Early Modern Period, 1890–1940
English Drama since 1940

English Fiction

English Fiction of the Eighteenth Century, 1700–1789
English Fiction of the Romantic Period, 1789–1830
*English Fiction of the Victorian Period, 1830–1890 *Michael Wheeler*
English Fiction of the Early Modern Period, 1890–1940
English Fiction since 1940

English Prose

English Prose of the Seventeenth Century, 1590–1700
English Prose of the Eighteenth Century
English Prose of the Nineteenth Century

Criticism and Literary Theory

Criticism and Literary Theory from Sidney to Johnson
Criticism and Literary Theory from Wordsworth to Arnold
Criticism and Literary Theory from 1890 to the Present

The Intellectual and Cultural Context

The Sixteenth Century
The Seventeenth Century
The Eighteenth Century, 1700–1789
The Romantic Period, 1789–1830
The Victorian Period, 1830–1890
1890 to the Present

American Literature

American Literature before 1865
American Poetry of the Twentieth Century
American Drama of the Twentieth Century
American Fiction, 1865–1940
American Fiction since 1940
Twentieth Century America

Other Literatures

Irish Literature since 1800
Scottish Literature since 1700
Indian Literature in English
African Literature in English
Caribbean Literature in English
Australian Literature in English
*Canadian Literature in English *W. J. Keith*

Already published

Author's Preface

This volume, in accordance with the aims of the series of which it is part, tries to be something different from traditional literary history. Such history, as with the *Cambridge History of English Literature*, provides useful information and may also give a valuable sense of literary development over a long period of time. But the tendency of such history is inevitably towards generalization and the loss of a sense of detail and individuality. Often, too, literary history has little to offer in the area of the relationships between literature and history. Yet anyone who attempts a book like the one which follows this preface is likely to have sympathy with the problems which confront the literary historian, for the problems of organization are acute. The chosen approach here – the generic one – allows, it is hoped, for some sense of development and comparison, while it is also an advantage that the approach conforms to an emphasis of the seventeenth century itself, the poetry of that century being very genre-conscious. But, of course, it needs to be remembered that the divisions used here are far from absolute. Satire and mock-heroic overlap; poetry of place and poetry of occasion merge at times; religious and secular lyric have much in common.

The effort to avoid merely listing authors and works in continuous prose has two chief effects. It means, first of all, selection, concentration, and, therefore, exclusion. Naturally, I have stressed what seems significant to me and I am particularly aware that I have emphasized the work of several poets who I think have been unjustly neglected (Carew, Cleveland, Cotton). Some readers are likely to feel that the dismissal of such as Traherne is too terse. The effort, however, has not been to say something about every poet of the century who has been felt by someone to have written a poem of merit, but to provide – and this is the second of the effects mentioned above – a suggestive account of a century's poetry and to give some idea of how this poetry relates to the century in which it was written.

Since it is my view that writers about seventeenth-century poetry have tended to avoid serious consideration of the relationship of the verse with the century's socio-political history, I have emphasized this, rather than the intellectual and purely literary context, although I am aware of the importance of both and also that my treatment of the socio-political history is no more than a sketch.

The main body of the text is intended to be 'open' rather than 'closed'. It is designed to be suggestive and stimulating rather than dictatorial, and in this sense is meant to teach. One thing which follows is that the Chronology, the General Bibliographies, and the Individual Authors – notes should be seen as important parts of the book, complementing, amplifying, and qualifying its arguments. They are designed to help the reader fill out the picture drawn in the body of the text. Eventually the reader should be able to create her/his own picture, although naturally I hope it will be identical with my own.

One other preliminary point needs to be made. The introduction begins with a section on seventeenth-century history. This is only an outline but it is an attempt to suggest the framework within which seventeenth-century literature is created. It is placed where it is because that framework seems to me to be particularly important for an understanding of the poetry of the century.

Many books and many conversations over a number of years have contributed to this book, and I should like to thank all unknowing helpers. More particularly I should like to thank my students and former students (especially Marta Grcar and Rosemary Heatley) for commenting on ideas used here; John Lucas, Simon Shepherd and Mick Wallis for their words and friendship; Michael Wheeler and David Carroll for their help and thoroughness as General Editors; and my wife, Maureen Bell, for all sorts of things.

George Parfitt

For Maureen, with my love

Introduction

1

Between 1600 and 1700 two British kings lost their thrones other than through natural causes. The overthrow of monarchs had happened earlier in British history (most famously with Richard II) but, despite the uncertainties of the Tudor claim to the English throne and the religious and political upheavals consequent upon Henry VIII's reformation, the sixteenth century managed to avoid dispossession, even though Edward VI came to the throne as a minor and the reign of Mary I meant both a Spanish consort for an English queen and the return of Catholicism as the state religion.

On the surface, the dispossessions of Charles I and James II are very different. Charles, after a trial by a parliamentary court which, reasonably enough, he refused to recognise, was formally beheaded in January 1649 ('justly condemned, adjudged to die, and put to death, for many treasons, murders and other heinous offences committed by him'[1]). Monarchy was abolished and a Commonwealth declared. James, heir to the throne to which his brother (Charles II) was restored in 1660, survived both the Exclusion crisis, brought on largely by his Catholicism, and the Monmouth Rebellion, but by 1688 a group of national figures had invited William of Orange to England. William landed at Torbay in November and on 13 December James fled England. Complex, even confused, discussions led to the naming of William and Mary (his wife and James's daughter) as monarchs in February 1689. Charles I had conceded little to his enemies, except militarily, and behind his execution lie the bodies of the Civil War dead. Moreover, the claims that Charles was dealt with constitutionally hold little water, it being nearer the truth to say that the constitution was remade to allow the monarch's trial and execution. By contrast, James was, on the surface, finally willing to conciliate and his fall involved virtually no bloodshed. And although James did not give up his claim to the throne his behaviour at the end of 1688 amounts to an abdication.

Yet these two throne-losses have links which are more important than the dissimilarities, so much so that it can be argued that the Civil War made the Glorious Revolution possible. Both events, in fact, are parts of a single process of questioning, defining, and redefining the roles of ruler and ruled in seventeenth-century Britain. To Burke the Revolution of 1688 and the

Declaration of Rights of 1689 mark the beginning of modern times, the triumph of a constitutional middle way in Church and State[2]. To a modern historian like J. H. Plumb the Restoration and Glorious Revolution mean the consolidation of power in the hands of the great landed magnates.[3] Monarchy survives, somewhat chastened by the Interregnum (which is one way of reading Charles II's Act of Indemnity of 1660 and his restraint over royalist appeals for restitution and revenge) but the bloodless substitution of William and Mary for James effectively establishes that the throne is in the power of the people.[4] When Dryden wrote *The Medal* (1682) he accused Shaftesbury of preaching 'to the Crowd, that Pow'r is lent,/But not convey'd to Kingly Government' (ll. 82–3): 1688 confirms the principle which the poet abhors, although the change of monarch was not, in any modern sense, effected democratically.

Democracy remains a smear word throughout the seventeenth century. Dryden, in *Absalom and Achitophel*, again attacking Shaftesbury (as Achitophel) claims that his aim is 'That Kingly power . . . might be/Drawn to the dregs of a Democracy' (ll. 226–7) and Dryden liked the latter line enough to use it again in *The Hind and the Panther* (1687). He is merely echoing a distaste which is voiced constantly, and not least by parliamentarians.[5] Democracy is part of the Leveller vision,[6] but the Army Debates at Putney in October and November 1647 show how unappealing the idea was to the parliamentary gentry.[7] The radicalism of the sects has had its issue since the seventeenth century (although its visions are largely unrealized even now) but at the end of that century radicalism seemed as defeated as absolutism.

If there can be said to be a single key moment in seventeenth-century British history, it must be when the axe fell on the neck of Charles I. One way of seeing the century can then be in terms of the questions, 'How did we come to this?' and 'How do we live in its aftermath?' From our twentieth-century perspective it is difficult to imagine how unthinkable the execution was. Monarchs had been rebelled against often enough, and violently disposed of, but not formally tried and executed. Moreoever, the Tudor century had seen obedience preached with an intensity and consistency which reflect both the weakness of the Tudor claim and the national desire for internal peace after the long broils of the Wars of the Roses. For their part, the first Stuarts codified the doctrine of divine right, relying upon the effect of those habits of obedience which the Tudors had laboured to inculcate. Rebellion was neither fashionable nor easy in seventeenth-century England; not least because few men could envisage a social order other than one where a monarch headed a social hierarchy. How, then, did England come to try and then execute Charles I?

In July 1642 Bulstrode Whitelocke, an intelligent and politically experienced man, found the slide into civil war nearly incomprehensible:

It is strange to note how we have insensibly slid into this
beginning of a civil war by one unexpected accident after another,
as waves of the sea, which have brought us thus far . . .[8]

He is aware of a drift from 'paper combats' to 'the question of raising forces, and naming a general and officers of an army',[9] and Whitelocke's 'paper combats' can be found featuring prominently in Anthony Fletcher's *The Outbreak of the English Civil War* (1981), a book which documents in detail national awareness of crisis and also the fears and frustrations of those who sought to resolve that crisis. Fletcher's account tends to support Conrad Russell's view that 'neither side really wanted the war, but both were too frightened of the other's intentions to trust any settlement', and Russell adds that 'Attempts to explain a deliberate revolution are inappropriate to a situation in which no deliberate revolution took place'.[10]

As we look back, centuries after the Civil War, we can discern patterns in the decades which precede it, but Whitelocke's feeling of an insensible slide is probably reasonably characteristic. Yet people were aware of a dangerous drift and some thought they knew what was causing it. Edward Ludlow felt the central issue was clear enough:

> The question in dispute between the King's party and us [was], as I apprehended, whether the King should govern as a God by his will and the nation be governed by force like beasts; or whether the people should be governed by laws made by themselves, and live under a government derived from their own consent.[11]

Ludlow sets government by a godlike king against government by consent, and his analysis (which, rephrased, could appeal to many royalists) is echoed whenever the issue is defined as being between the King's prerogative and Parliament's privileges. But the choice which Ludlow presents was not thought of as one between distinct constitutional models. What A. G. R. Smith says of the Jacobean situation holds true of the Caroline:

> . . . the dominant constitutional theory, accepted by king, Parliament and common lawyers alike, was of a balanced constitution which was founded on certain inalienable rights possessed by both Crown and subjects.[12]

Kingly prerogative and parliamentary privilege are both accepted: the disputes are about definitions and interrelationships. Moreover, specific disputes are often both important in themselves and for what they suggest about the state of relationships between the disputants. Thus the famous Ship Money dispute raised major issues about how far Charles's prerogative ran (and it is perfectly possible to argue that the King was attempting nothing illegal) but it is equally important in showing how little trust could be drawn upon in the 1630s.

This loss of trust cannot be explained in a formula. The personality of James I may have played a part (Elizabeth's more dazzling character could clearly baffle and enchant even tough Elizabethan parliament-men) as did fears of the influence of migrant Scots and of James's favourites. Then there is religion. The Gunpowder Plot (1605) both sums up and stimulates fears of Roman Catholic plans to overthrow the government, and in succeeding decades courtly softness on the Catholic issue is often seen as sinister complicity with such plans. John Pym's concern with 'the plot' may have been obsessive or just politically astute, but he was in touch with widespread apprehension which saw the King's court as focus for that apprehension. The tolerance of Romanists around the Catholic Henrietta Maria could only lend plausibility to apprehension.[13] Further, the rise of Arminianism within the Church of England – and especially Laud's appointment to the see of Canterbury in 1633 – seemed to many a king-sponsored move away from moderate Protestantism towards Rome, while the failure or inability of government to offer strong support in the continental Protestant fight against the Counter-Reformation could be seen in sinister terms.

Much follows from, and contributes to a loss of confidence. James seems to have had a strong liking for theory, and while his pronouncements about kingly power may well have been helpfully meant, the spelling out of prerogative could only have seemed provocative, especially granted his backing of men of mediocre backgrounds and talents. Men look more closely at what they see as their rights under James and, in so far as these are felt to be enshrined in Parliament, they object to what they see as kingly interference in Parliament's sittings and procedures – this being most fully dramatized with Charles's attempt to arrest the Five Members in the House of Commons in 1641.

Many other factors contribute to the loss of trust in the decades before the Civil War. Famine and plague play their parts, as do the varying fortunes of the gentry and their sometimes conflicting loyalties to central government and local interests.[14] Erratic and inefficient taxation is psychologically disturbing, as is the chronic inability to solve the problems of financing the monarchy. Mercantile ambition and self-confidence both provoke and respond to traditional hierarchic notions, while deep-rooted fear of the mob gains substance with London's increasing self-assertiveness.

Whitelocke's insensible slide, then, can be analysed, but we are left with a complex of causes rather than an explanation, and I suspect that the reasons for the breaking down of trust, and thus of the coming of civil war, inhere as much in the suspicious reading of kingly proclamation by opponents, and of parliamentary ordinance by king and court, as in any specific event. But even up to the trial and execution of the King, the bulk of people on both sides see the issue as one of how to operate the existing model (best seen perhaps as the idea of the nation most fully embodied as King-in-Parliament). As Russell reminds us, 'Parliamentary commissions were issued in the name of king and Parliament' during the Civil War itself, and he cites the parliamentary vice-admiral who saw himself (even in retrospect) as 'fighting to bring the king to his Parliament'[15]. Even Pym is content to see the King as the head, people as the body[16] – an image dear to James I. Structural change was a minority vision.

Yet the slide into war and the subsequent drift to Charles's execution, even if these are seen as essentially conservative phenomena, rather than revolutionary,[17] cannot, of course, conceal the facts that momentous changes were taking place and that contemporaries were aware of them. A king is defied, defeated, and executed; the office of monarchy is abolished, as is the House of Lords – and, in a sense, the facts matter more than the reasons. Even the short-lived successes of Levellers and Diggers have the enormous importance of having been able to happen. The field of what is possible, and seen to be possible, is enlarged.

So perhaps the most important factor in the often tentative and confused manœuvring of the pre-war period, of the Civil War itself, and of the Interregnum, is simply that power is seen to be transferable and alienable. Charles II seems to have realized this, but so did the opponents of his brother James. The most obvious beneficiaries of this realization are, in the short and medium terms, those who become the oligarchic power-holders and power-brokers of the late seventeenth and eighteenth centuries. But it is neither sentimental nor anachronistic for Marxist historians to honour the radicals of the middle years of the seventeenth century.

One major development since the Civil War has been the gradual separation of the secular and the religious, or at least of Church and State. Augustanism is primarily a secular phenomenon and in the eighteenth century 'enthusiasm' is a dirty word. Anglicanism becomes institutionalized to such an extent that strong spiritual impulses become located mainly in nonconformity, Catholicism, and in the pantheistic tendencies of Romanticism. The State continues to use religious sanctions, but in effect gives ground to secular moralities.

This is important for us in the attempt to understand the seventeenth century because such separation makes little sense for that period, so much so that efforts to discuss developments in secular *or* religious terms are misleading and misconceived. Contemporaries were quite capable of making distinctions between religious and secular impulses (as often when Donne is writing about love). Machiavelli and Bacon had not written in vain, and it is proper to see a tendency to separation in the course of the century, not least in the 'realism' of Hobbes and, towards the end of the century, in the cool dismantling by Locke of much of what is involved in spiritually weighted accounts of experience. But for most people, most of the time, the religious and the secular were felt to be, actually or ideally, one.

The Grand Remonstrance of 1641 provides a fine example of this intertwining. It talks of the 'root' of the crisis between King and Parliament as a 'malignant and pernicious design of subverting the fundamental laws and principles of government upon which the religion and justice of this kingdom are firmly established'. 'Government' is that 'upon which' both religion and justice are established, and when the Remonstrance goes on to list the 'actors and promotors' of the alleged sedition it speaks of 'Jesuited Papists', Arminian clergy, and of councillors and courtiers who work to 'further the interests of some foreign princes or states'.[18] We tend to see the Remonstrance as primarily a political document, but we begin to go wrong if we regard references to religion, papists, and 'the corrupt part of the clergy' as covers for essentially secular concerns. The Remonstrance's involvement with both papists and 'foreign princes' should remind us that fear of Catholicism is simultaneously political and religious. Spain is both a great political power and a great centre of Catholicism: it cannot be a political threat without being a religious one. Papal pronouncements might seek to reassure non-Catholics that religious toleration need not be seen as politically dangerous, but there is a stubborn refusal to accept this view: hence the failure of James II's Declarations of Indulgence, the efforts to pass the Exclusion Bill, and James's fall in 1688. Without violence a Catholic could not be monarch for long in seventeenth-century Britain. The office and the religion are not finally separable, and, of course, the Henrican reformation had formalized their union.

The Remonstrance's linking of government, religion, and justice is commonplace and it is not to be seen as merely a political formula. Pym's persistent anti-Catholicism was certainly a theme he used politically, but it is so potent because it draws upon deep fears of political tyranny, foreign domination, and, simultaneously, imposition of a 'superstitious' religion. Pym himself can be seen as both patriot and convinced Protestant, but he would probably have regarded the two as one. The same could be said of Cromwell. Hostile contemporaries are liable to call him 'atheist', and modern historians are understandably fascinated by the politics of his extraordinary career, but there is no good reason to doubt the sincerity of his searchings for divine help in his quest for political and military success. And, of course, reading the writings of such as Winstanley[19] is to see how scrutiny of the Bible can issue in political activism. There is nothing eccentric in Milton's career, nor anything perverse in seeing *Paradise Lost* as Civil War epic. The Elizabethan government had used the pulpit for political propaganda. Stuart governments did the same, while rightly fearing that puritan preachers were speaking an alternative politics as well as an alternative religion. So when Laud suppressed the London Feofees of Impropriation in 1633 he was acting politically as much as in the cause of High Anglicanism.

Religious controversy in the seventeenth century, then, is also political controversy. It can be seen in terms of introvert and extrovert tendencies: protestant emphasis upon the individual conscience and response to the Scriptures versus Catholic stress on authority and tradition. But governments which were not Catholic, yet which sought to strengthen central authority, saw, again correctly, that tendencies to religious separatism were politically dangerous, while almost every gentleman suspected that separatism in religion meant democracy in politics.

Separatism can be regarded as introversion, the wish of a minority to operate with minimal organization by the majority. But the first half of the century, in particular, also shows a longing for the identification of English Protestantism with the continental reformed churches, so much so that Stuart refusal to back, say, Gustavus Adolphus of Sweden effectively is a source of grief to many which is as much religious as patriotic. James I loved the title of peacemaker, while apologists for Charles I make much of the peaceful isolation of his kingdom. It can be argued that the foreign policies of these kings were necessarily pacific, or at least necessarily involved exercises in trimming. To be seen to be sympathetic with Spain or France is to risk the hostility of Protestant Europe (and of Protestant England) while to move decisively into the Protestant bloc is to alienate the major Catholic powers. Foreign policy in a moderate Protestant state with a significant Catholic residue could never have been easy in the seventeenth century. When writers like Daniel, Drayton, and Cowley think of civil wars they all see such wars as introspective (which, of their nature, they are) and they all contrast English society involved in internecine strife with glorious days of aggressive foreign policies, days of Henry V and Edward the Black Prince.

If one uses an index of this kind, the seventeenth century has to be considered a period of national humiliation rather than of triumph. Raleigh's execution in 1618 is, directly at least, the result of the failure of his Orinoco (1616) expedition, while the Amboyna 'massacre' (1623), the failure of Charles's trip to Spain (1623), the Cadiz fiasco of 1625, and the La Rochelle expedition of 1627 add up to a humiliating story of failure, at least by the standards of an aggressive foreign policy. The mock-apotheosis of such failure comes in 1667 when the Dutch fleet operated freely in the Thames and Medway, or in 1688, when the English turned to William of Orange in search of an alternative to James II.

The desire to have a successfully aggressive foreign policy can be seen in the pride, or relief, with which Marvell salutes the achievements of the only successfully aggressive ruler of seventeenth-century Britain – Oliver Cromwell – and again in Waller's efforts to make the inconclusive battle off Lowestoft in 1672 into a heroic victory. The roots of empire may be found in the colonization efforts of the century, but, within that century itself, defeat by the Dutch and failure to participate effectively in Europe are far more striking. Such failure may be attributed to the delicacy of England's position, or to Parliament's failure to match Protestant fervour with hard cash, or to jobbery and incompetence,[20] but the failure hurts in a way which explanation cannot salve.

It is really not at all surprising to find that the seventeenth century contains both the assertion of traditional worlds and the beginnings of new ones, this being in the nature of things. So there is no real paradox in suggesting that the century is both conservative and revolutionary, deeply wedded to old loyalties and old socio-political models, while also giving rise to new stresses and new models.

The fact that the old and the new coexist makes for complexity, and one reaction to complexity is to simplify. So it is, for example, that literary historians have used the Civil War to posit a break in culture. Stuart and Restoration can be kept largely apart by such constructs as the 'dissociation of sensibility'[21]; drama in the years between Charles raising his standard at Nottingham and his son returning to resume the monarchy can be largely ignored; the life-dates of religious poets can be forgotten. Such simplifications can serve a purpose, and culture *is* different in 1699 from what it was in 1600, but the clear-cut distinctions remain finally fictions.

Intimations of change begin to appear, however, early in the century. We tend to see Donne and Jonson as *the* poets of the early part of the century, and to contrast their work with that of Sidney and Spenser seen as *the* poets of high Elizabethanism. Similarly, we contrast city comedy and satiric tragedy as characteristically Jacobean with romantic comedy and 'serious' tragedy as typically Elizabethan. In doing these things we simultaneously register significant change and distort the record.

One way of suggesting significant change is to view the work of such as Donne, Jonson, Middleton, and Marston as a challenge to court hegemony. Sidney and Spenser may be regarded as the apotheosis of Elizabethanism, accepting and representing the Tudor emphasis on court; while the focus of Donne and the others is the city and the Inns of Court, their art celebrating witty scepticism and the rejection of conventions. Similarly, the growth of city comedy and of 'tragedy of court' emphasizes the importance of city and the vulnerability of the idea of court as centre of excellence. These are significant changes, but they are neither simple nor immediately decisive. In fact, they represent the selection deemed significant by later periods. We need, while being alert to the shifts, to notice that Jonson is deeply conservative, that much city comedy satirizes city aspirations, and that 'Elizabethan' verse is written well into the Stuart period.[22]

It should be added that there is a sense in which the Stuart period sees art becoming more courtly than Elizabethan art had been, or courtly in a different way. Under Charles I the English masque (most courtly of forms) reaches its peak, while King and courtiers are celebrated in paintings of a range unknown under Elizabeth and courtly lyric marks a retreat from Donne's depth into something more enclosed and complacent. Elizabeth's court can plausibly be seen as the focus for national aspirations, and one thinks of the Queen both as Gloriana and as the apparently accessible visitor to Tilbury docks and recipient of delegations from the House of Commons. By contrast, one thinks of Charles as Vandyke painted him and of the sublimation of Stuart ambition in Rubens's work on the ceiling of the Banqueting House, or one thinks of the symbolic dancing of royalty and courtiers as a magic, exclusive circle. In Dekker's *Shoemakers' Holiday* (?1599) the monarch is able to talk to Simon Eyre in a relaxed way and to assert a unity of purpose which to some extent binds city and king. In Jacobean masques whatever is allowed in from outside the magic circle is dominated by the awesome power of majesty.[23]

Yet even as Caroline culture emphasizes the greatness of courtly art, a more civic, more sober culture is continuing and developing. This can be seen in the durability of plain-style verse and in the development of plain-style prose, particularly within politico-religious controversy. Literary culture becomes more self-conscious even as a counter-culture gains ground.

In the period of the Civil War, Commonwealth, and Protectorate the urgency of the crisis dominates culture, but if we define that word broadly we can see the period as other than anti-culture. Obviously, a Parliament fighting a king and a government ruling without one are unlikely to promote a courtly culture, while it is deceitful to play down the hostility of some puritans both to secular and high religious art. But this does not mean that culture somehow vanished during the years between 1642 and 1660. 'High' culture survives, through the protection of cultured parliamentarians, among exiled royalists (especially in France) and among royalists and neutrals who remained in England. Such culture is not only preserved, but is produced in the period by such as Lovelace, Cowley, Shirley, Davenant, Suckling, Browne, Denham, Fanshawe, and Alexander Brome. But it is perhaps more important to notice that the decades in question also produce new developments in literary culture, with the growth of political satire, the establishment of newspapers, and the remarkable output of controversial prose. The latter is the most striking development: this is the age of Milton's prose, of Taylor, Edwards, Winstanley, and James Harrington. It is also the period when Clarendon's *History of the Great Rebellion* was begun and Hobbes's *Leviathan* was written.

Civil war, of course, formalizes conflict. Although many people found the question of loyalty difficult, and although many dealt with the issue by remaining as neutral as possible, there could be no doubt that there were two sides and choices to be made. Divisions in culture are evident before the war, as also are disagreements about the proper nature and function of art. As a result it is possible to speak of a tendency for culture in the reign of Charles I to become either decorative or utilitarian, provided we remember that much decorative Caroline art is decorative for an ultimately utilitarian purpose. During the war, and in the period of the Interregnum, this division continues, with the utilitarian principle dominating, through newspapers, pamphlets, and political verse satire, while the decorative serves mainly as a retreat for Cavaliers, although Marvell shows what could be done to unify the two principles even in times of acute stress. The cavalier retreat was, of course, a literal one for the exiled court in France, and can be seen especially in Cowley's lyrics.

French influence on Restoration culture has been much discussed, and affects not only drama and satire but also such things as manners and dress. But perhaps the most important fact is simply that exile stressed the division between court and country. When we speak of Restoration culture we are forcing unity upon something not truly united. The way in which Restoration comedy focuses upon genteel lives, with little or no inspection of what makes these lives possible, and the way in which these genteel lives are presented very largely as social events, in which dance, song, and theatre are parts of a social round which replaces work and service to the State, symbolize the isolation of courtly culture in the Restoration. The same emphases can be seen in the confident cross-references and namings of Restoration lyrics and in the impression given in Hamilton's *Memoirs of the Count de Grammont* that the world of court is the only world that exists. Rochester sees how empty this can be, but when he looks outside court he can see only more emptiness.

But, of course, court was not the only world. Although the vast majority of people in Britain in the latter part of the century remained outside both politics and literacy,[24] Augustanism was to be a civic culture rather than a courtly one, with its strengths in social verse satire, caricature, and the novel. The major figures tend to come from outside the ranks of the privileged (although anyone who had education and the vote at this time was relatively very privileged). It is the age of Pope, Defoe, and Richardson, not of Rochester, Howard, and Sedley; and the roots of this civic culture are to be found in the self-examinations of puritan spiritual autobiography and in the self-consciousness of Jacobean city comedy. The dominant modes of courtly Restoration literary culture are the lyric, the drama, and personal satire, whereas the equivalent Augustan modes are social satire and prose fiction.

2

The interaction of poetry with society in the seventeenth century is intricate, as such interaction always is, but it is possible to see – as we should expect – a set of connections, some more obvious than others.

The seventeenth century is, for instance, a great period for the lyric, both secular and religious. Since it is a period marked by constant religious controversy, and since such controversy is, in the seventeenth century, simultaneously spiritual and social, it is not surprising that religious lyric flourishes or that it is the creation not only of specialists like Herbert and Crashaw, but also of poets whose output is not primarily religious – poets like Carew, Marvell, and even Rochester. More broadly, the lyric mode suits a period in which poetry is mainly produced by people who do not earn their livings by writing it. Although not exclusively a court product, lyric is strongly influenced by court, and suits the courtly view of poetry as one of the social accomplishments of the gentry. There is, in fact, no major lyric poet of the century who works at any great distance from the genteel. Ben Jonson is perhaps closest, being certainly no gentleman, but his ideals are genteel in the best sense of that word. Moreover, lyric is not only socially convenient (its brevity suiting the amateur) but tends to be highly decorative. Brevity facilitates polish and the codification of themes and images, and it is in such codification and polish that the self-conscious image-making of courtly worlds is expressed. Lyric may also contain antitype as well as type. Being highly formalized, it can define opposition to its own formulae, and this critical possibility is a feature of seventeenth-century lyric, seen in Donne's serious playing with conventions, in Suckling's undercuttings of poses, in Marvell's presentation of smooth surfaces with shifting subsurfaces, and in Restoration lyric's expectation of the worm in the bud. Clearly, this element of doubt in secular lyric can be linked with the fears expressed in Donne's religious verse and with Herbert's sense of Man's sinfulness; while the motif of doubt in seventeenth-century verse as a whole is entirely unsurprising granted the upheavals which mark the period.

Such upheavals also make it likely that satire will be prominent, and one of the features of seventeenth-century poetry is how satire again becomes a notable social genre. In the Middle Ages, and with Skelton and Wyatt in the early Tudor period, satire is part of the active criticism of society, but most sixteenth-century satire is literary, rather than seeming the voice of real social disillusionment. But Ben Jonson shows how satire can be an important part of a social critique, and the period of the Civil War and Interregnum sees the establishment of political satire as a major literary mode. This is as we might expect, since satire is an obvious way of blackening opponents and of attracting and strengthening support for your own side. The seventeenth century keeps on testing allegiances – social, familial, and religious, often all at once – and satire, with its simplifications of experience, is an obvious way of defining choices. So for Cleveland satire is the inevitable form for his anger and hurt, as it is for Rochester's near-despair, while Dryden develops Jonson's perception that satire may be an important part of a poetic view of social experience. It is perhaps unnecessary to add that a prerequisite of successful satire is radical doubt about the stability and health of a society, or that the seventeenth century provides abundant reason for such doubt.

But doubt has other consequences than satire. It may, for instance, lead to an emphasis upon the transforming power of art, used ultimately to reassure, the prime example here being much Caroline verse (while much Restoration lyric might then be seen as a critical commentary upon the deluding aspect of transformation). Or doubt may encourage the contemplation of stability associated with the past. Historians reminded us of how potent images of Magna Charta and the Norman yoke are in the period.[25] Such images are part of the great effort to base contemporary politics on proofs of what the past had established. This reliance on authority and the past probably has something in common with ideas of the deterioration of the world with the passing of time[26], and it is striking that the commonest way of praising a new regime is in terms of reclamation: Astraea returns to earth; there is a new Golden Age; Charles II is a second Augustus.

In seventeenth-century poetry the impulse to look back takes two main forms. One is mainly decorative, the poetry of pastoralism and retreat, in which the present is transformed into the vaguely historical, as in much Caroline verse. But the second is the more complex and interesting, being an active effort to make the past influence the present. Such an effort may be directly historical, as in Jonson's reminders to James I in 'A Panegyre' (1603) or in Denham's contemplation of Henry VIII in 'Cooper's Hill' (1641–1668). Or it may be geographico-historical, as in country-house verse and Drayton's Poly-Olbion (1612, 1622). In such poetry the past is seen as inhering in the present – literally so, as at Penshurst and Appleton – and the poet is concerned with pressures which the present puts upon this inhering past. The idea of progressive evolution is not strong in seventeenth-century poetry: the present is commonly a matter of a struggle to preserve or to reclaim. Even Gondibert (1651) and Absalom and Achitophel (1681) are formally located in the past. This poetic emphasis parallels a socio-political stress, whereby both parliamentarians and monarchists consistently appeal to precedent, and whereby the accession of Charles II is a restoration.

A concern with the past takes interesting forms, too, when we think of the material chosen for large-scale works. The past may furnish examples of the glorious and the stable, but it may also offer material in which less reassuring patterns may be discerned. Early in the century both Daniel and Drayton write historical poems about civil war in England, while later Davenant concerns himself with civil strife in a notionally medieval Lombardy, Cowley with dissension between David and Saul – and Milton with the first civil war of all, that between Satan's forces and God's. Further, when Butler, in *Hudibras*, Dryden, in *Absalom and Achitophel*, and Cowley, in *The Civil War*, deal directly with rebellion in their own times, they all do so by feigning pasts. In Dryden's case, this is overt (placing contemporary issues in a biblical past) while with Butler and Cowley it is a matter of historically weighted reference (Butler's use of burlesque knight-errantry, Cowley's of epic). In relation to the links between literature and society, two points are especially important here. The prominence of the theme of rebellion in seventeenth century poetry obviously reflects fears and actualities of that century, while the location of the theme in time past parallels social concern with what the record of the past may be felt to show and suggest about present concerns and, oddly perhaps, the desire to avoid feeling isolated in the present by seeing contemporary problems as unique. Seeing, in the past, evidence both of dissent and stability is finally reassuring, for the lesson at a time of disunity might be that unity is possible, which is the theme both of Milton's epics and of Marvell's 'The First Anniversary' (1655).

There is one other aspect of this concern with the past which should be stressed. A major theme of seventeenth-century controversy is land, property. One way of seeing the breakdown between King and Parliament is in terms of who has the final say over control of the country, and in the seventeenth century this is a literal matter. The Civil War was decided by control of territory and thus of the support which territory can be made to yield, while issues of loyalty often took the form of choosing between the King's reading of how a locality should be governed and the views represented by local custom. Then the matter of the electorate is deeply involved with the land: Who decides who can vote? How vital is the property qualification? How far has king or magnate the right to place and control candidate and voter? The Diggers raised fundamental issues about the land, and the Army Debates at Putney are basically about property. Property is power in the seventeenth century, and although property is not necessarily land, there is a strong tendency for it to be so. It is no accident that Massinger's merchant, Sir Giles Overreach (in *A New Way to Pay Old Debts*) is so much concerned in land litigation (as, incidentally, was the mystic Henry Vaughan).

The land is also a major theme of seventeenth-century poetry. Country-house verse is obviously concerned with the power of property, and Jonson is as much interested in Penshurst's relationship with the land as with the house itself. *Poly-Olbion* is an epic of the land; 'Cooper's Hill' surveys it. Both Drayton and Denham associate history with territory, and Denham's poem is concerned with who controls it. Obviously, too, the poems spoken of above which deal with rebellion are involved with land: Satan's forces quickly build Pandemonium to register control over their new landscape, while Adam and Eve possess paradise by cultivating it. Marvell seems almost obsessed with location.

3

English poets of the seventeenth century could, if they wished, look back upon a rich and varied achievement in the sixteenth century. Broadly speaking, the sixteenth century had seen the continuation of features of native medieval verse together with developments based on classical and continental renaissance poetry. Moreoever, much of the sixteenth-century achievement came after 1580, which means that a young poet of the early seventeenth century could feel both that he had something established, but not exhausted, to work on and that he had something to react against. The seventeenth century itself was a period of such ferment that it challenges poets to find new ways to respond to experience, as well as ways of continuing to utilize the old.

Authority remains an important concept throughout the century, and in verse as much as anything else. Writers of epic and near-epic summon up the names of their great predecessors; Carew draws upon Catullus and Propertius, Du Bellay, and Ronsard; Oldham imitates Juvenal; Rochester 'alludes' to Horace. Just as political thinkers in the main appeal to precedents, so do the poets. The refinement of the decasyllabic couplet, for instance, is just that – the refining of a form already established in English by 1600, while the development of the ode by such as Cowley and Dryden is in self-conscious imitation of the classical Greek poet, Pindar. This is not, of course, to deny innovation as an element in seventeenth-century verse, but to say that innovation is mainly a matter of building on what already exists, adapting, refining, and naturalizing. Poets in the century work with and within conventions, and for our purposes 'conventions' can be defined as those sets of ideas about forms and attitudes which seventeenth-century poets drew upon. It should be added that it is wrong to see conventions as necessarily untruthful or inert. Stock views can be refined versions of truths, while stock formulations can be the basis for originality.

The lyric provides a good example of this. The sonnets of Sidney and Spenser can be taken to represent a definitive achievement in court-based love poetry – dignified, ornate, respectful of the lady.[27] These sonnets provide a set of attitudes and stylistic possibilities which are still active in 1700, but only as one extreme. The sixteenth century itself included another, a more sceptical, plainer manner which is strong in Wyatt, and also present in Gascoigne, Raleigh, and Sidney himself. This manner is summed up and developed by Donne, whose achievement in lyric offers another extreme, one which particularly attracts Suckling and Rochester, but which also affects Carew, Marvell, and Cowley. Naturally (and it is a sign of a healthy poetry) you find different blends of these extremes in different poets, but

Carew's courtliness is given edge by his awareness of Donne, while Rochester's lyrics, taken as a whole, ponder both the costume (Spenser) and what lies beneath (Donne). But it is Marvell, most of all, whose lyrics show the importance of tradition for originality in the seventeenth century. There can be hardly a statement in the whole body of Marvell's lyrics which lacks an analogue, yet the combination of statements and their realization in Marvell's enigmatic, terse forms constitutes his originality. Another perfect example of this type of achievement is Carew's 'The Spring', a lyric which is both totally derivative and wonderfully fresh. Another is Jonson's famous 'Drink to me, only', heavily dependent upon the Greek prose of Philostratus and completely Jonson's own.

Jonson is, of course, a notorious classicist, and classicism is recurrent in seventeenth-century poetry, in the use of Latin erotic elegy by Caroline courtly poets, in Milton's epic syntax, in Dryden and Oldham. Classical influence is thoroughly unsurprising, given the educational emphases of the century, but it is indirect as well as direct, drawing upon Jonson's example and, in the Restoration, upon French neo-classicism. Classical allusion was common enough before 1600 and continues (a guarantee of education among other things), while classical influence upon form can be seen in the ode, in formal verse satire, and in heroic and mock-heroic poetry. But perhaps the most interesting classical influence derives mainly from Jonson – the Horatian emphasis on humane, largely secular ethics, which recurs in country-house poetry and in much seventeenth-century occasional verse. At its best, in Jonson himself, in Lovelace and Cotton, this provides a defence against the stresses of the period. Elsewhere, as at times in Herrick, it is little more than an excuse for withdrawal from society.

Forms can be much more than skeletons. When, for instance, Oldham imitates Juvenal, he is alleging that the patterns which define experience in Juvenal's poems are applicable to his own times; that the two periods have much in common. And this, of course, is a satiric version of what is involved in speaking of the Restoration as Augustan, as Dryden does. Similarly, when Cleveland adopts a satiric mask close to those of the satirists of the 1590s he is both in touch with a version of Roman satire and is saying that the period of the Civil War is so degenerate and vicious as to demand Juvenalian treatment, rather than Horatian. The convention is itself a comment.

In the same way, to adopt epic style is to claim that the material you are using is of heroic stature, a claim that Wordsworth was to make for humble rural life much later when using blank verse for *Michael*. Thus Drayton, in *Poly-Olbion* and *The Barons' Wars* (1603), makes implicit claims about the status of his country by the level of his style and through his use of allusions, while Cowley, in *The Civil War* (c. 1644), uses epic conventions to indicate the significance of the war (and his interpretation of it). Milton's epics and Blackmore's make allegations through form and diction about the significance, respectively, of Bible and native mythic history. Conversely, mock-heroic uses epic conventions to indicate the lack of heroic status in the given material, as in Butler's version of the Civil War in *Hudibras* (1663–64, 1678) and Dryden's destruction of Shadwell in *MacFlecknoe* (1682).

This type of imitation can be found in much seventeenth-century verse and is an aspect of the importance of authority in the period. It also frequently suggests an alive response to the past. The element of imitation in Jonson, Marvell, and Milton is seldom fundamentally pedantic, even though a degree of pedantry or of unhealthy subservience can be seen in Cowley and Blackmore. At its best, what we are dealing with is a rich deployment of the past to analyse aspects of the present.

Forms – which are chosen and how they are used – have a social history as well as a literary one. The esoteric element in Donne's allusions and the hermetic code in Vaughan are ways of defining the audiences of their poems as exclusive, restricted to initiates, while the polish of a Carew lyric is a perfect example of the refinement of the Caroline court and a clear indication that the concerns of non-courtly life are largely excluded. Similarly, the balanced phrasing of Waller indicates confidence even in the face of difficulty, while the neat, short-line forms characteristic of Marvell dispute with the gaps in his syntax in a manner which expresses the tensions of the mid-century. In the Restoration, increasing polarization towards extremes of the heroic and the satiric is reflected in the bifurcations of Rochester and Sedley, and this polarization, when set against Donne's way of drawing disparates together and Jonson's efforts to make the decasyllabic couplet a form for all experience, can be seen acting out the self-conscious contradictions of the post-war years.

Most of the seventeenth-century poetry still read is sophisticated. Apparent exceptions (Denham's satirical ballads, Butler's *Hudibras*, Suckling's 'Ballad upon a Wedding') are usually deceptive, mock-popular rather than truly so. This is not to say that popular poetry did not exist. There is popular religious verse, folk lyric, and popular political satire. But the main body of seventeenth-century verse is distinctly literary, the product of the educated minority, and the main challenge to this dominance came, and was to come, in prose rather than verse.

One aspect of this sophisticated poetry concerns audiences. There is, throughout the century, a strong connection between poetry and courts, and with this a tendency for seventeenth-century verse to reflect courtly preoccupations, whether this takes the form of the confidence of much of Carew's verse or the brittle aggression of Rochester. Even where the poetry is not of the court, it most commonly shares priorities and attitudes of court, as often in Jonson; and where it is uncourtly, as with aspects of Donne and Marvell, it is far from popular. In an age in which the educated saw democracy as anarchic, a democratic poetry is scarcely conceivable. In fact, there is no major poet of the century who could reasonably be said to speak for the masses. Milton perhaps comes closest, but not in terms the masses would recognize. Voices of opposition can be heard, but the outsider element in Vaughan and Milton tends to be that of isolation rather than of mass aspiration. For that voice you have to turn to prose, to religious and political pamphlets; to Levellers and the voice of Rainborough in the Army Debates. No poet of the century speaks for the masses as Bunyan did in prose.

Yet it is important to avoid the suggestion that all seventeenth-century verse is élitist, for it clearly is not. Jonson was a very learned man and speaks of élite audiences made up of the understanding minority, yet his concerns are with all society and his manner is widely accessible. Poets like Drayton and Daniel, Wither and Cotton use a diction available to most of the technically literate; and the erotic attitudes of Suckling and Rochester are hardly esoteric (even where the craftsmanship is highly sophisticated). The courtly element in seventeenth century poetry needs to be seen as something which is comprehensible, at least in outline, beyond courts, while the century's verse includes roots which are not primarily courtly (as in Milton and Dryden) and we can also see a socio-urban tradition developing (in Jonson, Dryden, and Oldham) which is to dominate the eighteenth century. It should be added that the sophistication of religious poets like George Herbert and Vaughan should not make us ignore the appeal of their stress upon experience rather than doctrine.

Notes

1. *The Stuart Constitution 1603–1688*, edited and introduced by J. P. Kenyon (Cambridge, 1966), p. 339.

2. Edmund Burke, *Reflections on the Revolution in France*, 1790.

3. J. H. Plumb, *The Growth of Political Stability in England, 1675–1725* (London, 1967), *passim*.

4. Not, at this time, 'the people' in any democratic sense. Parliament, however, saw itself as representing the people, although the majority had no vote.

5. This distaste is ubiquitous, but a good smattering of expressions of it appears in *The Good Old Cause*, edited by Christopher Hill and Edmund Dell (London, 1949).

6. Historians still debate the question of just how broad a franchise Levellers and Diggers wanted, but there is no doubt that they sought a much wider one than then existed.

7. See especially the attitudes of Ireton and Cromwell. The best text is in *Puritanism and Liberty*, edited by A. S. P. Woodhouse (London, 1938).

8. Quoted in Hill and Dell, p. 236.

9. Ibid.

10. *The Crisis of Parliaments* (Oxford, 1974), p. 339.

11. Quoted in Hill and Dell, p. 255.

12. Alan G. R. Smith, 'Constitutional Ideas and Parliamentary Developments . . . ', in *The Reign of James VI and I*, edited by A. G. R. Smith (London, 1973), p. 164.

13. For details see Quentin Bone, *Henrietta Maria* (London, 1973). Pym (1584–1643) was perhaps the greatest manager of Parliament in the seventeenth century and was prominent in the impeachments of Buckingham

and Strafford (see J. H. Hexter, *King Pym*, Harvard, 1941). On Arminianism see C. Russell, *The Crisis of Parliaments: English History, 1509–1660.*

14. See J. S. Morrill, *The Revolt of the Provinces* (London, 1976).

15. Russell, p. 345

16. Russell, p. 346.

17. Russell, p. 341. See also Robert Ashton, *The English Civil War* (London, 1978).

18. Quoted in Hill and Dell, pp. 264–5.

19. Gerrard Winstanley's life is obscure. He lived from *c.* 1609 to *c.* 1660 and after his marriage was based in Surrey, leading a group of Diggers in establishing a colony at Cobham in 1649/50. See *The Law of Freedom and Other Writings*, edited by Christopher Hill (Harmondsworth, 1973).

20. See Patrick Collinson's review of Roger Lockyer's *Buckingham* in the T. L. S., 29 Oct. 1982, p. 1187. For incompetence see Pepys's *Diary*.

21. The phrase is T. S. Eliot's ('The Metaphysical Poets', 1921) and it refers to the idea that around the mid-century the integration of thought and feeling which Eliot identifies particularly in John Donne begins to disappear from our literature.

22. An extreme illustration of this last point is the poetry of Patrick Hannay (*Minor Poets of the Seventeenth Century*, edited by George Saintsbury, 3 vols, Oxford, 1921), I.

23. See Stephen Orgel, *The Jonsonian Masque* (Cambridge, Mass., 1967).

24. See Angus McInnes, 'The Revolution and the People', in *Britain After the Glorious Revolution*, edited by G. Holmes (London, 1969).

25. See, for instance, Christopher Hill, *The Century of Revolution* (London, 1961), esp. pp. 156–8.

26. See Victor Harris, *All Coherence Gone* (Chicago, 1949).

27. This is not always true in Sidney's case but applies to most of his sonnets.

Chapter 1
The lyric

The significance of Donne and Jonson

Sixteenth-century English lyric is usually now seen as a tale of two styles – the 'courtly' and the 'plain'[1] – and such a view has its uses, provided we remember that the styles are not always readily distinguishable. Most sixteenth-century poets were capable of working in both veins, and Sidney is an example of a writer who often mixes styles. Although, perhaps mainly because of Spenser, it has been traditional to see the courtly manner as dominant, recent work has reminded us of the importance of plain style, particularly in the poetry of Wyatt, Raleigh, and Gascoigne.[2] It is also important to remember that although accounts of seventeenth-century lyric emphasize either the newness of the Donne manner, or regard his poetry as bringing the plain style to the fore, the courtly mode continues to be found deep in the seventeenth century. Campion, one of the most neglected lyric poets of talent in our culture, is usually seen as Elizabethan, but his books of 'ayres' are chronologically mainly Jacobean, while the inclination of critics to read seventeenth-century verse in the light of Donne and Jonson has obscured how strong is the influence of Sidney upon such poets as Thomas Carew.

For most readers of seventeenth-century lyric, however, the story nevertheless starts with Donne. He began his writing career before the end of the 1590s and his secular verse, at least at first glance, seems to mirror fashionable genres of the late Elizabethan period – epigram, verse satire, epistle, lyric. But his poetry shows little interest in sonnet, allegory, or Ovidian epyllion: Donne is the 'new' poet of the late sixteenth century, alert to Martial, Juvenal, and the Roman writers of erotic elegy. Being such a poet it is not surprising that his secular lyrics show a turning away from sonnet and, indeed, from the most common Elizabethan lyric forms. Remembering that many of Donne's *Songs and Sonets* were written before Elizabeth's death in 1603,[3] Donne's 'novelty' can be seen by comparing his forms, and treatment of forms, with the habits of the anthology *England's Helicon*, which first appeared in 1600. Donne's rejection of sonnet in his secular poetry, together with his neglect of stock Elizabethan lyric forms, has led critics to present him as a new voice in the history of English lyric, and so we have had Leavis's famous remarks at the beginning of *Revaluation* and a Pelican *Guide to English Literature* volume called *From Donne to Marvell*.[4] Provided we remember that this sort of clarity is fiction, a matter of emphasis rather than the whole truth, the break which is suggested can be a useful tool, and we can begin to look at Donne's achievement in secular lyric by contrasting that achievement with sixteenth-century courtly lyric, while always remembering that there are clear anticipations of Donne's achievement in the sixteenth century and equally clear continuations of the courtly manner in the seventeenth.

Courtly lyric is social, public poetry. All poetry, of course, is public in so far as it presupposes an audience, but courtly lyric is public in a more specific sense than this. It is public in using, in effect, a plural rather than a singular voice, participating in the codes of address and behaviour of the social unit which is the court. Such lyric may be written from within the court itself, by such as Sidney, or may be an imitation of courtly codes by a poet from outside court, but what matters is that the voice is that of a group. This group, made up of the Elizabethan court proper, together with aspirants and snobs, is not numerically large, but its importance is not numerical. Court centres on monarch and represents (at least officially) the social, cultural, and political aspirations of society at large. To participate in court, even vicariously, is to be part of an élite and this involves knowing the codes and rituals of that élite. This suggests a private world rather than a public one, and Elizabethan courtly poetry is never public in the sense of actually being the voice of the population at large (any more than the Elizabethan homilies can properly be construed as expressing the nation's views about political obedience). But such lyric is public in two important ways, in voicing 'official' cultural values and aspirations (as defined by those with power and wealth) and in being accessible to any educated reader.

So Elizabethan courtly lyric, usually concerned with some aspect of love, works to fit the particular case (whether imagined or real) to the general or the ideal. Typically, Sidney's sonnet 'Queen Virtue's court'[5] presents Stella as absolute, in images which do not define her individual moral or physical nature, but which present her in terms of achieved ideals. This explains the famous conventions of language, attitude, and behaviour in the Elizabethan sonnet: the individual temperament and experience are valued in relation to the values and attitudes of courtly society. So we have generalization and the extreme. Spenser writes on the stock theme of his lady's eyes by invoking the standard absolutes of sun and moon, diamond and crystal, and, at the other end of the emotional spectrum, defines her stock cruelty with the standard image of the 'Tygre that with greedinesse/ Hunts after blood'.[6] This is, however, a double process. It operates by placing the particular in the context of the general, as a way of elevating the subject, but simultaneously it is a device to make the subject accessible to everyone who understands the relevant codes, which are esoteric enough to exclude the unsophisticated but open enough to admit a sizeable body of initiates. Inclusion calls for such literacy in verse as to allow response to the poem's patterning and to share in the field of ideas and beliefs which defines the lady's social and 'spiritual' power. Even the fact that courtly lyric is so much focused on love is significant here, since it implies leisure to contemplate and enact love, and to codify and refine its aspects, moods, and manifestations.

Donne, however, is not so much courtly as Inns of Courtly and the world of his lyrics moves sharply away from that of Sidney and Spenser. His work is marked by extreme variations of rhythm, by its range of imagery, linguistic shock effects, and a general air of iconoclasm. In the *Songs and Sonets* the effect, when these poems are set beside *Amoretti* or *Astrophel and Stella*, is paradoxical, in that the élite world of court is both expanded and contracted, a point best made with reference to imagery.

Rosemond Tuve has pointed out that to contrast the range and handling of imagery in Donne with the courtly Elizabethans can be misleading.[7] But whereas the courtly poets use imagery, from whatever source, to assert a high valuing of love, Donne uses imagery not only to sharpen the reader's awareness of categories other than love but to call into question the possibility, durability, and value of love itself, and his way of doing this takes love beyond court.

We can see such expansion, for instance, in 'The Canonization'. In stanza 2 it is argued that love does not have the influence often attributed to it:

> Alas, alas, who's injur'd by my love?
>   What merchants ships have my sighs drown'd?
> Who saies my teares have overflow'd his ground?
>   When did my colds a forward spring remove?[8]

And although Donne goes on to argue love's 'mystery', he is here, with typical concision, presenting love in the context of a harsh world of swamped merchant ships, perverted seasons, the plague, war, and litigation. It is the compression and linking of the images which create the sense of love in a context wider than that of court, rather than anything new in any of the individual images.

But there is also contraction here. In 'Queen Virtue's court' Stella is the embodiment of virtue, the realization of the courtly ideal. She defines and comprehends that world. Earlier, the Wyatt of 'Awake my lute' and 'They flee from me' had seen the poet-figure as isolated from courtly fashion, but court remains focal even for Wyatt: you get *exiled from* it. In 'The Canonization' lovers are divorced from the wider world, making 'A patterne' by withdrawal. And although the divorce is not here specifically from the court, it is so on other occasions. Thus, in 'The Anniversarie', 'our love [which] hath no decay' is set against the aging world of 'All Kings, and all their favorites,/All glory of honors, beauties, wits', and in 'Loves exchange' the poet-figure is contrasted with 'your fellowes' 'At Court' who 'Give th'art of Riming, Huntsmanship, or Play'.

Courtly worlds provide society and reassurance for a Sidney, and if for a Raleigh and a Wyatt they can be menacingly uncertain they are none the less central. Donne, however, has a greater sense of alternatives: court is one reference point but there are others. This may be partly for autobiographical reasons, since Donne was of a Catholic family and thus could not realistically aspire to court favour, but it is also, I think, because social and cultural alternatives are beginning to put pressure upon courtly exclusiveness. Donne is writing at a time of growing mercantile self-confidence, when the Inns of Court and the public theatres are expressing attitudes which challenge the authority of court (however obliquely) and when the House of Commons is beginning to develop independence from the control of court and monarch.

But if Donne's way with lyric includes the confidence to turn away from courtly modes, it is important to add that such turning away includes a heightened stress on the individual. The confident reference to understood categories of form, image, and allusion which is characteristic of both courtly and plain-style lyric in the sixteenth century is replaced by Donne with a more urgent and individualistic note. Wit and esoteric reference define a coterie for Donne (the world of the Inns of Court), but there is always the danger that the wit and esotericism will work to exclude all but the very few. Donne's lyrics contain both a tendency to isolation and a fear of this. The speed, frequency, and variety of his images suggest a compulsion to define and communicate which is something more internally urgent than the stylized pressures of the Elizabethan lyricist.

This urgency and individualism are manifest in several ways, but can usefully be seen in the context of sixteenth century court lyric.

Although the sonnet is capable of great subtlety, it provides a basically predictable pattern, while Elizabethan lyric at large makes heavy use of a small number of forms. By contrast, Songs and Sonets offers a variety of forms and the unpredictable play of stress, this producing the impression that the formal properties of each lyric are unique to the particular experience. Even formally, the Elizabethan lyric tends to work by moving the particular experience towards the generalized mode of expression (and is in this sense public), whereas Donne's treatment stresses the uniqueness of each experience. Moreover, Donne offers no sequence. Although Elizabethan sequences differ in narrative detail they all focus on a single lady and articulate a sustained relationship with her (Shakespeare's sonnets being a partial exception). Songs and Sonets, however, is neither made up of sonnets nor has any discernible narrative basis, but is a projection of moods and incidents united only by the poetic personality and style of the writer. The sequences are based upon the notion of fidelity and the belief that love is a difficult but worthwhile activity. Donne calls such views into question. The focal mistress is replaced by an indeterminate number of shadowy figures and the focus itself becomes the poet-lover. Some of Donne's finest lyrics stress the value of achieved love, but the urgency of the writing re-creates the tension and uncertainty of the achievement. The reader of Songs and Sonets cannot predict what will happen next, even within the individual lyric. In Donne's lyric world stasis is rare.

It has often been noted that Donne's lyrics do not provide much sense of the physical nature of the woman. This is also true of Wyatt, whereas the Elizabethan tendency is to present a picture in terms of conventional courtly ideas of female beauty. Further, Donne does not present a fixed context for his lyrics: the poetic affairs have no single locus comparable with the court. There is the poetic 'I' and there may be indications of location – a bed, a 'Pregnant banke' ('The Extasie') – but a reader's strongest sense is of the theatre of the poet's mind, and this is true even of a poem like 'Twicknam Garden', formally centred upon the house where Donne's friend, the Countess of Bedford, lived from 1608 to 1618. The reassuring context of court and of a single mistress has gone, to be replaced by the flux and variety of the poet's mind, which, as it reaches out for illustration and explication, may go anywhere.

Donne's lyric achievement is paradoxical. The impatience with standard poetic forms, language, and attitudes disrupts the closed courtly world of leisure and wealth, and thus Donne opens that world up, expands the context of poetic love. But the accessibility of the Donne world is reduced at times by the specialized nature of his allusions, whereby the abrupt directness of his openings may be countered by the enigmatic quality of poems like 'The Extasie' and 'Aire and Angels'. A reader is both drawn in and kept at a distance. The world of the poem is both larger and smaller than that of the Elizabethans, and rather than the poems being read on a grid of social and cultural expectations they define themselves on their own terms, and are in that sense private. But this is a shared privacy in so far as the emotional and psychological expression is such that it can be widely shared.

There is a solipsistic feeling to Donne's achievement in lyric. A world beyond the poet's mind is constantly suggested, being continually raided, but the poems return to that mind as if only it can be known to exist. No fixed social context is, it seems, possible and values are relative. Donne's images, moreover, are material ones, not transcendental: however far gold may be beaten to 'ayery' thinness it remains gold ('A Valediction: forbidding mourning'). The rhythmical variety, the wit, the constant questioning, all point the same way. Fixities and definites are very few. The ideal remains, but it is never more than precariously attained.

Much of what is suggested here about Donne's lyrics could be applied, with various degrees of usefulness, to poets like Wyatt, Raleigh, and Greville, but Donne is more emphatically apart from the courtly focus than any of this trio. It is tempting to make large claims for the social significance of *Songs and Sonets*, linking their doubts and hesitations with the larger world of late Elizabethan anxiety over the succession, or with still larger speculations about the 'new philosophy' and Jacobean pessimism. Some such connections may exist, but they cannot 'explain' Donne and we should be hesitant about defining the late sixteenth and early seventeenth centuries primarily in terms of Donne's poems and Shakespeare's tragedies. The turn of the century saw Dekker's *The Shoemaker's Holiday* as well as *Hamlet*, and Donne's scepticism is in part the fashionable melancholy of the Inns of Court and the formal verse satirists.

Yet, at his finest and remembering the chronological difficulties of *Songs and Sonets*, it is worth suggesting that Donne writes a poetry which both reflects developments in the society in which he is writing and anticipates tensions in later English society. A. G. R. Smith has argued that James I,

Parliament, and a lawyer like Coke were agreed that the sources of absolute power lay beyond Man, and that their disagreements were about what manifestations of that power were inherent in, respectively, monarchy, Parliament, and the law. Parliament and lawyers did not question the existence of metaphysical authority, but they concentrated upon its functioning in the physical circumstances of Jacobean England.[9] For his part, Donne is no erotic atheist. Love exists and is greatly to be valued, but attaining and retaining it is intensely difficult. And it is just this apprehension which marks much of the best writing of the early seventeenth century, which is anticipated by the more hectic and superficial 'new' poetry of the last years of the sixteenth, and which is more broadly characteristic of the last years of Elizabeth's reign and of the reign of James. Doubts and anxieties can, of course, be found in lyric poetry throughout the sixteenth century and seeming confidence in the seventeenth. We are dealing with matters of emphasis. The lyric norms of the 1580s are of élitist courtly confidence, while Donne's secular lyrics posit the passing of court as the only significant social and cultural centre. This remains a significant development even when we set Donne alongside his great contemporary, Ben Jonson, and remember that the work of the latter qualifies, as well as complements, that of the former.

Donne is, as poet, primarily a lyricist and his secular lyrics are always erotic. The situation with Jonson is, however, different, in that lyric is not so central to his poetry, nor love so exclusive a concern of his lyrics. This suggests a major difference between the lyrics of the two men: Donne's examine erotic love as the central value of life, and the intensity of Donne's best work makes this much more than conventional hyperbole. Since Donne examines love as a series of relationships with mistresses, and especially since he considers such relationships principally as they relate to the ego, his lyrics seem intensely individual, even withdrawn. Jonson's lyrics, on the other hand, appear in masques, plays, and (singly or in clusters) as parts of *The Forest* (1616) and *Underwoods* (1640). This and the fact that not all the lyrics are erotic means that it is artifical to take a Jonson lyric out of context, since, in context, it is likely to shade into, or stand in a critical relationship to, other types of poetry. As a whole, Jonson's verse offers an ethical critique of his society, and his lyrics are a part of this.

If, moreover, for purposes of comparison, we take Jonson's lyrics and consider them alongside Donne's, the differences are more immediately apparent than the similarities. Although, for instance, Jonson is a master of intricate forms, he is far more likely than Donne to use simple, traditional ones (even Skeltonics) while his lyrics (whether formally simple or complex) seldom convey Donne's sense of uniqueness, intense immediacy, and individuality. There is not the same drama of openings, the same shiftings of tone, nor such evident rhythmical variety. This suggests a less intensely personal, less 'committed' lyric, and Jonson does indeed use the persona in a different way from Donne.

At times Jonson writes a very pure lyric, one reminiscent of Campion or of the best Elizabethan songs, and this type of lyric is particularly common in Jonson's masques, where the poet is creating a sense of ideal worlds. Song lyrics like 'O how came Love' or 'Now, my cunning lady moon'[10] are a type of perfection, indicating and enacting worlds in which quiddities of personality and behaviour no longer operate. They work at a level of generalization which is a feature of many of Jonson's other lyrics. Thus 'Against Jealousy' is a theme poem. It has an 'I' but it is a thoughtful, rather abstract account, not seeking to create that sense of particular occasion which Donne would bring to it. Again, both poets have lyrics called 'The Dream'. Donne's opens 'Deare love, for nothing lesse then thee/Would I have broke this happy dreame' – where a reader is at once drawn into the position of overhearing direct address to the woman and where there is a sense of particular occasion ('*this* happy dreame'). Jonson begins 'Or scorn, or pity on me take,/I must the true relation make,/I am undone tonight;/Love in a subtle dream disguised,/Hath both my heart and me surprised' – where there is more distance from the 'event' and where love is personification rather than relationship.

But a tendency to generalization and idealization is matched in Jonson's lyrics by a counter tendency to the specific and the local. The emphases blend in 'To the Same: Song. To Celia', where Jonson's version of the Catullan theme of multiple kisses includes

> Till you equal with the store,
> All the grass that Romney yields,
> Or the sands in Chelsea fields,
> Or the drops in silver Thames.

Here the exultant multiplication and erotic contemplation make the particular glamorous, but, conversely, the English place-names anchor the extravagance. Or there is the fine 'My Picture Left in Scotland'. The opening has the same poised, reflective tone as 'The Dream' and the poem uses standard Elizabethan material (Cupid's blindness, adoration, rejection, emphasis on the eyes). But Jonson particularizes and reverses these by an idiosyncratic version of the self:

> she hath seen
> My hundreds of grey hairs.

Jonson's way with erotic extravagance is most fully developed in the lyric sequence *A Celebration of Charis*. The fourth poem, 'Her Triumph', is a perfect example of Jonson's kind of idealization, and the last stanza is one of the finest pieces of lyric in English. But it is presented as the work of a poet-figure seen, with the wryness of 'My Picture . . .', as humiliated and rejected:

> So that there, I stood a stone,
> Mocked of all: and called of one
> (Which with grief and wrath I heard)
> Cupid's statue with a beard,

Or else one that played his ape,
In a Hercules his shape.
(*Charis*, 2)

Charis is later persuaded to describe the sort of man she could love and does
so to 'ease' herself of the poet-figure's importunities, describing a possible
lover quite unlike the bearded persona. This lover is a model of male beauty
and virtue, and Charis finishes with fine feminine independence: 'But
. . . if short he came,/I can rest me where I am' (*Charis*, 9). The beauty,
pride, and aspirations of Charis elevate her, and the poet-figure is out-
classed, but the sequence ends not with Charis's victory but with the re-
flections of 'Another Lady':

What you please, you parts may call,
'Tis one good part I'd lie withal.

If we take the elements of *Charis* and compress them we have something
similar to a Donne lyric: the desire to celebrate, together with uncertainty
about the possibility of love and fear that love may be only sex. But Jon-
son's treatment is less compressed and urgent. He can create comic versions
of self, write lyric debates and poems from the woman's perspective,
whereas Donne seems always to be writing one part of a dialogue. Of the
two, Jonson is perhaps the less 'revolutionary', the more content to use
Elizabethan forms and the more interested in developing the idealized el-
ement of that lyric. Even his sense of humour may owe something to Sid-
ney. But Jonson's awareness of alternatives to idealization suggests an
important link with Donne, a link which is essentially to do with implied
criticism of the courtly.

Donne, in a sense, largely bypasses courtly ideals. These, as epitomized
in Castiglione's *The Courtier*, are decent and moderate, but enclosed. They
presuppose the superior value of courts and that courtly ideals are both
absolute and satisfying in society, and they are conducive to that moral
beauty which Sidney is often seen as representing and which is commu-
nicated so well in Surrey's 'Norfolk sprang thee . . .'.[11] But Castiglione and
those influenced by him were seeking to make courtiers into a type of
gentleman which most people were not and could not be. Another way
of putting this would be to say that the ideal of the courtier keeps on being
challenged by the actualities of courts, as can be seen if *The Courtier* is put
alongside Machiavelli's *The Prince*.[12] A Sidney may show what might be
achieved, but what of a Raleigh or an Essex? What happens when we think
of Castiglione's ideals in the context of Wyatt's experiences at the court of
Henry VIII or of Surrey's sense of the axe?

I suggested above that Donne is less courtly than Inns of Courtly. He
brings to love the play of a wit which is brilliant, far-reaching, and sceptical
– and the world of Castiglione cannot bear too much inspection by such
wit. Donne does not see love as necessarily centred upon court or as best
expressed in the context of courtly ideas and ideals. In his verse secular love

is central, but personal rather than social. By the prevailing standards of the sixteenth century Donne is revolutionary in his removal of love from court and all it implies.

Jonson's position is perhaps more complex. As a whole, his work is courtly in that the ethics he supports are often seen as embodied in persons of the court. But it is interesting that Jonson tends to admire people who are more than courtiers – administrators and others active in society at large – while he is also acutely aware (perhaps because himself an outsider) of courtly actuality falling short of courtly ideals. In the masques, Jonson's songs may present courtly ideals, but antimasque often introduces a critical perspective on this, in the manner of *Charis*. Moreover, the type of humour and the versions of self which we also find in Jonson's lyrics necessarily involve some critical play upon the courtly ideals often presented. Such elements allow one to argue that, like Donne, Jonson is using lyric not as a direct expression of court but as part of that broad reassessment of traditional values which is an aspect of early seventeenth-century experience.

Some versions of 'Cavalier'

Donne and Jonson did not, of course, write in isolation. They knew each other and they knew many other writers, of various types and manners. 'Followers' of Donne and Jonson would know their work, but not only their work, and literary influence is seldom a simple, pure, or direct matter. It follows that such labels as 'School of Donne' and 'Tribe of Ben' need to be treated with some scepticism. But it remains true that the history of English lyric in the seventeenth century can usefully be seen in the dual context of the overlapping and complementary achievements of these two poets.

Although Donne and Jonson seldom write lyrics which touch directly upon political issues, or even obvious social problems, their lyrics are nevertheless socially and politically revealing, for in raising questions about courtly ideals they are indirectly questioning courtly dominance and a commitment to courtly modes. Robert Herrick, however, is often treated as if his verse lies beyond social and political considerations, as if he is a kind of Cavalier-in-aspic, a writer quietly polishing up miniatures while safely tucked away at Dean Prior in Devon.

Herrick, in fact, obtruded briefly upon the political world when he took part, in 1627, as a chaplain to Buckingham in the expedition to the Isle of Rhé, and twenty years later he was politically acted upon when expelled from his vicarage for his support of the monarchy, but during most of this period, and again from 1660 until his death in 1674, he was well away from the political centre. His poetry is mainly the product of the 1630s and 1640s, that is, of the period of the rise and fall of Laud and Strafford, and of the disputes between King and Parliament which led up to the outbreak of civil war. These are among the most vital and disturbed decades in English history, but a typical selection of Herrick's lyrics would scarcely suggest as much.

Hesperides, published in 1648, contains the bulk of Herrick's verse (the chief exception being his religious lyrics, published in 1647 as *Noble Numbers*). The collection is reminiscent of Jonson's *Epigrams*, showing the same preference for the couplet and displaying a broad range of themes and moods. Herrick is best remembered as the author of such lyrics as 'Delight in Disorder' and 'To Anthea lying in bed', but *Hesperides* has much else in it, including satirical epigrams –

> Sudds Launders Bands in pisse; and starches them
> Both with her Husband's, and her own tough fleame
>
> ('Upon Sudds')

– and ethical banalities –

> Two parts of us successively command;
> The tongue in peace; but then in warre the hand.
>
> ('The Hand and Tongue')

Yet Herrick's own introductory poems suggest a focus chiefly upon love and the country:

> I Sing of Brooks, of Blossomes, Birds, and Bowers: . . .
> I write of Youth, of Love . . .
>
> ('The Argument')

This is presented in explicitly pastoral terms:

> There with the Reed, thou mayst expresse
> The Shepherds Fleecie happinesse:
> And with thy Eclogues intermixe
> Some smooth, and harmlesse Beucolicks.

Included in this pastoral pose, and echoing Horace, is the argument for retreat, the 'happy life'. City and court are places of 'critics' and 'contempts', and so staying peacefully at home is to be recommended:

> That man's unwise will search for Ill,
> And may prevent it, sitting still.
>
> ('To his muse')

Such an argument had already produced fine English poetry, in Wyatt's satires and in the *Faerie Queene*; while the contrasting of country with court is, of course, central to Jonson's 'To Penshurst' and 'To Sir Robert Wroth'. Pastoralism remains strong in seventeenth-century verse and, in Herrick's time, was quite capable of incorporating and analysing a variety of themes and issues. Moreover, the 1630s and 1640s were ideal decades for considering the respective value and values of the rural and the urban. The debate on residence, the issue of the relation between local and central government, the overlapping problem of the gentry's choice between direct reliance upon the monarch for betterment or upon local power and tradition, and the socio-religious regionalism which we see clearly in the Civil War itself, are all issues which press upon literary tradition.

But in his lyrics Herrick is seldom concerned with such issues, either directly or (like Marvell) indirectly. Having told us that he is to sing 'of Brooks, of Blossomes', of Love and 'cleanly-Wantonnesse', that is in the main just what he does. But Herrick's material is seen not only in pastoral terms but anthropomorphically ('I write/How Roses first came Red, and Lillies white') and mythically ('I sing/The Court of Mab, and of the Fairie-King' – 'The Argument'). In Herrick's poetry, the actual is always being transformed. This, of course, happens by definition in art, but in Herrick we are constantly aware of the transmutation. Also, miniaturization is doubly a feature of his verse. He favours the brief lyric and often a short line, but he also likes to concentrate upon part of a whole, as in 'The Rock of Rubies' (Julia's lips and teeth) or 'Upon the Nipples of Julia's Breast' (self-explanatory). This playful specialization emerges also in Herrick's enjoyment of little poems about the sportive Cupid.

Jonson once, rather harshly, said of Spenser that he 'writ no language'. (*Discoveries*, ll. 2237–8). Herrick writes a clear, if rather precious, English, but his poems seem oddly lacking in atmosphere. There are persistent themes – mutability, transience, the relationship between Art and Nature – but there is little resonance and little rootedness. Herrick does have literary roots (and scholarship makes much of his classical background), but can find no way of writing satisfactorily of the English countryside. Until Clare and Crabbe this is perhaps significant chiefly for what it suggests about the interests and angles of vision of English poets, most of whom are not interested in the countryside as such. Wyatt and Jonson are concerned with the idea of country and the ideals associated with this. Like Spenser and the Shakespeare of *As You Like It* they use pastoral and see country in value terms which are themselves sophisticated and distanced from the actuality of labour. Herrick operates similarly, but what he values is aesthetic rather than richly ethical; and this is so, I think, because Herrick connects things mainly at a trivial level. Stephen Musgrove makes much of the relationship of microcosm and macrocosm in Herrick's verse,[13] and one can see what he means, but the relationship is seldom felt in the writing. These are famous lines:

> Gather ye Rose-buds while ye may,
>   Old Time is still a flying:
> And this same flower that smiles today,
>   To morrow will be dying.

> ('To the Virgins, to make much of Time')

Typically, Herrick fails to give any weight to his theme. 'Time' is just flatly 'Old', while, in the final stanza, the marry/tarry rhyme does scant justice to the loneliness of solitary ageing:

Then be not coy, but use your time;
    And while ye may, goe marry;
For having lost but once your prime,
    You may for ever tarry.

He lacks almost completely the proper *frisson*, caught for instance in George Turberville's 'The Lover exhorteth his Ladie to take time . . .'.[14] It is almost as if Herrick's versions of *carpe diem* are so famous because so comfortingly trivial: it is hard to see how they could threaten either physical or mental virginity. Yet such lack of engagement and urgency are everywhere in Herrick and this prevents resonance. The final stanza of 'To His Mistresse' runs:

You have broke promise twice
    (Deare) to undoe me;
If you prove faithlesse thrice,
    None then will wooe ye.

Think of Donne on infidelity, or even of Suckling's feeling for the decay of woman's beauty in a man's world.

Herrick did more than withdraw from London to Devon: his lyrics suggest that he withdrew from life to art. Much later Tennyson was to be told that Man cannot live in art,[15] but Herrick seems to have tried, and whereas in Donne withdrawal seems a necessity, in Herrick it seems a pose. This is not a matter of where Herrick lived, nor even of his subject-matter, but one of treatment. Herrick fragments experience without enacting the need to do so, and here again Marvell's lyrics provide a telling contrast. The effect is pretty and trivial.

It is clear that the early seventeenth century was a period in which intelligent synthesis of experience was difficult. It was conceptually possible. Charles I, Cromwell, Laud, and Pym all had visions of socio-religious unity, and Bacon could imagine a coherent programme of scientific achievement. But practice was something else. These are decades of conflict and uncertainty, reflected in the great literature of the period; in Donne and in Jonson's non-dramatic verse, and in the drama of Shakespeare, Jonson, and Middleton. We shall also see this in lesser figures.

Herrick does suggest something of these problems. His long residence in Devon, his concentration on the rural, his miniaturization, all symbolize something of the pressures upon unity in the 1630s and 1640s. And if Herrick could have thought and felt with any passion he might have made something significant of all this. George Herbert retired – albeit with initial reluctance – to Bemerton without losing interest in the state of his nation, and Lovelace was to show how the rural and the miniature could be made into a valid critique of *his* nation. Herrick has some feeling for contraries and can render them with delicacy and precision:

An erring Lace, which here and there
Enthralls the Crimson Stomacher:

A Cuffe neglectfull, and thereby
Ribbands to flow confusedly.

('Delight in Disorder')

His poetry is often reminiscent of other men. 'Delight in Disorder' is de-
veloped from Jonson's 'Still to be neat', while his fondness for 'fairy' re-
minds one of Drayton, and the articulation of lyrics like 'The Eye' suggests
Sidney. But what is more significant is what is largely ignored, especially
the urgency of Donne and the 'gravitas' of Jonson.

If it is part of the stock picture to think of Herrick pottering life away
in Devon, it is equally conventional to think of such poets as Thomas
Carew, Richard Lovelace, and John Suckling as 'Cavaliers', and to under-
stand that term as connoting a thoughtless and faintly debauched way of
life. Herrick may be Cavalier in terms of such a definition, but he lived
mainly away from the centre of the nation's life, while the poets just named
are of that centre, all three of them courtiers. But it should be noted that
if the stock view of 'Cavalier' is correct then clearly something was wrong
in the nation, for, if the court was central, it should not be thoughtless and
faintly debauched.

In fact, the conventional view is not accurate enough to be of much use,
containing too much legend and not enough fact. The court remained the
symbolic centre of the nation in the years before the Civil War (this role
being defined in court masques and paintings) but during the war the court
was one of two centres, the other being Parliament (which saw itself as
embodying the essential monarchic power, even while fighting the mon-
arch) and the speed with which the two centres were identified at the war's
outset indicates that the court was not the nation's sole real focus in the
years before the start of the war. Moreover, the Cavalier/puritan antithesis
often hardens in a misleading way, one which ignores the problems of
definition of the word 'puritan' itself, travesties the term, and fails to recall
how many people were desperately unsure where their true loyalties should
lie. Still more harmfully, for our purposes, the term 'Cavalier' is misleading
in relation to Carew, Suckling, and Lovelace, partly because it suggests that
they are more similar than they are and partly because it defines their writ-
ings through terms which misdescribe them.

So-called Cavalier poetry tends to be best remembered as lyric, and the
brevity of lyric fits the idea of the amateur, knocking off a song to impress
mistress or friend. A poem like Carew's famous 'A Song' ('Aske me no
more where Jove bestowes') seems a perfect example:

Aske me no more where Jove bestowes,
When June is past, the fading rose:
For in your beauties orient deepe,
These flowers as in their causes, sleepe.

But one has only to read a Carew lyric carefully to realize that the idea of
the careless, light-hearted amateur will not do. Suckling called Carew's
verse 'hard bound' ('The Wits'), and Carew is very seldom either vacuous

or careless. 'A Song' is not a casual, superficial compliment. What it does
is to take the lyric convention whereby natural forces are seen to originate
within the mistress and to make the conventional compliment a real valuing
of beauty through the quality of the craftsmanship. Thus, when the poet
explains where the nightingale 'hastes' 'when May is past' – 'in your sweet
dividing throat,/She winters and keepes warme her note' – the oblique
eroticism of 'dividing' and the fostering indicated by 'sweet' and 'warme'
have a beauty which makes the quality of the writing the true compliment.
Carew usually works like this, by reanimating conventions through the
accuracy and imaginative quality of the writing. It is the precision of detail
and the sympathy for words in their connections with things which make
'The Spring' such a fine poem and its ending more than conventional:

> only shee doth carry
> June in her eyes, in her heart January.

Carew writes a poetry which constitutes a case for the Caroline court. It
is clear, to any reader of his verse as a whole, that his concerns go well
beyond erotic licentiousness, but it should also be clear to any attentive
reader of his lyrics that Carew's poise and craftsmanship produce a poetic
texture which has cultural strength. This, in turn, may say something
about the tragedy of the Caroline court: the intelligence of such as Carew
and Vandyke cannot bridge the gap that was opening up between the court
and the country at large.[16]
   Carew wrote fine poems about both Donne and Jonson, and his poetry
draws intelligently on both. His friend, Sir John Suckling, also learns from
both men, but what he learns is revealing. To him Jonson's example seems
mainly to mean neatness and polish in lyric (although fillers and lazy in-
versions in such poems as 'The Invocation' indicate un-Jonsonian ama-
teurishness) while Suckling's interest in Donne is chiefly with the more
'insolent' and cynical of the *Songs and Sonets* (see, for example, 'Upon the
black spots worn by my lady D. E.'). Suckling finds brutality, even vi-
ciousness, all too easy in such poems as 'Profer'd Love Rejected' and 'The
Deformed Mistress' and it seems characteristic that he parodies the won-
derful last stanza of Jonson's *Charis*, 4 as

> Hast thou seen the Doun ith'air
>   when wanton blasts have tost it;
> Or the Ship on the Sea,
>   when ruder winds have crost it?
> Hast thou markt the Crocodiles weeping,
>   or the Foxes sleeping?
> Or hast view'd the Peacock in his pride,
>   or the Dove by his Bride,
>   when he courts for his leachery?
> Oh so fickle, oh so vain, oh so false, so false is she!

>   ('A Song to a Lute')

Suckling's sensibility often seems coarse and deadened, and whether this is innate or environmental it is tempting to see it as illustrative of a divided and fearful nation, his poetry a lyric counterpart of Cleveland's satire and the vicious personalization of Civil War propaganda. It is certainly terminal lyric in its refusal or inability to show trust, and so sex becomes strip-tease ('His Dream') or perversion ('A Candle'), while the claim to value another person betrays itself through rhythmical banality ('Non est mortale . . .'). Far more than Carew, Suckling is a poet who turns in upon love and then turns upon it in bitterness and frustration. Donne's lyrics depend upon love: that is, they rely on it, even where the poetry calls into doubt the possibility of love's permanence. Suckling concentrates on love, needs it, but cannot consider trusting it, or anything else. So his is the lyric of the defeated and isolated, and he cannot even envisage isolation *with* a lover. For Suckling love is the solo activity of the voyeur and masturbator, and his lyrics matter because at moments the emptiness comes convincingly through, with the Jacobean feeling for corruption in

> A quick corse me-thinks I spy
> In ev'ry woman; and mine eye,
>   At passing by,
> Checks, and is troubled, just
> As if it rose from Dust.
>
> ('Farewel to Love')

Or there is the sense of the futility of the finally sensual here: 'this once past,/What relishes? even kisses loose their tast' ('Against Fruition (I)').

Although Suckling was almost certainly dead by 1642, he is often seen as the quintessential Cavalier, but often the laughter is hollow, the gaiety close to hysteria. Suckling, it seems, poses as he does because for him there are no solid values in the court of Charles I. It is hardly surprising to learn that he killed himself.[17]

Richard Lovelace is different again. Carew died in 1639, before the outbreak of the Civil War; Suckling seems to have poisoned himself in Paris, probably in 1641; Lovelace, who was imprisoned for his support of the King, lived until 1658, by which time the crown had been offered to Cromwell.[18] He is thus the only one of the three who, as a royalist, had to work out a way of coping with the establishment of a regime with which he could have had no sympathy.

A glance at Lovelace as he is usually represented in anthologies might suggest that he coped with life by adopting a careless, libertine manner:

> Why should you sweare I am forsworn,
>   Since thine I vow'd to be?
> Lady it is already Morn,
>   And 'twas last night I swore to thee
> That fond impossibility.
>
> ('The Scrutinie')

Elsewhere carelessness is technical:

This knew the wisest, who
From Juno stole, below
To love a Beare, or Cow.
('A Paradox')

But Lovelace is seldom convincing when he follows Suckling, and he cannot get near Carew for eroticism. Often, in fact, he seems more like Sidney than anyone else, in poems like 'Love Conquer'd' and 'A loose saraband', and he shows more awareness of major Donne that Suckling does:

Though Seas and Land betwixt us both,
    Our Faith and Troth,
  Like separated soules,
    All time and space controules:
Above the highest sphere wee meet
Unseene, unknowne, and greet as Angels greet.
('Song. To Lucasta, Going beyond the Seas')

This stanza provides a clue to one of the emphases which make it inadequate to speak of Lovelace as 'Cavalier', for his concern with 'soul' is not shared by Carew or Suckling. The love he writes of in the famous 'To Lucasta, Going to the Warres' involves 'the Nunnerie/Of thy chaste breast, and quiet minde', while the equally famous 'To Althea, From Prison' also associates love with innocence and quiet:

Stone Walls doe not a Prison make,
  Nor I'ron bars a Cage;
Mindes innocent and quiet take
  That for an Hermitage;
If I have freedome in my Love,
  And in my soule am free;
Angels alone that sore above,
  Injoy such Liberty.

'Nunnerie', 'chaste', 'quiet', 'innocent', 'Hermitage' – the words together describe ideals very different from conventional views of the cavalier. Whereas Suckling tears at love as if to find freedom in nihilism, Lovelace looks to love for quasi-religious serenity.

In fact, although Lovelace is often technically sloppy, he is a serious poet in his awareness of values other than those of sexual love. He makes efforts, albeit rather naively at times, to compare love's value with other values, and to that extent is not a complacent representative of a smug court. His attractive bird and insect poems show this in their mixture of amusement with sober consideration of lessons to be learnt from other species. And it is this awareness of, and sympathy with, things beyond the courtly that enables Lovelace to write 'The Grasse-hopper'. Here there is identification with the insect's hedonistic freedom – 'The Joyes of Earth and Ayre are thine intire' – but also with the melancholy of transience – 'But ah the

Sickle! Golden Eares are Cropt'. The grasshopper teaches humankind, and so the poet addresses his friend, Charles Cotton:

Thou best of Men and Friends! We will create
A Genuine Summer in each others breast

and can build to his conclusion:

Though Lord of all what Seas imbrace; yet he
That wants himselfe, is poore indeed.

The dignity and stress upon self-knowledge and friendship are Jonsonian, but they are also Lovelace's own. 'The Grasse-hopper' is a poem of what can be saved from defeat, but it is also a commentary upon what had led to that defeat.[19] Charles's court had, pre-war, too often mistaken seeming peace for real and flattery for love: Lovelace had come to understand something of this.

The idea of making a 'Genuine Summer' is clearly consistent with the language of nunnery and hermitage in the poems to Althea and Lucasta quoted above. In 'To Lucasta, Going beyond the Seas' the desire for peace is in an erotic context; in 'To Althea, From Prison' the context is philosophical, reminiscent of Boethius; in 'The Grasse-hopper' it is political. But in each case the desire is for a 'paradise within' and the articulation is generalized, reflective, with limited dramatization and limited individual self-analysis. Lovelace seems concerned to place his own experiences within general categories of behaviour.

In lyric poetry of the middle of the seventeenth century, Lovelace, the 'Cavalier', is perhaps closer to Marvell, the 'Puritan', than to Suckling or Carew, but even so the differences are more striking than the similarities. Like both Herrick and Lovelace, Marvell has a fondness for the diminutive ('On a drop of dew', 'The picture of little T. C.') and for ideas of retirement. But the worlds of Marvell's lyrics are consistently more complex than those of Herrick and Lovelace. The latter has a feeling for basic contrasts (parting/togetherness; physical constraint/psychological freedom; hedonism/permanence) and such contrasts can readily be found in Marvell's lyrics. In fact Marvell is almost always a binary poet – from the explicit pairing of 'A Dialogue between the Resolved Soul and Created Pleasure' and 'A Dialogue between the Soul and Body' to the contrasts between art and nature in 'The Garden' and between the small and the large in 'Upon Appleton House'. Then there is the tension between active and passive principles in, for example, the violence which erupts in 'The Nymph complaining . . .', the blasting of the garland in 'The Coronet', and the burning energy of meteor-Cromwell in 'An Horatian Ode'. But there is also in Marvell's lyrics a theatricality which reaches back to Donne and is more central than in Carew, Herrick, or Lovelace. The essential difference can be seen in 'The Garden'. The poem contemplates the contemplative poet-figure: we, as readers, observe that figure in the poem's landscape, are aware of its meditations, and are not asked to identify with it to the exclusion of critical distance. By comparison Lovelace seems to present poet-figures which speak directly for the poet, without ironic distancing.

Clearly, the lyrics of Suckling, Lovelace, and Marvell all reflect disturbance. With Suckling this expresses itself almost as nihilism, while Lovelace – aware of violence, transience, defeat – is yet more able to contemplate the creation of 'A Genuine Summer'. Marvell, however, is more radical than this. He not only creates in binary terms, but in terms of the almost necessary threatening of one thing by another (as the innocence of fawn and nymph is threatened by the troopers) and he will even evoke violence as solution – as with the plea to God to 'disentangle all his winding snare;/Or shatter too with him my curious frame' ('The Coronet') and the call to 'tear our pleasures with rough strife,/Thorough the iron grates of life' ('To His Coy Mistress').[20] Marvell makes tight, polished forms, but characteristically threatens them with violent vocabulary and disconnective connectives. And the threatening of formal peace by formal violence mimes the Marvell world, in which Nature's bounty overturns the poet-figure, where the Mower mows himself, and where Cromwell is warned of the lessons of violence.

This world of disruption can be understood in more ways than one, and I do not see Marvell's lyrics as political allegories, or indeed as allegories at all. Rather they are symbolic poems, along the lines of 'The Ancient Mariner' and Browning's 'Childe Roland'. As such, however, they speak of their period. Marvell's lyrics are 'about' threatened identity and roles; but Marvell seldom achieves resolutions or confirmations of roles. His mode is of questions, appeals, and imperatives. This reflects, very precisely, vital issues of the period – To whom do I owe my loyalties? As the socio-political conflicts develop, and the issues become more complex, do I change my loyalty? As the traditional model comes apart, where do I find a role? In 'The First Anniversary . . .' Marvell elaborates the image of 'contignation', and this image seems one which the poet wants to believe in, but can only doubt. Marvell represents perfectly a world which executed a king in 1649, only to offer the throne to a commoner in 1657, and to restore the monarchy in 1660.

Edmund Waller provides a marked contrast. He was born in 1606, when the Elizabethan dramatist John Lyly died, when Coke was Lord Chief Justice, the Red Bull was built, and Drayton's *Eclogues* were published. He died in 1687, when Dryden's 'Song for St Cecilia's Day' and *The Hind and the Panther* were printed, as was Newton's *Principia*, and when James II issued his first Declaration of Indulgence. His lyrics are mainly a product of the 1630s and may be seen as offering a bland version of Carew's courtly manner. Dryden tells us that Waller 'first made writing easily an art' (in the preface to *The Rival Ladies*, 1664) and it is not difficult to see what he meant:

> You gods that have the power
>   To trouble, and compose,
> All that's beneath your bower,
>   Calm silence on the seas, on earth impose.

> Fair Venus! in thy soft arms
>   The God of Rage confine;
> For thy whispers are the charms
>   Which only can divert his fierce design.
>
> ('Puerperium', ll. 1–8)

Waller likes simple forms and regular rhythms, a typical poem being neat and logical, direct and confident. He also conveys the impression of speaking generally and of representative experiences. Usually his themes are stock amatory ones, the farewell to love ('Love's Farewell'), *carpe diem* ('To Phyllis'), inconstancy ('The Mutable Fair'), and they are presented with more clarity than pressure, so that the impression is one of good breeding, of love as a pleasant way of passing the time:

> Now will I wander through the air,
> Mount, make a stoop at every fair;
> And, with a fancy unconfined,
> (As lawless as the sea or wind)
> Pursue you whereso'er you fly,
> And with your various thoughts comply.
>
> ('To the Mutable Fair')

We accept this as an agreeable fiction, the style denying the propositions at every turn. The feeling in Waller's lyrics is consistently that the positions typical of Donne, or even Suckling, are being smoothed, made decorous, as in 'To Amoret', when Waller uses the image of woman as food:

> Amoret! as sweet and good
> As the most delicious food,
> Which, but tasted, does impart
> Life and gladness to the heart

or when, in 'Of Love', woman is seen as horse:

> Who first the generous steed oppressed,
> Not kneeling did salute the beast;
> But with high courage, life, and force
> Approaching, tamed the unruly horse.

When Donne or Suckling uses such language the effect may be offensive, but there is a strong sense of individual psychological truth, whereas with Waller there is an impression of social game. He plays his games well, and a typical Waller lyric is polished, insidiously intelligent, witty, and graceful, but the appeal is limited. In their different ways, Marvell and Carew both suggest that the lyric experience relates to a life outside art, but in Waller this is only the case if we read life as art. His verse creates the sense of a society at leisure, one in which experience is readily contained within simple verse forms and a standardized vocabulary, a society both privileged and made etiolate.

If Waller's lyrics present the more complacent outlook of the Carloine court, Cowley's suggest that the mid-century court-in-exile could survive the upset of civil war with some equanimity. His verse conveys the impression that he is operating as representative of a coterie, and his main lyric collection, *The Mistress* (1647), seems to have been written for the exiled English court in France, as a set of exercises on stock themes.[21] There is, as with Waller, the sense of Donne tamed:

> I Came, I Saw, and was undone;
> Lightning did through my bones and marrow run;
>   A pointed pain pierc'd deep my heart;
> A swift, cold trembling seiz'd on every part;
>   My head turn'd round, nor could it bear
>   The Poison that was enter'd there.
>
>   ('The Thraldome')

And as with Waller there is a gap between what is being claimed and the manner of the claim. Cowley's lines are theatrical but not dramatic.

Like Suckling, Cowley finds it easy to catch the clever, insolent tone of insult which is one of Donne's voices (as in 'Inconstancy' and 'Answer to the Platonicks'), but where, as in 'All-over, Love', he follows the finest Donne he fails to match the earlier poet's sense of urgency. He seems to be pretending to self-analysis and conveys little of that unstable complexity which Donne communicates. It is difficult to avoid feeling that love, in Cowley, is a matter for conversation and reasonable discourse, and that the nature and characteristics of love are agreed upon by initiates for the purposes of civilized social intercourse, whereas for Donne and Marvell research and contemplation are vital if the experience is to be understood. Suckling finds erotic experience disturbing at times, but Cowley sees in it the material for urbane wit:

> Though you be absent here, I needs must say
> The trees as beauteous are, the flowers as gay . . .
>
> Five years ago (says Story) I lov'd you,
> For which you call me most Inconstant now;
> Pardon me, Madam, you mistake the Man;
> For I am not the same that I was than.
>
>   ('The Spring', 'Inconstancy')

Cowley is a standardizer, and being an intelligent and technically accomplished one, he is, at his best, impressive:

>   Can that for true love pass,
> When a fair Woman courts her glass?
> Something unlike must in Loves likeness be,

His wonder is, one, and Variety.
For he, whose soul nought but a soul can move,
   Does a new Narcissus prove,
      And his own Image love.

                                             ('Platonick Love')

His lyrics, like Waller's, enact a retreat from individualism. In a sense, theirs is a lyricism of confidence, of the celebration of agreed standards, and of the view that the erotic impulse may be civilized, even pacified. But it is also worth pointing out that the implied scale of the civilization is small and undemanding. Marvell enacts the effort to retain neatness and order in the face of anarchic forces, while Donne's syntax and allusions suggest that the truly civilized are specialists and few. The lyrics of Waller and Cowley, however, create an audience of amateurs. They use allusion, but not testingly, to include the cultured and to ignore all others: the horses of their imagery are merely 'generous' and the food only 'delicious'. Another way of making the same point is to say that these intelligent and skilful poets create isolated societies. Waller, much more than Carew, embodies Caroline complacency, while Cowley suggests a world curiously detached from the strains of the political situation in England. Whereas Suckling's intimations of a loss of value in experience and Lovelace's knowledge, in 'The Grasse-hopper', of what defeat can mean relate their verse to a sense of the actual which goes beyond court, the lyrics of Waller and Cowley seem just polite fictions.

Restoration lyric

'Politeness' is scarcely the word for Restoration lyric, which is perhaps best known for its obscenity. Yet while obscenity is more prominent in Restoration lyric than it was earlier in the century, such lyrics show a greater range than might at first appear. There are, for example, many poems like Sedley's 'Song' which, in three neat quatrains, presents a pleasant picture of pastoral:

My humble Love has learnt to live,
   On what the nicest Maid,
Without a conscious Blush, may give
   Beneath the Myrtle-shade.[22]

But Sedley's poem is slightly more complex than it first seems, for the lover has had to learn to survive on limited returns and the poet, in the first stanza, shows awareness of a cynical norm in the assessment of love:

Phillis, Men say that all my Vows
   Are to thy Fortune paid;

> Alas, my Heart he little knows
> Who thinks my Love a Trade.

While Dryden has a number of lyrics which do no more than tunefully pre-
sent pastoral commonplaces (poems like 'Roundelay' and the dialogue
'Celimena, of my heart') Sedley tends to put pastoral in the context of some
element which questions or redefines it, as in another of his songs:

> Smooth was the Water, calm the Air,
>   The Evening-Sun deprest,
> Lawyers dismist the noisie Bar,
>   The Labourer at rest,
>
> When Strephon, with his charming Fair,
>   Cross'd the proud River Thames,
> And to a Garden did repair,
>   To quench their mutual Flames.

This is a knowing world, not an innocent one, and it is recognizably
contemporary.

Such lyrics work by accepting traditional ways of projecting and valuing
love (as the pastoral stresses innocence and natural sexuality) while adjust-
ing it to provide a critical perspective. In a similar way some Restoration
lyrics are conscious that love may be seen as a game which the lovers agree
to play:

> Prethee Cloe, not so fast,
> Let's not run and Wed in hast;
> We've a thousand things to do,
> You must fly, and I persue;
> You must frown, and I must sigh;
> I intreat, and you deny.
>   (John Oldmixon, 'To Cloe')

But the playing may be interrupted by a response which stresses reality.
So the poet-figure in Thomas Flatman's 'The Slight' claims to have be-
haved in a wholly decorous manner:

> I did but crave that I might kiss,
>   If not her lip, at least her hand.

This, the poet-figure argues, was an 'inoffensive libertie', and he is shocked
by the response:

> Shee (would you think it?) in a fume
>   Turn'd her about and left the room,
> Not she, she vow'd, not she.

The rejection of the proffered kiss is not surprising, but what is interesting is the location of the poem in a clear social context, the slightly colloquial 'fume', and the poet-figure's colloquial phrasing of his surprise.

Such awareness of alternatives to a wholly conventional world is a strength of some Restoration lyrics, and there are a large number of poems which develop this awareness. Sackville, for instance, in the song 'Methinks the Poor Town . . .' offers 'bonny Black Bess' as an alternative to the artificial world of Phillis, Cloris, and of the 'fools, who at once can both love and despair,/And will never leave calling them cruel and fair!' Sackville gives his lyric a contemporary setting which goes as far as to include names from real life, and he also uses a verse form which has more to do with popular verse than with courtly lyric. Alexander Radcliffe pushes this sort of awareness towards an extreme which perhaps anticipates Swift's satirical juxtapositions:

> While Duns were knocking at my Door,
> I lay in Bed with reeking Whore,
> With Back so weak and Prick so sore,
>   You'd wonder.
>
> I rouz'd my Doe, and lac'd her Gown,
> I pin'd her Whisk, and dropt a Crown,
> She pist, and then I drove her down,
>   Like Thunder.
>
> ('The Ramble')

With Radcliffe lyric becomes virtually indistinguishable from satire, but he is only presenting in extreme form the scepticism which marks a lot of Restoration verse. This scepticism is found in Flatman, for example:

> Let the wine, and the sand of his glass flow together,
>   For Life's but a winter's day;
>   Alas from Sun to Sun,
> The time's very short, very dirty the weather,
>   And we silently creep away.
>
> ('The Unconcerned')

And in Cotton:

> Come, ply the Glass then quick about,
>   To titillate the Gullet,
> Sobriety's no charm, I doubt,
>   Against a Cannon-Bullet.
>
> ('Clepsydra')

The brevity of mundane existence and the finality of a bullet are not new themes, but Restoration lyric can find little to set against them. In place of concepts of Christian or pagan eternity, or of the intensity of physical life which Donne and Marvell can offer, these poets articulate only drink and sex, often with the awareness that, as Suckling says, 'even kisses lose their taste'. In Rochester's best writing this attitude has real gravity:

> The present Moment's all my lot,
> And that, as fast as it is got,
>   Phyllis, is wholly thine.
>
> Then talk not of inconstancy,
>   False hearts, and broken vows;
> If I, by miracle, can be
> This livelong minute true to thee,
>   'Tis all that heaven allows.
>
>   ('Love and Life')

Rochester's expectations are low, and his vision of peace is both simple and difficult to assess:

> When, wearied with a world of woe,
>   To thy safe bosom I retire
> Where love and peace and truth does flow,
>   May I contented there expire,
>
> Lest, once more wandering from that heaven,
>   I fall on some base heart unblest,
> Faithless to thee, false, unforgiven,
>   And lose my everlasting rest.
>
>   ('A Song')

This reads as if the poet has heard of 'love and peace and truth' rather than having experienced them, while the secular heaven of the final stanza dominates the metaphysic which its vocabulary gestures towards.

Restoration lyric is a paradoxical achievement. It is often formally very confident, but its statements are of doubt and disbelief. These doubts are sometimes communicated with force, and the seeming flippancy of much Restoration lyric can be seen either as reflecting culpable refusal to think or as something which lies beyond thought, whereby engagement seems scarcely worth while. Games are played because this is a way of passing the time. Often these poets cannot offer any hope of 'paradise within' or 'Genuine Summer'. Their awareness of the forces which threaten peace and meaning suggests the great tensions of Marvells's best work, but they seldom write to this standard and at times this seems to be because that would in itself be too great an act of faith or caring. The Restoration marked a qualified and short-lived victory for the traditional world of the monarchy, but it could not obliterate the period of the Commonwealth and Protectorate, and the reassertion of tradition was on new terms. Charles II's Declaration of Breda recognizes this, but many Cavaliers found the new world disconcerting. Restoration lyric marks both the victory and its cost – the victory in the confidence of its manner; the cost in the doubts which rive its matter.

Religious lyric

Few seventeenth-century poets are only religious poets, and few poets of that century fail to produce some religious poems. In literature as in life the seventeenth century offers secular and religious responses which are so mixed as often only to be distinguished artificially by analysis. In the case of John Donne, the first significant name in an account of the religious lyric in the period, continuities and overlaps between his secular and religious achievements have surprised some writers and readers, but in so far as the intertwining of impulses just mentioned is valid there is nothing surprising in the phenomenon. On the contrary, overlap and continuity are what we should expect.

Donne's first *Holy Sonnet* ('Thou hast made me . . .') contains fourteen first person singular pronouns, an emphasis which is maintained throughout these poems, while the figure projected by way of these pronouns is very much a dramatic one:

> Spit in my face you Jewes, and pierce my side,
> Buffet, and scoffe, scourge, and crucifie mee;
>
> today
> In prayers, and flattering speaches I court God:
> To morrow I quake with true feare of his rod.
>
> (*Holy Sonnets*, XI, XIX)

The figure is seen in a variety of postures, but typically as being thirsty, derided, in need of instruction or seduction; and expresses a variety of emotions, but typically pleading, fear, uncertainty. The writing shows a strong tendency to project hypothetical situations in a syntax which may undermine the assertions being made, a syntax of appeal and condition: 'Oh let this last Will stand'; '. . . let myne amorous soule court thy mild Dove' (*Holy Sonnets*, XVI, XVIII). The language used is striking in its violence, especially in its verbs, and for the streak of erotic vocabulary; while the experiences are presented in a way which puts sonnet form under a great deal of pressure:

> What if this present were the worlds last night?
> Marke in my heart, O Soule, where thou dost dwell,
> The picture of Christ crucified, and tell
> Whether that countenance can thee affright,
> Teares in his eyes quench the amasing light,
> Blood fills his frownes, which from his pierc'd head fell.
>
> (*Holy Sonnets*, XIII)

Donne's religious poetry is certainly a record of belief. God not only exists for Donne, but exists with an immediacy and intensity which are startling. However, the God in Donne's religious lyrics is characterized by force and sternness rather than by love and serenity; and, in awareness of God's 'sterne wrath' (*Holy Sonnets*, IX), the poet-figure can only plead, reason, and, sometimes, bluster:

> so I say to thee,
> To wicked spirits are horrid shapes assign'd,
> This beauteous forme assures a pitious minde.
>
> (*Holy Sonnets*, XIII)

God's existence is never in doubt, but there are radical doubts and fears about God's nature, and the poet-figure has great difficulty in trusting the God in whom he must believe. As the poet himself says, he has 'a sinne of feare, that when I have spunne/My last thred, I shall perish on the shore' ('A Hymne to God the Father'), and this sin is discernible even in what appear to be the latest of the poems.

This poetry has been discussed in relation to contemporary practices of meditation,[23] and it seems clear that Donne was aware of and used such practices. But these practices do not explain the nature of the verse, and there is little evidence to suggest in the verse the serenity which should finally be achieved through meditation. In fact, Donne's religious verse has exactly the same instability which marks his erotic poetry. The fears and hesitations may plausibly be linked with what we know of Donne's life, and specifically with the career of a man born into the Roman faith who converted to Anglicanism, it seems, with anguish and for a number of reasons, not all of which seem primarily religious.[24] Yet, in some ways, Donne's religious nature seems Protestant rather than Catholic. It is, for example, the case that both Catholicism and Laudian Anglicanism stress the congregational. Thus the Laudian John Cosin claims that 'private holiness at home will not serve' and sees true worship as manifest only when 'the whole congregation together . . . come[s] and with one heart and one mouth [s] forth His most worthy praise'.[25] Protestantism does not wholly deny the importance of the congregation, but it does play down the collective ceremonial experience, stressing instead preaching, improptu prayer, and individual study of the Scriptures. One of the great products of this type of Protestant stress was spiritual autobiography, and Donne's religious poetry can be seen as work of this kind. Clearly, his poems have little sense of the congregational, if we mean by this the sense of the poet-figure as representative of or part of the community. Instead we have projections of the solitary figure in dialogue with a God of power and awe. The poet-figure scrutinizes and interrogates this God, seeking assurance of salvation in the puritan manner, but scarcely finding what is sought. Donne can imagine the Crucifixion intensely, and can transfer the sense of its pain and humiliation to himself, but he cannot imagine the Resurrection with equivalent weight or transfer it to self. By the standards of Bunyan's *Pilgrim's Progress* (the masterpiece of spiritual autobiography) Donne makes Christian's spiritual journey but without the arrival at the Heavenly City. Donne's career and poetry tell us a lot about religion in the early seventeenth century. He ended his life as Dean of St Paul's in the Anglican communion, having by his own account found it difficult to balance the claims of Catholicism, puritanism, and moderate Anglicanism (e.g. in *Satyre*, III). Moreover, Donne's search for truth (and the quality of the poems is the guarantee of the urgency and genuineness of the search) involves scrupulous self-examination and careful consideration of the nature and manifestations of the deity. All of this is typical of the high level of religious commitment which marks the controversies of the period.

But although Donne's work does represent aspects of seventeenth-century religious experience in striking form, he is too individual a poet to be strictly representative, either of seventeenth-century religious experience or of its poetry. Yet there has been an unfortunate tendency to see the religious poetry of the century almost solely in terms of Donne's achievement.

There is, for instance, no doubt that George Herbert learnt from Donne, but there is equally no doubt that he presents a very different sensibility. What Herbert learnt from Donne is mainly technical – which is obviously important – and can be seen particularly in the use of direct openings:

> Lord, with what bountie and rare clemencie
>   Hast thou redeem'd us from the grave![26]
>
> ('Ungratefulnesse')

and

> Broken in pieces all asunder,
>   Lord, hunt me not,
>   A thing forgot.
>
> ('Affliction (iv)')

There is also the Donne-like stress upon the first person pronoun:

> I know the ways of learning; both the head
> And pipes that feed the presse.
>
> ('The Pearl')

and

> Why do I languish thus, drooping and dull,
>   As if I were all earth?
>
> ('Dulnesse')

Herbert's confident colloquialisms and use of mundane imagery may also owe something to Donne, but in the final analysis his poetry remains a distinctive achievement.

In this context, the full title of Herbert's collection is significant: 'The Temple. Sacred Poems and Private Ejaculations.' The subtitle suggests a blending of the private with the communal, while the main title represents both the idea that the individual human is a microcosmic temple of God and that the poems which make up the collection are themselves a church. And although *The Temple* (1633) as we have it is structurally incomplete, there is reason to regard the individual poems as contributions to the expression of an overall religious experience which is as much representative as individual. Thus a reader enters the collection by way of 'The Church Porch', and it is notable that that poem is marked by general religio-moral precepts and admonitions:

> Envie not greatness: for thou mak'st thereby
> Thy self the worse, and so the distance greater.
>
> ('The Church Porch' ll. 259–60)

It is also noticeable that, on entry to the church, one of the first poems we meet is Herbert's wonderful contemplation of Christ crucified, 'The Sacrifice'. Whereas Donne contemplates the Crucifixion with terrified fascination, Herbert indicates the bafflement of Christ at Man's obduracy towards the grace of his sacrifice. Moreover, the poet-figure is not prominent in Herbert's poem: the focus is upon Christ with a singleness which we never find in Donne. This provides a context for protest in Herbert's writing. When we come to 'The Reprisall' and read 'I have consider'd it, and finde/There is no dealing with thy mighty passion', we respond by way of the sequence, understanding the passion in terms of 'The Sacrifice' and 'The Thanksgiving' (which ends, 'Then for thy passion – I will do for that – Alas, my God, I know not what'.) Herbert is as aware as Donne of the distance between Man and God, but he is not terrified by the awareness, as Donne so often is, and his verse enacts confidence even where it is articulating the distance:

> Yet by confession will I come
> Into the conquest. Though I can do nought
> Against thee, in thee I will overcome
> The man, who once against thee fought.
>
> ('The Reprisall')

Donne finds it virtually impossible to make that transfer from 'Against thee' to 'in thee'.

The Temple thus offers interplay between the poet-figure and the architecture and furnishing of the church building, and this involves a congregational element which is rare in Donne. Such interplay is clear in poems like 'Redemption' and the last of the lyrics called simply 'Love', where the parabolic use of the poet-figure generates a sense of poet as representative Christian, so that the poem becomes both an act of worship and an object which can be used by others in contemplation of their deity. In 'The Dedication' Herbert asks God to 'Turn their eyes hither, who shall make a gain:/Theirs, who shall hurt themselves or me, refrain', and this sense of the collection as meant to be of service to others indicates precisely the role of poet/priest as pastor which is defined in Herbert's prose manual *The Country Parson*.

Herbert sets his 'private Ejaculations' in the public context of the church as building, and his collection responds to the physical and communal objects of the congregational life of the believer. Thus, his stress is different from the focus on self which we find in Donne, but it is also important to emphasize how little Herbert has to say about doctrine in these poems. The stress is upon the need to respond to the love and mercy of God and upon the aid given here by the traditional objects and ceremonies of worship. The quiddities of doctrine receive little attention, and the emphasis is inclusive rather than exclusive.

There is, therefore, a sense in which Herbert's verse seems to stand at a distance from the controversies which characterize religious experience in the early seventeenth century. But this issue can be approached from a different angle. Herbert's verse is both caring and charitable, concerned to present that which is spiritually essential, at the expense of that which is doctrinally indifferent. Thus, although the poems are not themselves controversial, they do relate to controversy, standing as an enactment of an Anglicanism which emphasizes inclusion. It is, in this sense, a presentation of the practical latitudinarianism of the Elizabethan settlement. In another way, Herbert's verse is the projection of what should be possible, given recognition of the love of God. The pity of it is that Herbert's vision has lamentably failed to dominate the history of Christianity, and, more specifically, that his care and charity have so often, in Anglicanism, deteriorated into mediocrity and sentimentality.

What Herbert offers, therefore, is a sophisticated blend of the personal and the typical. It is a useful simplification to associate the former with what Donne represents in his religious verse, while it is commonly assumed that the latter is the product of Herbert's feeling for his priestly role. Donne projects images of self in colloquy and conflict with God, and it seems appropriate to think of him as preacher rather than pastor. But Herbert's poems are extensions of the idea of the shepherd, and to that extent the 'private Ejaculations' are made to serve the pastoral role: the personal and the traditional become one. But it should be added that this difference from Donne does not make Herbert's poetry eccentric. The emphasis upon what Herbert may have learnt from Donne has drawn attention away from his connection with another type of religious poetry which has been largely forgotten because of the stress upon 'metaphysical' verse which marks twentieth-century accounts of seventeenth-century poetry.[27] The type of verse to which I am referring is represented by poets like Wither, Quarles, and Breton, and it is a tradition which has been unjustly neglected.

Donne's 'Goodfriday, 1613. Riding Westward' has a title which suggests both a particular time and a specific situation, and it begins with lines which, characteristically, offer an intellectual proposition:

> Let mans Soule be a Spheare, and then, in this,
> The intelligence that moves, devotion is,
> And as the other Spheares, by being growne
> Subject to forraigne motions, lose their owne.

These lines lead to the introduction of the poet-figure:

> Hence is't, that I am carryed towards the West
> This day, when my Soules forme bends toward the East.

And the poem concludes with typical emphasis upon the needs of the poet-figure itself:

> Burne off my rusts, and my deformity,
> Restore thine Image, so much, by thy grace,
> That thou may'st know mee, and I'll turne my face.

When George Wither writes about the same day in the Christian year his title is 'Good Friday' and his opening is very different:

> You that like heedless strangers pass along,
>   As if nought here concernéd you to-day,
> Draw nigh and hear the saddest passion-song
>   That ever you did meet with in your way:
>   So sad a story ne'er was told before,
>   Nor shall there be the like for evermore.[28]

In so far as Donne's poem has a story it is of the poet-figure's journey, while Wither offers the narrative of Christ's Crucifixion; and in place of Donne's first-person figure we have a neutral, impersonal voice, one which draws simple moral lessons from the account:

> Our sins of spite were part of those that day,
>   Whose cruel whips and thorns did make him smart;
> Our lusts were those, that tired him in the way,
>   Our want of love was that which pierced his heart;
>   And still, when we forget or slight his pain,
>   We crucify and torture him again.

Wither writes a clear, generalized verse which presents his material directly, with a minimum individualization of the poet's voice:

> This favour Christ vouchsaféd for our sake:
> To buy us thrones he in a manger lay;
> Our weakness took, that we his strength might take,
> And was disrobed that he might us array.
>
> > ('Christmas Day')

The emphasis upon the general is also seen in Wither's interest in versifying liturgy, as in 'The Lord's Prayer' and 'The Ten Commandments'. His religious verse suggests confidence in God and in the basic patterns of faith: there is little feeling of a sensibility under stress or of a mind which finds the mysteries of faith particularly mysterious. Such features may reflect nothing more than limitations of imagination and intelligence, but it would be condescending to suggest this, for Wither's clarity and metrical and rhythmical control are products of intelligence, and I prefer to suggest that his religious verse is evidence that quiet faith was possible even under the pressures of the early seventeenth century.

Francis Quarles is more likely than Wither to make use of a first-person figure and he is also more interested in wit:

> I love the World (as Clients love the Lawes)
> To manage the uprightnesses of my Cause;
> The World loves me, as Shepheards doe their flockes,
> To rob, and spoile them of their fleecy lockes;
> I love the World, and use it as mine Inne,
> To bait, and rest my tyred carkeise in:
> The World loves me: For what? To make her game;
> For filthy sinne; she sels me timely shame.
>
> (*Pentelogia*, 'Fraus Mundi')

But Quarles also has a simplicity and directness which link him with Wither and make a contrast with Donne:

> The world's a Printing-house: our words, our thoughts,
> Our deeds, are Characters of sev'rall sizes:
> Each Soule is a Compos'ter; of whose faults
> The Levits are Correctors: Heav'n revises;
> Death in the common Press; from whence, being driven,
> W'are gather'd Sheet by Sheet, and bound for Heaven.
>
> (*Divine Fancies*, IV.3)

Donne might well appreciate the wit of the comparison, but he would not have developed it in this systematic way, nor would he have been likely to use the plural pronouns which Quarles employs.

Neither Wither nor Quarles writes strongly individualized verse, and this makes it easier for their writing to have a representative aspect, something evident in Quarles's 'Mors Christi':

> And am I here, and my Redeemer gone?
> Can He be dead, and is not my life done?
> Was he tormented in excess of measure,
> And doe I live yet? and yet live in pleasure?

Quarles articulates concern, whereas Donne would be more likely to communicate near-despair, and the manner indicates final confidence of a kind Donne rarely shows:

> Since thou art dead (Lord) grant thy servant roome,
> Within his heart, to build thy heart a Tombe.
>
> ('Mors Christi')

Such writing has strong connections with sixteenth-century traditions, in its plainness, impersonality, and moral stress, but it also suggests a context for George Herbert. Donne's communication of the urgency of achieving personal salvation and the techniques he used to communicate this are indicative of the strains of religious life in the early seventeenth century. They fit in well with the intensity of religious controversy and with the socio-political dimension of such controversy (see Introduction, pp. 5–6). But the poetry of such as Wither and Quarles, a poetry which, without being naive, is not sophisticated in a courtly sense, indicates that it was possible in the period to feel and express a sense of community and confidence neither exclusionist nor narrowly self-interested. Both men make extensive use of the Scriptures, but neither strains at gnats of interpretation and both have something of Herbert's feeling for the vital importance of love and charity. Such verse as theirs offers relatively little to the practical critic: its quality is of the surface and there is little feeling of subsurface. But this is weakness only if we insist that nothing but the highly individualized has value, for Quarles and Wither represent the strength of a tradition.

This may indicate something of folly of speaking of seventeenth-century religious lyric as if it were solely an exercise in Donne's manner. The field is richer and more various than this suggests, as is indicated by the poetry of Henry Vaughan, who lived through almost three-quarters of the century and who saw himself as a follower of Herbert. In his main volume, *Silex Scintillans* (1650, 1655), the links with *The Temple* are obvious enough, to be seen in titles, verbal echoes, and choice of verse forms. But this clear influence can be misleading, for if Herbert draws on Donne while achieving individuality, Vaughan reminds us of Herbert because of details, but writes very few lyrics which, as a whole, read as if they could be by Herbert. What happened when a poet tried, respectfully and without individuality, to imitate Herbert can be seen in Christopher Harvey's *The Synagogue* (1640).

Herbert is usually involved with the operation of God's grace on earth, and he is, paradoxically, an earth-directed poet, in that he concentrates upon the transformation of man's earthly life through the achievement of reconciliation of man and God, and that his vision of heavenly existence is presented in earthly terms, as with the feasting image of 'Love (III)'. Consequently, Herbert's poetry is strongly ethical. Man's conduct on earth is of vital importance, and Herbert shares this stress with Jonson (who, however, feels little need to use Herbert's religious context). Vaughan is more truly visionary, conceiving of the afterlife as something essentially *other*, and his glimpses of this other make him impatient of earthbound existence. Vaughan seeks union with God, away from the dross of such existence, and he conceives of this union in terms, above all, of radiance and of dichotomies between earthly life (which he associates with death and darkness) and heavenly (as associated with light and life).

Vaughan is very much a poet of images, specifically of pairings of images which present his fundamental vision of contrast in terms of day and night, sun and cloud, fire and ashes. The result is poems such as 'They are

all gone into the world of light' which use such contrasts as the funda-
mental principle of organization:

> They are all gone into the world of light!
> And I alone sit ling'ring here;
> Their very memory is fair and bright,
> And my sad thoughts doth clear.
>
> It glows and glitters in my cloudy brest
> Like stars upon some gloomy grove,
> Or those faint beams in which this hill is drest,
> After the Sun's remove.

Associated imagery of hatching and of animal and vegetable growth in-
dicates Vaughan's sense of human living as being closely identified with
organic nature (which is why he is sometimes seen as proto-Romantic) and
his feeling that contact with the world of spirit is analogous to birth.
Vaughan is, of course, known as a poet in touch with hermetic traditions,
and the hermetic belief that real truth is something covered by the com-
monplace is reflected in Vaughan's idea that truth is a light which breaks
through darkness. But it is important to add that the poetic importance of
hermeticism in Vaughan's work is easily exaggerated. He is not an intel-
lectual poet and his fundamental attitudes are available to any reader who
can respond to the basic contrasts.

Since Vaughan is concerned to embody his vision of the spiritual and
his joy in that vision, and since he is also intensely aware of how readily
this vision is frustrated by Man's fallen nature and consequent binding to
earth, the whole pitch of his poetry is unlike Herbert's. Moreover, since
Vaughan is trying to trap visionary moments he cannot be expected to
work through Herbert's kind of precision. His use of detail is often less
exact and his dominant unit of meaning is the stanza rather than the line.
And whereas one of the most marked features of Herbert's writing is his
feeling for the completeness of the individual lyric, Vaughan is much less
able to achieve this kind of autonomy. He can write quite brilliantly:

> I saw Eternity the other night
> Like a great Ring of pure and endless light,
> All calm, as it was bright,
> And round beneath it, Time in hours, days, years
> Driv'n by the spheres
> Like a vast shadow
>
> ('The World')

Here the calm certainty, almost matter-of-factness, of the vision is some
guarantee of truth, but Vaughan seldom writes whole poems of uniform
quality.

As these remarks may have suggested, Vaughan has a strong sense of
sin and evil, but he has little interest in how these express themselves in

this life. They are of interest to him because they inhibit union with God in the radiance of eternity, while the urge to pull clear of the dross of earthly life means that Vaughan, by definition, will show little interest in the ethical. It should be added that his poems also show little concern with the doctrinal or congregational. His poet-figure is representative only in so far as it is not highly individualized, but it represents only those who share, or imaginatively can share, his visionary bias. Typically, the figure is alone with its experiences.

It is tempting to see Vaughan's type of religious lyric as the expression of frustration with the whole world of seventeenth-century doctrinal controversy, for he is equally distant from the ceremonial stress of Roman Catholicism and Laudian Anglicanism, and from the austerity of extreme puritanism and the simplicities of all those who sought a return to the alleged purity of the early Church fathers. These emphases all have social implications, while Vaughan's verse is almost wholly non-social. He goes even beyond the concept of the community within the State to express a manner of living which precludes almost all sense of society. Vaughan's life was another matter. He married twice, practised medicine, showed a strong litigious streak, and was well aware of the Civil War. In that context his verse must be seen more as a projection of what he sought than as expression of his own biography. As such, however, his achievement is in strong contrast with the varieties of communal religious lyric found in Herbert, Wither, and Quarles, and it shares isolation (if almost nothing else) with Donne. But it might also be said that although Vaughan projects a vision of the individual isolated from society in solitary communing with the spiritual, this does have something in common with the emphasis of the separatist sects. Such sects share Vaughan's rejection of established social patterns and it could be argued that their concern with the small community of saints is similar in nature to Vaughan's embodiment of the individual communing with the spiritual world. At times we can see a similar emphasis in Marvell, but the latter has the stronger sense of the need to return from 'green shade' to the 'dial' of the 'skilful gardener' ('The Garden').

Vaughan's special interest was in the secret world of hermeticism, while Richard Crashaw is the main English seventeenth-century Catholic poet, Catholicism still being the dominant single Christian faith. But the two poets have in common a spiritual rather than an intellectual emphasis, a stress upon the visionary and a shared liking for repetition. Moreover, both poets – obviously enough – write lyrics which reject the material world in favour of the transcendental, and although this is what we should expect in religious verse the approach differs in different cases. Donne, for instance, certainly seeks union with God, but concentrates upon the present state of his relationship with the deity. Herbert looks forward keenly to union yet stresses the here and the now, while conveying confidence in the future. As for Milton, his emphasis is historical and political rather than mystical, while the visionary stress of Vaughan and Crashaw takes very different forms. Yet these forms can be associated with the socio-political crisis of the mid-century in England. Vaughan deals with that crisis by withdrawal; Crashaw by identifying himself with the international Catholic community.

No poet of the seventeenth century is more difficult to assess than Crashaw. It seems at times as if there is no problem, because sometimes there seems no need even to mention him. What can be made of an epigram like 'Blessed be the paps which Thou hast sucked'?

> Suppose he had been Tabled at thy Teates,
> Thy hunger feeles not what he eates:
> Hee'll have his Teat e're long (a bloody one)
> The Mother then must suck the Son.[29]

Or what is to be said about the crippling lack of control, intelligence, and self-criticism in 'Upon Lazarus his Teares'?

> He scornes them now, but, o, they'll sute full well
> With th' Purple he must weare in Hell.

To associate such writing with Donne, as examples of wit, or to link it with the continental baroque tradition (that is, with the emotional extravagance of such as Bernini)[30] is only to offer a historical note on taste, and does not explain Crashaw's technical weaknesses, such as the looseness of sense and rhythm in long poems like 'The Weeper'. But the matter is made more complicated when we remember that Crashaw's secular verse, although minor, is perfectly competent:

> Who ere shee bee,
> That not impossible shee
> That shall command my heart and mee;
>
> Where ere shee lye,
> Lock't up from mortall Eye,
> In shady leaves of Destiny.
>
> ('Wishes. To his [supposed] Mistresse')

It is also relevant to remember that Crashaw was an inveterate reviser, a writer who recast poems so thoroughly that the revisions are often essentially new poems. While the chronology of Crashaw's poetic career is often difficult, it is reasonable to believe that the poems in *Carmen Deo Nostro* (1652) which are not revisions were his last poems, and these show him moving away from his witty style to a more individual and worthwhile manner.

Wit, in fact, was never Crashaw's strength. He is notorious for writing

> Two walking baths; two weeping motions;
> Portable, & compendious oceans
>
> ('The Weeper')

– and it says something about the erratic nature of Crashaw's development
that these lines appear in the 1648 version of 'The Weeper' and are not
found in the earlier, 1646, version. But we may begin to understand his
way of writing when we start to see that his madder moments are not just
flashes of idiosyncrasy but usually developments fundamentally consistent
with the lines of emotion and thought which make up his poems. 'The
Weeper' belongs to a tradition of poems about Mary Magdalene, but
Crashaw shows little interest in Mary herself and his poem is more
directly about tears. The opening stanza of the 1646 version indicates the
manner:

> Haile Sister Springs,
> Parents of Silver-forded rills!
> Ever bubling things!
> Thawing Christall! Snowy Hills!
> Still spending, never spent; I meane
> Thy faire Eyes sweet Magdalene.

Crashaw, even more than John Cleveland, is a poet of synonym. In this
first stanza, tears move from being 'Springs' to becoming – weakly –
'things', then 'Christall' and 'Hills', while the second stanza transforms
tears to heavens, stars, seeds – all within 12 lines of a 138-line poem. And
the movement from one synonym to the next is by association rather than
reason, although Crashaw will argue with himself about the adequacy of
his images and play wittily with them. So, in the fourth stanza, he plays
with the idea that Mary, being earthbound yet weeping upwards, must
weep against gravity:

> Upwards thou dost weepe,
> Heavens bosome drinks the gentle streame.
> Where th' milky rivers meet,
> Thine Crawles above and is the Creame.

This, in turn, leads to the picture of cherubs breakfasting on Mary's tears:

> Every morne from hence,
> A briske Cherub something sips.

When Crashaw's interest in the extreme takes over he is inclined not
to resist the impulse to extravagance, and gives the impression of being
unconcerned about control and technical precision. But he does have the
problem that he is committed to finding verbal expression for the finally
ineffable (the necessary problem of the mystic). In the 'new' poems of *Car-
men Deo Nostro* he begins to find a more adequate style for his concerns.
The best way of indicating this is perhaps in relation to the poem 'To the
name above every name . . .'.

This is not a poem of detailed argument or intellectual density. Instead,
and typically, it takes a fairly simple 'plot' and drenches it in synonyms so

that individual words seem relatively unimportant when compared with the stress on sound and repetition. This emphasis is borne out formally, as the couplet-base is progressively departed from as the poem proceeds, but the departure is functional, miming the increasing excitement as the poem moves to its climax. Syntax is also mimetic, rhetorical rather than logical: an emotional response to a metaphysical experience is played out in the technique of the writing. But what is achieved is not the denial of meaning so much as the creation of contemplative verbal meaning. So, for instance, commonplace adjectives are used in pairs, which become motifs, whereby earth is dull, dark, sad, and humble, while heaven is represented by adjectives of scope, size, and power. Nouns and verbs are chosen from a narrow range of possibilities and, through repetition, particular words come to have solidity and become the basic 'facts' of the poem. So 'To the name . . .' is beyond paraphrase: its meaning is its whole, the representation of the name of Jesus by all its words and rhythms.

Donne and Herbert both use imagery to suggest that aspects of their religious experience are like particular features of secular life, and this is the method of simile. But Crashaw operates by drawing the reader into a melodic experience which is the enactment of the imagined sense of being in God's presence. Simile is neglected because the poem is not saying that the experience is like anything secular. What is aimed at is enactment. Through redistribution of the normal relative values of sound and sense a visionary experience is achieved which would not otherwise be possible. The nature and reality of the vision are the unity and harmony of the poem itself.

It is artificial to divide the religious and secular lyric as I have done in this chapter, and as critics so often do. All the poets here considered as religious writers wrote secular verse as well, while few seventeenth-century poets failed to produce at least occasional religious lyrics. At times, too, it is not easy to say just where the dividing line lies, as is the case with Carew's fine poem to George Sandys ('To my worthy friend Master Geo. Sandys'). It would, in fact, be very strange if, in the seventeenth century, the categories were as distinct as convenience would have us pretend, granted the interpenetrability of the religious and the secular in the life of that century, a point well exemplified by a number of poems in *The Rump*,[31] which move from the strictly political to the strictly religious with no discernible self-consciousness. When we remember this we can begin to see also that it is a distortion to consider the religious lyric of the period only in the context of religious tradition and that of religious art, for religious experience in the seventeenth century is simultaneously social experience, and the individual articulation of tradition is itself a social statement. So the strong impulse of Vaughan and Crashaw to create some sense of oneness with a transcendental state should be seen not merely as an exercise in religious tradition or as an indication of individual sensibility (although both are relevant) but also as revealing responses to the socio-political worlds in which they lived.

There is another general point to be made. The tendency to see Herbert,

Vaughan, and Crashaw in the context of Donne has served both to disguise major differences between them and to produce a kind of chronological shrinkage. Crashaw belongs to a different period from Donne and Herbert, while Vaughan lived into the 1680s. Donne and Herbert are pre-Civil War poets, while Crashaw's *Steps to the Temple* was not published until 1646 (the year in which the First Civil War ended) and Vaughan's *Silex Scintillans* first appeared in 1650 (when the future Charles II was defeated at Dunbar). Nor, of course, does religious lyric cease to be written as the century goes on.

There are critics who would say that this point should be made through discussion of such as Thomas Traherne and John Norris, and in one sense this is fair, since both men did write religious lyric in the latter part of the seventeenth century, but the problem is that neither is any good as a poet. Their example, therefore, suggests either that the last decades of the century were inimical to good religious lyric or simply that no poet of talent chose to work the field (which may amount to the same thing). What is, I think, clear is that the kind of energy and conviction which make the best religious lyric of the first half of the century cannot be found in such lyrics in the second half. There is not space here to consider why this is so, but it can be suggested that the religious impulse in the Restoration period is diverted, into the serious doubts of the best of Rochester or into the secularized religion of Dryden.

Notes

1. See Douglas L. Peterson, *The English Lyric from Wyatt to Donne* (Princeton, 1967).

2. See Peterson, and *An Anthology of Sixteenth Century Poetry*, edited by Robin Hamilton and Simon de Lancey (Nottingham, 1981).

3. The fullest recent discussion of the dating is Helen Gardner's. She suggests that *Songs and Sonets* was 'mainly written' after 1597, but her grouping indicates a substantial pre-1603 bloc (*John Donne: The Elegies and the Songs and Sonets*, Oxford, 1965, pp. xlvii–lxii).

4. F. R. Leavis, *Revaluation* (London, 1936); *A Guide to English Literature*, III, edited by Boris Ford (Harmondsworth, 1956).

5 Philip Sidney, *Astrophel and Stella* (London, 1591), sonnet 9.

6. Edmund Spenser, *Amoretti* (London, 1595), sonnets 9, 56.

7. Rosemond Tuve, *Elizabethan and Metaphysical Imagery* (Chicago, 1947).

8. *Donne: Poetical Works*, edited by H. J. C. Grierson (Oxford 1933). For modern criticism of Donne's poetry see Individual Authors – notes. The relationship between his verse and the period to which he belongs has not been particularly well treated, but for suggestive comments see R. C. Bald, *John Donne: A Life* (Oxford 1970) and John Carey, *John Donne: Life, Mind and Art* (London, 1981).

9. Alan G. R. Smith, 'Constitutional Ideas and Parliamentary Developments . . .', in *The Reign of James VI and I*, edited by A. G. R. Smith (London, 1973), p. 164.

10. The best recent discussion of Jonson's lyrics is in Richard Dutton, *Ben Jonson: to the First Folio* (Cambridge, 1983).

11. *Henry Howard, Earl of Surrey*, edited by Emrys Jones (Oxford, 1964), p. 32.

12. Baldassare Castiglione (1478–1529) and Niccolo Machiavelli (1469–1527) can be seen as representing two faces of Italian humanism. Castiglione's is graceful and optimistic, Machiavelli's cynical and opportunist.

13. Stephen Musgrove, 'The Universe of Robert Herrick', *Auckland University College Bulletin*, no. 38, English Series no. 14 (Auckland, 1950).

14. *An Anthology of Sixteenth Century Poetry, p. 101.*

15. R. C. Trench: 'Tennyson, we cannot live in Art', quoted in Christopher Ricks, *Tennyson* (London, 1972), p. 92.

16. See Graham Parry, *The Golden Age Restor'd* (Manchester, 1981).

17. Although there is some doubt about the manner of Suckling's death, the evidence makes suicide the most likely method.

18. There is some doubt about the date of Lovelace's death, but the probabilities favour 1658.

19. See D. C. Allen, 'Richard Lovelace: "The Grasse-hopper"', in *Seventeenth Century English Poetry*, edited by W. R. Keast (Oxford, 1962), pp. 280–9.

20. The Donno edition reads 'iron grates', but there is a strong case for 'iron gates'. This discussion of Marvell's lyrics is necessarily very brief, particularly since the poems have been much debated. Perhaps the best books for starting-points for more detailed study are J. B. Leishman's *The Art of Marvell's Poetry* (London, 1966) and Rosalie Colie's *'My Ecchoing Song'* (New Jersey, 1970).

21. See Arthur Nethercot, *Abraham Cowley, The Muses Hannibal* (Oxford, 1931).

22. For ease of reference quotations from Restoration lyrics are, unless otherwise indicated, taken from *The Penguin Book of Restoration Verse*, edited by Harold Love (Harmondsworth, 1968). Restoration lyric has not yet attracted much good criticism, but see J. Wilson, *The Court Wits of the Restoration* (London, 1967).

23. See especially L. L. Martz, *The Poetry of Meditation* (New Haven, 1954), pp. 107–12.

24. See Carey, *John Donne: A Life.*

25. Quoted in David Trotter, *The Poetry of Abraham Cowley* (London, 1979), pp. 61–2.

26. For Herbert criticism see Individual Authors – notes. L. C. Knights's essay 'George Herbert' (*Explorations*, London, 1946) remains one of the best introductions to his poetry.

27. See, for example, the account in Helen White, *The Metaphysical Poets* (New York, 1936).

28. Wither and Quarles both work in the emblem tradition. On emblems see Rosemary Freeman, *English Emblem Books* (London, 1948). The public

emphasis of the emblem helps explain the relative impersonality of their work.

29. A. Warren (*Richard Crashaw*, London, 1939) and R. Wallerstein (*Richard Crashaw*, Madison, 1959) both deal with the problems Crashaw presents, but neither manages a convincing vindication of his practice.

30. Giovanni Bernini (1598–1680), baroque sculptor, painter, and architect.

31. *The Rump* (London, 1662).

Chapter 2
The poetry of place

Introduction

All poems involve some sense of place, whether geographical or psycho-
logical. This chapter is mainly concerned with poems of geographical place,
which for the seventeenth century means emphasis upon the antithesis be-
tween country and court/city, an antithesis which reaches back to Horace
and beyond, and one which is made complex by other antitheses which
play across and beside it: the tensions between city and court, the contrast
between wild and cultivated nature, and that between contemporary nature
and nature in the past.

It is possible, and fruitful, to see seventeenth-century history in England
as a dialogue between three terms – city, court, and country – and in the
poetry of that century the terms interact with a rich thematic and icono-
graphic tradition which draws in such earlier poets as Theocritus, Virgil,
and Horace, and such myths as those of Eden, Arcadia, the Golden Age,
and the New World. When court, city, and country are in harmony you
have, naturally, unity, and unity is a major concern of seventeenth-century
governments. Political unity means that the interests of all social orders are
seen to be one and to be represented by the existing social and political
institutions,[1] and, of course, there is seventeenth-century art which presents
such unified societies. Thomas Dekker's *The Shoemaker's Holiday* does so
around 1600, and Jonsonian masque is partly designed to project images
of the court as the focus of society as a whole, with other aspects of society
harmoniously and hierarchically ordered in relation to that focus.[2] But the
history of the seventeenth century is of this image largely failing to rep-
resent actuality accurately, although the terms of court, city, and country
continue to be those which define the disputes. Naturally, the interests of
these components of the State overlap and interpenetrate all the time, but
that is not to say that the interrelationships were always, or even often,
harmonious. The career of the great merchant Lionel Cranfield, for in-
stance, includes his efforts to reorganize the monarchy's chaotic finances,
but if this represents an attempt to harness mercantile fiscal insights to the
needs of the crown it is also something which made Cranfield very un-
popular within court and brought about his fall.[3] Again, the charter of the
city of London gave it a pride and degree of autonomy which was of vital

importance before, during, and after the Civil War, being something which Parliament was able to use against court and king.[4]

Something of the complexity of the relationships between court, city, and country can be seen in the place of the country house in the poetry and society of the century. Standard images of the relationship between monarch and people as being like that of the head and body or of father and children,[5] can be linked with the view of the country gentry, in their country houses, as being *in loco regis*, deputies for the monarch or extensions of monarchic power. This suggests a line which runs from country via country house (gentry) to court (king) in the way described in Charles I's proclamation of 1632, where we are told that when the gentry resided at their country seats 'they served the King in several places according to their degree and ranks, in aid of the government, whereby, and by their house-keeping in those parts, the realm was defended and the meaner sort of people were guided, directed and relieved . . .'.[6] But country houses, even if recently built, had their roots in a tradition which this view of their social function disguises, the tradition of baronial houses, a tradition of something other than simple subordination to the wishes and needs of monarchy; and in so far as the aim of governmental legislation in the seventeenth century was an increase of effective central control it was of limited success. Alongside the theory of common interest focused on king and court, we have to put the evidence of local and class interest which emerges when we look, for instance, at the so-called gentry controversy, or at the complex pulls of loyalty before and during the Civil War between fidelity to monarch and fidelity to regional traditions and interests,[7] or at pre-war disputes about financing government. And since Parliament is the chief forum for debate of such issues we can construct a different line from that proposed earlier, one which runs from country via country house to Parliament (rather than to king/court). The reality of the conflicts suggested here is to be seen, for example, in the importance of regionalism, in uses of the word 'country' itself, and in Conrad Russell's comments on parliamentary armies before the New Model.[8] Plumb is surely correct to see, as a key issue in the search for political stability, the control of regions by central government[9] – and that can be viewed as a matter of country versus city and/or court.

Naturally enough, these issues play an important part in shaping the poetry of place in the seventeenth century, and it should be added at once that such poetry is largely written by poets of court and city rather than of country.[10] Moreover, such poetry is of restricted range, representing mainly the voices of the 'haves'. It could be said that poetry of place is as important as it is in the seventeenth century because place is so often conterminous with property, and property means power. It is with the poetry in such a political context that I shall be most concerned, whereas the bulk of secondary writing about the poetry of place has interested itself either in the relevant thematic and iconographic traditions, or in relating poem to landscape, or in the ideals embodied in such poems.[11] These enquiries have helped understanding of the poems, but the social and political dimensions have not been fully considered, despite Raymond Williams's argument that country-house poems, operating through exclusion, uphold oppressive social behaviour, and despite Mark Girouard's stimulating comments on the class significance of architecture.[12]

If it is true that all poems at least suggest some sense of place, it is also true that within groups of poems differences of setting, whether overt or implied, will be significant. We notice something important when we become aware that George Herbert's verse is church-centred, while Vaughan's is nature-centred. But we are concerned here chiefly with poems in which place is the subject, or a major part of the subject, and this, above all (at least in the first part of the century) means the poetry of country house.

But why does country house dominate poetry of place like this? One answer might be that for such as Jonson and Carew the country house complements the focus upon monarch imaged in the masque. Another would be that the poets are merely reflecting the identification of greatness with property. Another would lie in the fact that these houses dominate the poetry of place because such houses dominate rural social life (as the 'big house' was to continue to dominate rural society for a long time) and because they are therefore of great social importance. Summing up these ideas simply means repeating the formula whereby place = status = power, and suggesting that the poets follow the formula. But we shall not fully understand the poetry of country house unless we see it in the context of place poetry at large, and so we shall be concerned also with pastoral and edenic poetry, with patriotic place poetry, and with poetry of the city.

Country, country-house, and erotic topography: to Andrew Marvell

Most of the poems we shall be considering concern themselves with a limited location within Britain, but, in his *Poly-Olbion* (1612, 1622), Michael Drayton produced an epic of place. *Poly-Olbion*, organized as thirty 'songs' in twelve syllable couplets, is a celebration of England, marked from the beginning by a strong patriotic note. So, in his first line, the poet defines his task:

> Of Albions glorious Ile the Wonders whilst I write.

England is 'this most renowned Ile', 'this Iland Fortunate', 'ever-happie Iles', 'Ye happie Ilands set within the British Seas' l. 8, 26, 62). And although it may seem odd to describe sections of several hundred lines of couplets as 'songs', the term is appropriate to Drayton's celebratory purpose, for no so far as 'song' indicates a lyric expression of delight it points to Drayton's pleasure in what he is doing. This pleasure is both aesthetic and historical. 'Aesthetic' is an appropriate word because one of the most striking features of *Poly-Olbion* is the sense of the poet enjoying his command of his medium. The confident, relaxed handling of metre and language is, for instance, evident in Drayton's use of botanical terms in the thirteenth song (about Warwickshire):

> Valerian then he crops, and purposely doth stampe,
> T'apply unto the place that's haled with the Crampe.
> As Century, to close the wideness of a wound:
> The belly hurt by birth, by Mugwort to make sound.
>
> (XIII. 213–16)

Although *Poly-Olbion* is discursive the poem has a firm structure, one cot-erminous with England itself, and Drayton feels able to draw on a broad range of material and language.

This range constitutes a kind of historico-geographical account of Eng-land and makes the poem much more complex than it may at first seem. So the relaxed style and apparently casual voice are seen, as a reader pro-ceeds, to be deceptive, for from the beginning Drayton places England in the challenging context of classical myth:

> . . . check the surlie Impes of Neptune when they chide,
> Unto the big-swolne waves in the Iberian streame,
> Where Titan still unyokes his fiery-hoofed Teame,
> And oft his flaming locks in lushious Nectar steepes,
> When from Olympus top he plungeth in the Deepes.
>
> (*Poly-Olbion*, I. 18–22)

Such references, however, come cheek by jowl with native place-names:

> Thou Ligon, her belov'd, and Serk, that doost attend
> Her pleasure everie howre; as Jethow, them at need, . . .
> Yee seaven small sister Iles, and Sorlings . . . . . .
> From fruitfull Aurney, neere the ancient Celtick shore,
> To Ushant and the Seames . . .
>
> (I. 54ff)

In a sense Drayton is creating a map which relates England to the classical world, and this is in itself an oblique assertion of how he values his subject, an assertion that England is valuable at the level of the Graeco-Roman myths. But Drayton's map has both extent and depth. Its history includes its native myths, sung by 'sacred Bards' who preserve'th 'ancient Heroës deeds' and 'the British rites' taught by Druids (I. 31, 32, 35).

Drayton's celebration of England as place, then, has a patriotic emphasis reminiscent of Spenser's attempt to show that native myth has the quality of epic and that the vernacular can embody such myth, but the 'argument' to the first song also suggests a further dimension:

> The sprightly Muse her wing displaies,
> And the French Ilands first survaies;
> Beares-up with Neptune, and in glory
> Transcends proud Cornwalls Promontorie.

Drayton's survey begins outside England, and what he celebrates is a richly varied yet unified land, with its own culture and history. And this stands in striking contrast to the epic of rebellion which both Drayton and Samuel Daniel wrote, in which, among other things, they lament the way in which civil strife prevents the time-honoured activity of warring with the French (see Ch. 4). *Poly-Olbion* is a poem of a peaceful and unified kingdom, confident in the protection of the sea.

But it is important to repeat that Drayton's England is a richly textured place, given solidarity and mass by the poet's feeling for details of native myth, strongly English vocabulary, place-names, and social issues. *Poly-Olbion* achieves mass by extending to the natural boundaries of the kingdom, while simultaneously recalling the layers of history and prehistory which belong to the land; and all this is caught and presented in the poet's feeling for the language of his country. When, therefore, Drayton ends his long poem with the lines,

> . . . by her double Spring, being mightie them among,
> There overtaketh Eske, from Scotland that doth hye,
> Faire Eden to behold, who meeting by and by,
> Downe from these Westerne Sands into the Sea doe fall,
> Where I this Canto end, as also therewithall
> My England doe conclude, for which I undertooke,
> This strange Herculean toyle, to this my thirtieth Booke.

there is a satisfying sense of the drawing together of the main elements of a complex. This includes the feeling that Drayton has earned the possessive adjective 'My' and that it is more than fortuitous that his final specific place-name is Eden. Yet the quality of Drayton's achievement is that his Eden is made more than fantasy or nostalgia: his feeling for detail anchors the poem in the history which makes up the island's present.

Drayton has something of Jonson's feeling for social unity. In *Poly-Olbion* this takes the form of a patriotic view of England which avoids the silliness and blindness of so much patriotism because the poet is consistently intelligent. But while that intelligence makes the poem an attractive version of truth, it is important to add that the century did not provide another convincing account of a united England. Also, of course, *Poly-Olbion* is only a part of the truth and what Drayton sees tells us as much about his desires and interests as about anything else, his perceptions relating simultaneously to the growing antiquarian interests of the sixteenth and early seventeenth centuries,[13] the patriotic concerns of high Elizabethanism, and the uncertainties commonly called Jacobean. The first eighteen songs were published in 1612. In that year the younger Cecil died (which provides a significant break with Elizabeth's reign) and so did Prince Henry, in whom so many had invested their hopes of a new Arthurian era. It is also the year in which Jonson's *The Alchemist* was first published. In that play place is highly important, but in it place is concentrated upon the town house of one gentleman and that house is plague-infected. There is a great distance between that and Drayton's vision of a whole and healthy England. By the time that the rest of *Poly-Olbion* was published (1622) England's unity and self-confidence had had to face the Somerset scandal, the rise of Buckingham, the execution of Raleigh, the falls of Suffolk and Bacon, and the Protestation of Rights. In such a context, Drayton's poem seems a great and moving ideal, and its truthfulness lies in its ability, reminiscent of Jonson's 'To Penshurst', to make that ideal feel both desirable and attainable.

This element of the ideal provides a link between Drayton's poem and the versions of place found in pastoral, the latter offering something between the account of England as a whole and the selected places found in country-house poems. Pastoral can be both a general state and have details specific to a particular region, but it is also as much a projection of moral values as it is an account of physical place, the latter usually being the embodiment of the former, whereas in *Poly-Olbion* the account of place suggests the values inherent in the imagined England.

It is an elementary error to believe that pastoral rapidly became an anachronism in the seventeenth century. The example of Donne and the 'realism' of much Jacobean drama might suggest as much, but the early part of the century is notable partly because of the strength of its pastoral verse, a good example being William Browne's *Britannia's Pastorals* (1613–16). Its opening lines have similarities with Drayton, but also interesting differences:

> I that whileare neere Tavies straggling spring,
> Unto my seely Sheepe did use to sing,
> And plaid to please my selfe, on rustick Reede,
> Nor sought for Baye, (the learned Shepheards meede)
> But as a Swaine unkent fed on the plaines,
> And made the eccho umpire of my straines:
> Am drawne by time, (although the weak'st of many)
> To sing those layes as yet unsung of any.
> What neede I tune the Swaines of Thessalie?
> Or, bootlesse, adde to them of Arcadie?
> No: faire Arcadia cannot be compleater,
> My praise may lessen, but not make thee greater.
> My Muse for loftie pitches shall not rome,
> But only pipen of her native home:
> And to the Swaines, Love, Love rurall Minstralsie,
> Thus deare Britannia will I sing of thee.[14]

Like Drayton, Browne chooses to concentrate on his native island, while the reference to Tavy suggests that his poem may share with *Poly-Olbion* an interest in the details of native place. The patriotic element is also drawn out almost at once:

> High on the plaines of that renowned Ile,
> Which all men Beauties Garden-plot instile

and at times Browne brings in the kind of detail which marks Drayton's poem:

> Yea, on the Oake, the Plumbe-tree and the Holme,
> The Stock-dove and the Blackbird should not come,
> Whose muting on those trees doe make to grow
> Rots curing Hyphear, and the Miseltoe.
>
> (p. 19)

But whereas Drayton works from a geographical sense of place and transforms this through style into an artful map, it is clear even from his first verse paragraph that Browne's main focus is the artifice of pastoral. The poet immediately adopts the fiction of the poet-shepherd who sings to his 'seely' sheep, plays on his rustic pipe, and presents himself as humble singer of humble theme. A consequence of this is that the formal situation of England, and, more specifically, the local precision suggested by the Tavy reference and its accompanying note,[15] are largely displaced by the conventional geography of literary pastoral. 'Displaced' may not be quite accurate. It might be more precise to say that pastoral provides the dominant context within which Browne places passages of greater realism, as here:

> A Hunts-man here followes his cry of hounds,
> Driving the Hare along the fallow grounds:
> Whilst one at hand seeming the sport t'allow,
> Followes the hounds, and carelesse leaves the Plow.
>
> (p. 42)

Browne's motives are celebratory-aesthetic and *Britannia's Pastorals* does not offer direct analysis of the contemporary state of England, but it is suggestive that this sort of pastoral vision, presented with some real imaginative life, is prominent in the poetry of the early seventeenth century. It offers a view of 'where we want to be' which involves transforming actual landscape into pastoral norms, and it also, obviously, involves suppressing the urban realities of London and the slowly increasing mercantile aspects of English life. If, then, Drayton offers an appealing account of English history as a vision of a happy and unified kingdom, Browne is offering an attractive vision of England as Arcadia. And, instead of speaking of either as evasions of reality, both can be seen as visions of what a healthy society might be. This, I want to suggest, is also a major emphasis of the country-house poem.

The country-house poem is essentially the invention, in English literary history, of Ben Jonson, who, typically, works up hints, phrases, and themes from several classical writers (notably Horace, Juvenal, and Martial) which are merged with Jonson's sense of England to constitute a new English genre. It is not easy to say why the country-house poem emerges when it does, although as we have seen it is possible to suggest why it comes to dominate the poetry of place, but it coincides with a period of activity in the building of great houses and, suggestively, with a time when country aristocracy and gentry were, it seems, tending to drift to London, to a

degree which clearly worried central government, which relied on such
people for local administration of law and order.[16] When, therefore, a
Jonson or a Carew wrote in praise of a country house and its inhabitants he
could easily be seen as voicing attitudes which endorse government policies,
this being a view of country-house poetry which has struck and irritated
Raymond Williams.[17] But before we look more closely at what versions of
place such poems present, it is important to remember that the term
'country house' includes various types of dwelling-place and that, as
suggested earlier, its social function is ambivalent.

Any individual country-house poem should be read as both general and
specific. 'Country house' embraces dwellings as relatively modest as Pen-
shurst and as vast as Hardwick, and it includes houses deeply rooted in the
Middle Ages as well as those built in the late sixteenth and early seven-
teenth centuries and others radically altered in that period (thus Burghley
extended Theobalds, while Hatton created Holdenby as a building on the
scale of Hampton Court – and he was a bachelor). Moreover, country
houses were lived in by such great traditional lords as the earls of Derby
and Worcester, by gentry long associated with a particular area, and by
'new' men like Hatton and the Cecils, but also by the households of these
groups (in the 1580s Derby's household was as large as 140[18]). What fol-
lows from this is that we should not assume that a particular country-house
poem is necessarily a blanket endorsement of the whole complex and var-
iety indicated here. Nor, remembering the ambivalence indicated earlier,
should we assume that a country-house poem is necessarily a sycophantic
document or an attempt at narrow verisimilitude.

Jonson's 'To Penshurst' (1612) is the poem which establishes the genre,
and its famous opening provides two clues as to how that genre can work.
First of all, there is the critical dimension:

> Thou art not, Penshurst, built to envious show,
> Of touch, or marble; nor canst boast a row
> Of polished pillars, or a roof of gold:
> Thou hast no lanthorn, where of tales are told;
> Or stair, or courts; but stand'st an ancient pile,
> And these grudged at, art reverenced the while.
> Thou joy'st in better marks, of soil, of air,
> Of wood, of water: therein thou art fair.

This is criticism through historical and moral discrimination. Penshurst is
'an ancient pile', and by contrast the 'polished pillars' and 'roof of gold' are
seen as rather flashy modern features, while the dialogue between terms
like 'envious' and 'grudged', on the one hand, and 'reverenced' and 'better',
on the other, provides a parallel moral contrast. It is clear that Jonson is
offering an endorsement of a particular house (and perhaps type of house)
rather than a general eulogy of country houses.

But if the specificity of these opening lines indicates, as it does, that the
poet is concerned with a limited and individual place, the references in the

immediately following lines to dryads, Pan, Bacchus, nymphs, sylvans, and fauns demonstrate another important feature of the poem, its idealizing aspect. Some commentators have seen details like these and the strange passage of the fish as little more than decoration, put in perhaps to raise the tone of the poem. This view seems to be put forward in the cause of claiming that 'To Penshurst' is a naturalistic poem, at least at heart. But if we notice how the blend of the naturalistic and the idealized parallels the combination of detail and commentary which is found in *Poly-Olbion*, we may argue that Jonson is not offering a naturalistic account of the Sidneys' house at Penshurst.

Jonson does offer details, and it has been shown that his poem provides an accurate account of the setting and layout of the house.[19] This much is hinted at very early in the poem, with the references to 'Thy Mount' and to 'That taller tree, which of a nut was set,/At his great birth, where all the muses met', and this specificity is an important part of the poem's purport, providing a convincingly firm and local texture. But that aspect of 'To Penshurst' coexists with others, like the critical perspective established at the opening and never forgotten, and the classical and hyperbolic details glanced at above. These features extend the significance of the local detail in two main and important ways. The critical perspective continually emphasizes the valuable special nature of Penshurst within the tradition of the country house. Thus Jonson's opening stresses suggest that there is a category opposite to this house, and there is a close parallel when Jonson is speaking later of hospitality at Penshurst:

> I not fain to sit (as some, this day,
> At great men's tables) and yet dine away.
> Here no man tells my cups.
>
> (ll. 65–7)

And, of course, this kind of discrimination is magnificently summed up at the poem's end:

> Now, Penshurst, they that will proportion thee
> With other edifices, when they see
> Those proud, ambitious heaps, and nothing else,
> May say, their lords have built, but thy lord dwells.

What this amounts to is something which, in terms of ideas of place, can be contrasted with Drayton. He presents a version of a unified England, and it is this unity which gives satisfaction. In contrast, Jonson presents his version of Penshurst as a desirable exception to the norm. When he writes that

> though thy walls be of the country stone,
> They are reared with no man's ruin, no man's groan,
> There's none, that dwell about them, wish them down
>
> (ll. 45–7)

there is again this idea of the exceptional, but there is also a sense of 'country' which is different from Drayton's, for the humane influence of Jonson's Sidneys is explicitly local. It pertains to their 'country', and that here means the immediate environs of the house. Jonson's poem does not suggest that this is a microcosm of English society in the early seventeenth century, and so Drayton's England might be said to have shrunk in Jonson's poem to Penshurst (and whatever other Penshursts there may be).

But the idealization mentioned (Jonson's equivalent to the idealization of pastoral in Browne) takes the matter further, for it indicates that Jonson's Penshurst is not offered as a simple literal version of actuality. Certainly Jonson works from the actual – hence the detail – but it is transformed through style, so that while Penshurst is surrounded (so the critical perspective says) by moral and aesthetic corruption, it is in itself perfect as a version of Jacobean ideals of familial and social behaviour. The pattern of classical and biblical allusions enforces this point: the literal Penshurst is transformed, partly through this pattern, into a model of how life should be lived. Where the poem differs importantly from Browne's pastoralism is that its ideals are so firmly bedded in specific detail that the combination of detail and ideal amounts to a persuasive version of what should be possible for mankind. The ideals, and their fictional enactment, follow so convincingly from the concrete detail that we are drawn, through Jonson's art, to suspend cynicism and to believe, however temporarily, that this life must be achievable.

Through selection, then, Jonson creates a version of history which is finally a moral mirror. The aim seems to be to draw a reader to see in that mirror what should be possible, rather than to claim that what the mirror is reflecting is mimetic of the real Penshurst, let alone of society at large. In so far as this is an accurate account of how the poem works, it can be seen to have similar purposes to those of Drayton and Browne. All three poems are offering artistic versions of society, and they thus provide linked possibilities for the poetry of place as the century progresses.

Browne's *Britannia's Pastorals* has been looked at as an example of early seventeenth-century pastoral, and while pastoral need not be escapist it obviously does contain the possibility of escapism. By the seventeenth century, pastoral innocence could be taken to include sexual innocence (seen as equivalent to free love), one version of this being the fiction of a return to Eden, where, since the race was sinless, sex itself must be free of guilt. So we find that poets of the early seventeenth century who wish to write erotic verse often do so by creating Edens, the locale being the excuse for concentrating upon sex, while largely ignoring those moral issues which actually bear upon sexual concerns.

Thomas Randolph wrote several pastoral poems, and the title of his 'A Pastoral Courtship' suggests something along the lines of his own 'Eglog to Mr. Johnson'. But 'A Pastoral Courtship' is pastoral eroticism, and its pose of innocence is just a pose. In this Eden place is ideal and ideally suited to the poet-figure's purpose:

> Behold these woods, and mark my Sweet
> How all the boughes together meet!

> The Cedar his faire arms displayes,
> And mixes branches with the Bayes.
>
> (ll. 1–4)

In this place there is positive harmony, which is accentuated by the account of what is absent:

> There lurks no speckled Serpent here.
> No Venomous snake makes this his rode,
> No Canker, nor the loathsome toad.
>
> (ll. 26–8)

But this setting is also marked by a lack of detail. The trees of the opening lines are all obvious properties for this drama, and the adjectives they are given are general ones (fair, lofty, sturdy). Similarly, Randolph's serpent is predictably speckled and his snake venomous. But this serpent/snake is mentioned as absent, to indicate that the setting is Eden before the Fall.

Moreover, in 'A Pastoral Courtship' place exists, in the poem's fiction, to serve humankind. This is a microcosmic version of the Ptolemaic universe, the idea being similar to Jonson's fish in 'To Penshurst', which rejoice in serving man. So here the trees are seen as if 'all ambitious . . . to be/Mine and my Phyllis canopie!' and the flowers of the third verse paragraph have the same function: 'These for thee/Were meant a bed.' This subordination of Nature to Man later becomes a strategic merging of the two, whereby the woman is seen as the extension of Nature:

> the spring remains
> In the fair violets of thy veins:
> And that it is a summers day,
> Ripe Cherries in thy lips display.
> And when for Autumn I would seek,
> 'Tis in the Apples of thy cheek.

And again

> Come let me touch those breasts, that swell
> Like two faire mountains, and may well
> Be stil'd the Alpes
>
> ('A Pastoral Courtship', ll. 9–10, 21–2, 51–6, 65–7)

This involves a strategy by which Nature's co-operation is indicated and then, by way of the natural epithets, it is indicated that the woman, being now natural, should be also co-operative:

> These for thee
> Were meant a bed, and thou for me.
>
> (ll. 21–2)

In addition, however, the displacement which substitutes mountains for breasts and apples for cheeks allows for another displacement, this time of the morality of seduction, for who questions a person's right to scale a mountain or eat an apple?

What this means in the context of the poetry of place becomes clearer in another erotic poem of about the same time (the 1630s), Thomas Carew's 'A Rapture'. The title incorporates two of the poem's chief themes, suggesting both the ecstatic state of the erotically aroused poet-figure and the imagined possession of the woman by this male figure.[20] (There are, incidentally, moments when a reader is reminded, disconcertingly, of Volpone's attempt to seduce/rape Celia.) Both elements are there in the opening couplet:

> I will enjoy thee now my Celia, come
> And flye with me to Loves Elizium.

The setting, like Randolph's, is one of generalized natural co-operation:

> a bed
> Of Roses, and fresh Myrtles, shall be spread
> Under the cooler shade of Cypresse groves:
> Our pillowes, of the downe of Venus Doves.
>
> ('A Rapture', ll. 35–8)

The last line quoted is the giveaway, where fantasy has replaced any pretence of actual place. And, as in Randolph, what place there is is secure:

> There, no rude sounds shake us with sudden starts,
> No jealous eares, when we unrip our hearts
> Sucke our discourse in, no observing spies
> This blush, that glance traduce.
>
> (ll. 99–102)

But Carew takes further than Randolph the merging of the natural with the human, and in 'A Rapture' the activity of the bee is made a metaphor of sexual activity:

> So I will rifle all the sweets that dwell
> In my delicious Paradise, and swell
> My bagge with honey, drawne forth by the power
> Of fervent kisses, from each spicie flower.
> I'le seize the Rose-buds in their perfum'd bed.
>
> (ll. 59–63)

Here again both of the title's main implications are enacted. The location is the woman's body as paradise, and the language is that of aggressive seduction, verging on rape. But the idea of the woman's body as paradise (not in itself particularly unusual) sums up a strategy by which the formal place of the poem ('Loves Elizium') has shifted to become the body of the woman herself, a *place* where the poet-figure's 'tall Pine, shall in the Cyprian straight/Ride safe at Anchor, and unlade her fraight' (ll. 85–6).

But Carew is a much finer poet than Randolph, and his handling of place in 'A Rapture' is more complex. On the one hand, as we have seen, he produces a sequence in which the place of the poem gradually becomes conterminous with the woman's body, and this undermines the importance of the formal setting, while allowing for the compliment that the woman is indeed equivalent to Elizium or Eden:

> thee that art my Paradise.
> Thou art my all.
> ('A Pastoral Courtship', ll. 50–1)

But when Carew writes of the security of the setting, in the passage which begins 'There, no rude sounds . . .' (l. 99), his references are not to snakes and spiders but to a world of spies, rivals, and bribed chamber-maids, the world, in fact, of Donne's elegies. This, in turn, reminds us of the figure of honour at the poem's beginning and end, a figure which is seen as a massive obstacle to be evaded or overcome. 'A Rapture' both seeks to use Edenic place as fantasy and is confronted by other places which will not allow themselves to be finally banished, so that the poem ends with an impatient, perhaps embittered question:

> Then tell me why
> This Goblin Honour which the world adores,
> Should make men Atheists, and not women Whores.

I do not mean by this that 'A Rapture' is a consciously critical poem, but it is disturbing and revealing in ways foreign to Randolph because Carew has found it impossible to create an undisturbed fantasy of place. His Eden is not truly prelapsarian, being troubled by memories of other places.

Libertine poems such as the two just discussed are clearly a long way away from Jonsonian country-house poetry. But just as style can transform the literal house into an embodiment of ideals, and as it can invent Edenic settings for imagined copulation, it can, rather strangely, draw country house and Edenism into a single poem, as it does with Edmund Waller. Waller has two poems called 'At Penshurst' and they show how civilization can become elegant triviality.

For Jonson, Penshurst was a country house where humane values were expressed both through the symbolism of the architecture and the behaviour of the Sidneys. However we regard the value system which underlies these expressions, there is no doubt that they are seen by the poet as humanly desirable, conducive to harmony and stability. When, however, Waller places two poems at Penshurst all the setting suggests to him is a tamed version of Randolph's Eden. Interestingly, while Jonson sees the tree planted for the birth of Philip Sidney as memorial of 'his great birth, where all the muses met' ('To Penshurst' l. 14), Waller is both more specific and more restrictive. So, in 'While in the park I sing', (c. 1635) we have:

>   why dost thou falsely feign
> Thyself a Sidney? from which noble strain
> He sprung, that could so far exalt the name
> Of love, and warm our nation with his flame;
> That all we can of love, or high desire,
> Seems but the smoke of amorous Sidney's fire.

Sidney is mentioned again in Waller's other 'At Penshurst' (c. 1635) poem ('Had Sacharissa lived when mortals made') where the stars said to have shone at his birth are seen as 'The monument and pledge of humble love'. Rather than symbol of a way of life, Sidney is here only a symbol of a type of lover. Further, generalizations have replaced Jonson's specificity. Instead of a detailed sense of place giving substance and solidarity to a system of behaviour and values felt to be conducive to a full and harmonious life, there is only place as something generalized so as to allow for formalized love-complaints. Oddly, although Waller sets these complaints in what is formally a real place, he actually creates a setting which is more fantastic than those of Carew and Randolph. Thus he begins one of these poems with a speculation:

> Had Sacharissa lived when mortals made
> Choice of their deities, this sacred shade
> Had held an altar to her power.

and goes on to offer an elegant version of the idea of Nature's subservience to mankind:

> If she sit down, with tops all towards her bowed,
> They round about her into arbors crowd;
> Like some well-marshalled and obsequious band.

But while Carew was unable to banish worlds beyond his imagined Elizium, and while Randolph has at least a feeling for sexual urges, Waller can offer only a muted whimper:

> His humble love whose hope shall ne'er rise higher,
> Than for a pardon that he dares admire.

Carew has the male arrogance to treat the female body as a natural object, to be rifled if at all possible, and he presents this by seeing the body as only equivalent to the natural phenomena found in the setting. Waller, however, finishes up with his poet-figure in a position which merges him with the plants which bow and organize themselves in obeisance to Sacharissa.

It is not, however, really accurate to suggest that Waller is creating a simple fantasy, for what emerges from these poems is place used for the lightly disguised presentation of a specific situation in the real world. Waller, that is, is writing to Dorothy Spencer, Countess of Sunderland,

and decorum means that he cannot approach her as if she were Carew's Celia or Randolph's Phyllis. This is not so much a matter of the woman being real or imagined as of the poets' sense of themselves and their roles. Carew and Randolph project poet-figures which dominate, even violate, while Waller presents a seventeenth-century version of poet-lover as courtly worm, a version which happens to reflect fairly accurately Waller's position in relation to the court. Further, if this position involves taming the erotic impulse, it also means that Jonson's view of the poet as free to comment widely upon society and social behaviour has largely gone. With it has vanished the concern with the country house as a significant social organism.

Neither Randolph nor Waller uses place to articulate a direct view of social or moral issues, although the former does offer superficial logic in relation to moral questions and the latter creates poems which are revealing in relation to the poet's social role. But I have suggested that Carew's 'A Rapture' does have, possibly unconsciously, a sense of other places which puts some pressure upon his attempt to create a location which is free of the constraints which define normal life. To that extent 'A Rapture' is the richest of these poems, but its richness does not extend to a sense of place as something both detailed and national, as in *Poly-Olbion*, or as rooted in a particular locale, as in 'To Penshurst'. To see how such a feeling for place develops from Drayton and Jonson we need to turn to Robert Herrick and to Carew's country-house poems.

Pastoral often seems a city-dweller's version of country,[21] and Herrick was more urban than rural so far as temperament went. But there were aspects of life in Devon which he came to appreciate and his verse provides both pastoralism and native rural detail, together with a persistent moral element and a strong awareness of classical values. Herrick is often seen with more sentimentality than accuracy, and it is important to note that he is a poet with a considerable number of masks and a breadth of technical competence, so that deciding what the poet believed or most valued is not as simple as selections in anthologies often hint. But one of his poses involves the traditional idea of country as retreat. So, in 'A Country life: To his Brother, Master Thomas Herrick', we read:

> Nor are thy daily and devout affaires
>   Attended with those desp'rate cares,
> Th'industrious Merchant has; who for to find
>   Gold, runneth to the Western Inde,
> And back again, (tortur'd with fears) doth fly,
>   Untaught, to suffer Poverty.
>   (ll. 63–8)

Such 'desp'rate cares' are contrasted with 'The Countries sweet simplicity' where Thomas Herrick has retired 'To grow the sooner innocent' and where he has learnt, we are told, to 'keep one Centre' and 'to confine desires' (ll. 4, 6, 15, 16).

But although country is seen as the proper setting to learn and to prac-
tise the Horatian values of moderation, and although the poem does contain
some detail ('Making thy peace with heav'n, for some late fault,/With
Holy-meale, and spirting-salt', ll. 59–60), the effect of the whole is of an
exercise rather than of the result of experience. There is little sense of
specific place, while the style generalizes and prettifies, with its 'Damaskt
medowes' and 'Purling springs', with its 'brisk Mouse' and 'green-ey'd
Kitling' (ll. 43, 45, 124, 123). Also, there is something glib about the way
in which the moral tags are slotted into the argument:

> Thus let thy Rurall Sanctuary be
>   Elizium to thy wife and thee;
> There to disport your selves with golden measure:
>   For seldome use commends the pleasure.
>
> ('A Country Life', ll. 137–40)

In fact, Herrick's feeling for the country is picturesque rather than in-
ward, and he has a constant urge to change the natural into the tidied pas-
toral. Thus 'The Hock-Cart' has such detail as 'Flailes . . . Fanes . . . Fatts',
but it also has 'Rurall Younglings' and 'frollick boyes' (ll. 40, 16, 43), while
Herrick's love of melody for itself seemingly weakens the impact of an
important perception in this poem, the awareness that rural life, for the
farm worker, is basically hard, a life of oppression sweetened by such fes-
tivals as harvest home only because it is in the interest of masters to soften
the realities on select occasions:

> And, you must know, your Lords word's true,
> Feed him ye must, whose food fils you.
> And that this pleasure is like raine,
> Not sent ye for to drowne your paine,
> But for to make it spring againe.
>
> (ll. 51–5)

Yet 'The Hock-cart' is a success of a type rare in Herrick, for here the
decorative surface works ironically. The festivities are articulated, as also
in 'Corinna's going a Maying', in what may seem a lightweight celebration
of the rural, but here with awareness of underlying realities.

Herrick is often spoken of as if he were the voice of a particular part
of England. But this can only be seriously maintained at the biographical
level, for Herrick generalizes his country to the point where it becomes
representative of the countryside at large. In Herrick, country can become
as much an idea as a location and in this he resembles Vaughan, who trans-
lates specific topography into a spiritual landscape. Herrick is not a poet
of place in the way in which John Clare was to be, nor, despite his use of
town/country antitheses, does he share Jonson's feeling that a particular
location may embody an important alternative to what is seen as a pre-
vailing way of life. In fact, Herrick usually simply transfers Horatian values
to a generalized English landscape which he presents in verbal terms that

tidy actuality. As a result his poems of place usually lack tension, 'The Hock-cart' being an honourable exception.

There are some similarities between Herrick's poems of place and Carew's two country-house poems, 'To Saxham' and 'To my friend G.N. from Wrest' (*Poems*, 1640), but Carew offers an account which is finally more substantial than Herrick's, perhaps because he is working with specifics, even though Jonson is also very much in mind. 'To my friend G.N. . . .' is a verse epistle to a particular person (of whom we know nothing), beginning with direct address –

> I Breathe (sweet Ghib:) the temperate ayre of Wrest
> Where I no more with raging stormes opprest,
> Weare the cold nights out by the bankes of Tweed

– and ending in a similar way:

>   Thus I enjoy my selfe, and taste the fruit
> Of this blest Peace, whilst toyl'd in the pursuit
> Of Bucks, and Stags, th'embleme of warre, you strive
> To keepe the memory of our Armes alive.
>
> (ll. 1–3; 107–10)

Somewhat allusively, Carew indicates an occasion, his return from the expedition to Berwick against the Scots in May/June 1639, and this occasion provides him with contrasts of climate and life style. The peace and warmth of Wrest are set against the conflict with the Scots and the inhospitable bleakness of 'the bankes of Tweed', and it is in terms of these located contrasts that Carew praises the house and its owners.

His terms of praise are clearly Jonsonian – 'pure and uncompounded beauties', 'usefull comelinesse', 'a house for hospitalitie' ('To my friend G.N. . . .' ll. 19, 20, 24) – and Carew also uses Jonson's architectural contrast between 'prouder Piles' and the 'reall use' shown at Wrest (ll. 53, 55). For Carew, as for Jonson, place is important in its manifestation and nourishing of humane behaviour. In pastoral and in Herrick there tends to be a glib suggestion that country is almost inevitably beneficial, and although Jonson and Carew do convey something of this attitude, they have far more to say about how the natural and the human interact. Both poets work inwards, from accounts of setting to the buildings themselves and then to the owners. According to Carew, the natural setting of Wrest serves humanity ('farre more genuine sweetes refresh the sense', l. 18) and the house itself has a similar function – 'But built a house for hospitalitie' (l. 24).

Because of its epistolary form and because of the contrasts with which he works 'To my friend G.N. . . .' has the strength of the particular. It does not pretend to be a microcosm of the country at large, either in the sense of country-as-countryside or of country-as-state. In Carew's country-house poems there is a strong feeling for peace, which, in 'To Saxham', seems under threat. So he imagines the house at winter time, with the weather cutting a visitor off from 'That beautie which without dore lyes'.

But the result is the realization that 'thou within thy gate,/Art of thy selfe so delicate; . . . As neither from, nor to thy store/Winter takes ought, or Spring addes more' (ll. 2, 5–10). Like Wrest, Saxham is a centre of generosity, ungrudging and outward looking, but in both poems Carew is aware of other situations, and that which is valued is valued at least partly because it is not seen as the norm. And, of course, in the socio-political context of the 1630s the stability of such houses could be seen as a desirable but threatened aspect of an unhappy society.

Carew is a conscious stylist and, as a result, whatever his intentions may have been, his country-house poems are very clearly artefacts, rather than essays in mimesis. But, unlike Herrick's, Carew's constructs have discernible roots in particular actualities and they therefore function rather as Jonson's 'To Penshurst' does. That is, the poems create their own imagined worlds, which bear on actuality, offer commentaries on it, but do not attempt to reproduce it. Rather, the poems provide a version of human life which is to be seen as desirable, and perhaps attainable, but not as a settled achievement. It may have been an error for Jonson and Carew to focus upon the country house as offering, when artistically interpreted, the best hope for social harmony, but that does not mean that what they offer is complacent.[22]

Jonson and Carew are both, we have seen, aware that the houses which they praise stand in opposition to tendencies which the poets see as regrettable, and both men are clear about those tendencies, identifying them with extravagance. It would be possible to extrapolate from the type of building which these poets attack and to identify the undesirable with the showy building and rebuilding which often accompanied the arrival of the 'new men', going on to link this with a conservative reading of socio-economic forces. However blind a reader may feel (with the benefit of hindsight) such responses to be, they are both clear and consistent. But when we look at the last great country-house poem of the century, Marvell's 'Upon Appleton House' (c. 1652), we find ourselves contemplating something altogether stranger and more disturbing.

The headnote for this poem in E. S. Donno's edition of Marvell's verse tells us something of the complex of traditional materials which bears upon it, referring a reader to classical sources, native developments, and to 'Elements of other genres . . . and numerous topoi.'[23] A number of couplets early in the poem, taken in isolation, strike a familiar note:

> Within this sober frame expect
> Work of no foreign architect . . .
> But all things are composed here
> Like Nature, orderly and near . . .
> Humility alone designs
> Those short but admirable lines . . . .
> ('Upon Appleton House', ll. 1–2, 25–6, 41–2;)

But 'Upon Appleton House' is something more than a synthesis of traditional elements, and its unique quality is, I think, tied up with what happens in this poem to the idea of alternative ways of life. Characteristically, Marvell thinks in binary terms. For him, almost any statement seems to require its opposite. But in 'Upon Appleton House' the opposites go to create a world in which little is as it seems, little stays still under the observer's eye. Donno properly speaks of country-house poems as 'designed to describe and praise a house, a family and a way of life', and Marvell's poem may well be designed (in the sense of intended) to do just this, but when we ask ourselves exactly what is praised in the poem as a whole, there is difficulty in finding clear answers. This is partly because Marvell uses an apparently discursive structure:

> While with slow steps we these survey, . . .
> We opportunely may relate
> The progress of this house's fate.

and

> And now to the abyss I pass
> Of that unfathomable grass.
>
> (ll. 81, 83–4, 369–70)

It is also because of the constant shifts of focus and scale, which appear in the poem from its beginning and which the poet himself comments on when he notes 'No scene that turns with engines strange/Does oftener than these meadows change' (ll. 385–6). Then there is the difficulty created by Marvell's way with metaphor, through which things usually held to be distinct are associated. So flowers are seen in military terms, with teasing word-play:

> Then flowers their drowsy eyelids raise,
> Their silken ensigns each displays,
> And dries its pan yet dank with dew,
> And fills its flask with odours new.
>
> (ll. 293–6)

At almost the centre-point of the poem we come to what seems to be its key question. At the end of a stanza which takes the garden at Appleton and expands it to include the whole kingdom ('Oh thou, that dear and happy isle/The garden of the world ere while') the poet-figure asks

> What luckless apple did we taste,
> To make us mortal, and thee waste?

The next stanza adds:

> Unhappy! shall we never more
> That sweet militia restore,

When gardens only had their towers,
And all the garrisons were flowers.

                              (ll. 321–2, 327–32)

Jonson's Penshurst and Carew's Wrest can be seen as versions of paradises
preserved within fallen worlds, but Marvell seems unable to offer this kind
of solution to his own question, for in 'Upon Appleton House' the enemy
is as much within as without. Not only is the poem's topography change-
able and hence deceptive, but Fairfax himself is presented with something
of the tension found in Marvell's famous account of Cromwell in 'An
Horatian Ode', and although Maria Fairfax is eulogized the eulogy scarcely
provides a solution. Maria is given the power of the lady of so many erotic
lyrics:

    'Tis she that to these gardens gave
    That wondrous beauty which they have,

and her quality is explicitly associated with her education at Appleton:

    This 'tis to have been from the first
    In a domestic heaven nursed.
                              (ll. 689–90, 721–2)

Here, in the poem's closing stanzas, Marvell offers some positives. Maria
Fairfax is a model to other virgins and her virginity will at some point in
the future be taken 'for some universal good' (l. 741). Meanwhile, in emu-
lation of her, the grounds of Appleton House shall stand as ideals:

    That, as all virgins she precedes,
    So you all woods, streams, gardens, meads.

Then Appleton becomes an explicit microcosm, a 'lesser world' which fig-
ures 'heaven's centre, Nature's lap,/And paradise's only map'. But the
whole feeling of the poem is that paradise is elsewhere. In the now of the
poem's world things are strangely inverted and disturbing, and we end not
with assertion but with a withdrawal:

    How tortoise-like, but not so slow,
    These rational amphibii go!
    Let's in: for the dark hemisphere
    Does now like one of them appear.
                              (ll. 751–2, 765, 767–8, 773–6)

   In so far as Marvell has drawn together a body of linked traditions it
is, finally, to suggest that they can no longer, or not now, operate effi-
caciously. For Jonson the example of Penshurst could, through art, be
made to seem a realizable ideal: for Marvell Appleton, at best, can only

remind us of what the ideal may once have been. Jonson focuses upon a particular place and gives it solidarity, but when Marvell contemplates such a place it insists on shifting with 'engines strange'. But this is scarcely surprising when one remembers how strange were the engines that were changing English society in the mid-century.

Denham and Cotton; city and country

John Denham's 'Cooper's Hill' provides another commentary on seventeenth-century instability, not only because of its treatment of theme but also because of its formal properties. Denham is not writing a pure poem of place, but uses topography as the focus for a discussion of relationships between king and people. He seeks a heightened conversational style and develops the couplet towards the smoothness and balance of Augustan verse:

> O could I flow like thee, and make thy stream
> My great example, as it is my theme!
> Though deep, yet clear, though gentle, yet not dull,
> Strong without rage, without ore-flowing full.[24]

But 'Cooper's Hill' involves difficult questions of text. Brendan O Hehir prints four different versions of the poem, dating the earliest as 1641 and the latest 1668, and comparisons between the different versions make it clear that variants are not just the result of the poet's search for the most appropriate phrasing, but also represent alterations in Denham's analysis of his material. These alterations may, of course, indicate deep shifts in Denham's thinking or judicious reactions to changing socio-political conditions in the period between 1641 and 1668; and the difficulty of writing a poem about the relationship between rulers and the ruled in the mid-century is clear when we recall that 1641 saw the debate on the Grand Remonstrance, the execution of Strafford, and the abolition of the Star Chamber, while by 1668 Charles II had been on the throne for some eight years. A full discussion of 'Cooper's Hill', therefore, would involve treating it as several poems rather than one, a situation reminiscent of *Piers Plowman*. But the 1668 version of the poem can at least serve as representative of a late form of Denham's thinking.

In all its versions 'Cooper's Hill' is a poem responding to crisis, and as such can be linked with 'Upon Appleton House'. Marvell's poem, through its title, suggests the country-house tradition, and, like 'To Penshurst', presents a commentary which involves mediation between the past and the present, together with a dialogue between the house itself and its setting, both immediate and national. Denham, however, although his poem is

concerned with buildings among other things, has a title which indicates
that the natural feature, the hill itself, is to be his focus, rather than any
man-made object, while his opening hints that the poet may, fictionally,
establish himself on the hill as his vantage point:

> Sure there are Poets which did never dream
> Upon Parnassus.

This hint is misleading, in that 'Cooper's Hill' is itself an object of con-
templation, but it is accurate in indicating the scope of the poet's survey.
Whereas Jonson and Carew in their country-house poems work centripe-
tally, Denham uses Cooper's Hill more as a perspective point and scans the
scene as a landscape. Moreover, the landscape of his poem is both geo-
graphical and conceptual:

> By taking wing from thy auspicious height,
> Through untrac't ways, and aery paths I fly,
> More boundless in my Fancy than my eie.
> (ll. 10–12)

In 'To Penshurst' or 'To Saxham' the poet's eye steadily contemplates a
single suggestive object , while in 'Upon Appleton House' the survey, more
quizzical and discontinuous than with Jonson or Carew, yet remains fo-
cused upon the single place. In Denham's poem, however, the eye is more
active, ranging freely across the physical and mental landscape, relating
distinct things in a way which anticipates Coleridge's plastic imagination[25]:

> My eye, which swift as thought contracts the space
> That lies between.
> (ll. 13–14)

Denham is concerned to give depth and meaning to his landscape. He be-
gins by associating Cooper's Hill with Parnassus, and throughout he in-
cludes classical allusions, so that Charles and Henrietta are seen as Mars and
Venus, Philippa of Hainault is Bellona, and the Thames transcends Eri-
danus (ll. 40, 79, 193). Clearly, this is an attempt to indicate that Denham
sees his material as of major importance, and it helps create that sense of
depth in time which was mentioned earlier as a feature of 'Upon Appleton
House'. This aspect of 'Cooper's Hill' is further underlined by the inclusion
of English history. Thus the Philippa/Bellona link comes in an extended
survey of native kings, a survey which, exemplifying Denham's method,
rises from contemplation of Windsor as a place within his landscape.

The ranging aspect of Denham's eye, when associated with the historical
perspective just mentioned, is reminiscent of *Poly-Olbion*. Penshurst and
Wrest may be offered as metonymies of what England might ideally be,
but Denham's images of the swift contracting eye, of the hunt and of riv-
ers, indicate a different strategy and a more dynamic one. Also, while the

scope of Denham's poem suggests Drayton, there is the important difference that the latter's reference point is the idea of England as a beloved geographical and historical entity, while Denham's is the specific landscape involving the hill itself. This topography is simultaneously a geographical locus and a context for discourse.

For Denham topography is such a context in two main and overlapping ways. Firstly, the geographical locus is the context for discourse in a passage such as the selective survey of English monarchy which begins at line 65:

> Not to look back so far, to whom this Isle
> Owes the first Glory of so brave a pile.

Interestingly, the passage has its roots in the consideration of Windsor as place and is introduced as an essay on the history of the castle. This becomes a critical account of history, and in that sense the place acts as a focus for the discussion. Beyond this, it is important to note that Denham presents English monarchy as in the classical heroic tradition: the 'Gods great Mother . . . cannot boast . . . More Hero's than can Windsor' (ll. 61–3). As we absorb the poet's account of kingship, and particularly the passage on Henry VIII, it becomes clear that this is more than decoration or chauvinism. It is a way of stressing the importance of the socio-political issues.

But at the same time as Windsor provides Denham with a geographical focus, a location for his account of kingship, it offers him a metaphor of harmonious social relationships. This is made clear some twenty lines before that account begins. Windsor is first named at line 39:

> Windsor the next (where Mars and Venus dwells,
> Beauty with strength) above the Valley swells
> Into my eye, and doth it self present
> With such an easie and unforc't ascent.

The prospect offers 'such a Rise, as doth at once invite/A pleasure, and a reverence from the sight', and it is to be read as 'Thy mighty Masters Embleme, in whose face/Sate meekness, heightened with Majestick Grace'. Moreover, the location is natural: the site has been 'Markt out for such a use, as if 'twere meant/T'invite the builder, and his choice prevent' (ll. 34–56). The topography images the nature of the King and implies the harmony of the contented kingdom.

Such deployment of topography as metaphor is hardly surprising in a century which regards nature as a book to be read for significance, and Denham's usage can be connected with such diverse responses as Lovelace's interest in ants and grasshoppers as insects which have lessons to teach mankind and the convention in love lyric by which flowers and trees are animated by the mistress. But what is striking in the case of 'Cooper's Hill' is Denham's effort to make the treatment of topography-as-metaphor consistent with topography as something observed and yet reflective of the complexity of his material. For although there is clearly in 'Cooper's Hill' the iconography of flattery – in, for example, the equation of Charles and Henrietta with Mars and Venus,[26] and in the association of the Stuarts with the very origins of the State – Denham's poem is not only a panegyric, and its way of being more involves analytic deployment of topography as metaphor.

It is clear throughout the poem that Denham wants there to be a critical perspective. This is evident when he introduces a town/country contrast, in the discussion of the religious policy of Henry VIII (which he explicitly links with the contemporary situation) and in the warnings of the perils of greatness (a lesson typically deduced from the natural world). Further, the account of Henry is complex in that it moves between criticism of his motives and of the complacency of Tudor monastic life. The complexity is developed in the final section of the poem in the images of hunting and river.

The long passage about hunting is too elaborate and tricky to analyse fully here.[27] It is consistent with Denham's use of the literal that the passage begins as an observation rooted in topography. The 'spacious plain' (l. 223) is a meeting-place for deer and there, the poet says, he has seen the King come to hunt. This leads naturally to the account of hunting, but it is immediately clear that this is no simple description. The deer have been 'read' even before the account really begins, for they 'shew how soon/Great things are made, but sooner are undone' (ll. 239–40). Further, there is complexity inherent in the situation itself. In so far as the hunt is led by the King (who finally kills the stag) we expect the account to emphasize the King's greatness, but the stag is itself a common symbol of royalty and its (alleged) heroic virtues, and the stag is explicitly presented as hero ('Cooper's Hill' l. 313f).

The problem, then, is what the stag represents here. Obviously, so long as the King in the account represents the actual King (and it would be lunatic to suggest anything else) the stag cannot, at least in any obvious sense. So what is meant by the stag, with its curious mixture of bravery and cowardice, evasiveness and force? Clearly, it is a challenging presence, and metaphorically must relate to something which resists the King before finally offering itself to be killed by him, if only when no other resource offers itself. All I can suggest here is that Denham is articulating his sense of tensions within the State. If so, the response is psychologically precise even though the symbol is itself finally enigmatic, in that it could indicate some respect on the poet's part for oppositional elements or even something along the lines of Cleveland's distressed use of the idea of the King's two bodies (in 'The King's Disguise'). It is possible that, as Denham revised his poem, the hunt metaphor proved too rich for clarity, or that its implications seemed best kept covert, or that the poet lacked the ability to work out those implications fully. What is most important, however, is that this instance of topography as metaphor is almost Marvellian in its figuring of the difficulties of the conflicts of the mid-century.

Just how enigmatic Denham's hunt is can be seen at its end, and with its teasing application. Killed by the King, the stag is 'glad to dy./Proud of the wound'. At one level this is so because it has died by the royal hand. But its own blood is a 'Purple floud', the imperial colour, and although the poet uses the terms 'innocent' and 'happy' for this hunt, he contrasts it with another which took place 'of old, but in the self-same place'. Here Denham's usual strategy of uniting place and time leads him to juxtapose the Charles-hunt with an earlier metaphorical one where 'Fair liberty pursu'd, and meant a Prey/To lawless power, here turn'd, and stood at bay', this being the occasion of Magna Charta:

> Here was that Charter seal'd, wherein the Crown
> All marks of Arbitrary power lays down.
>
> (l. 325f)

The echoes and potential significance of this passage are almost without end. It can be read as offering a flattering contrast (as the latter hunt being 'more Innocent, and happy' might suggest) but it is difficult to avoid feeling some connection between the stag of the Magna Charta hunt, which is explicitly 'Fair liberty pursu'd', and that of the Caroline occasion, and the parallel is also disturbingly incomplete. For whereas the Charta hunt ends in compromise, the Caroline finishes with the stag's death. And, of course, even the comparatives of l. 323 ('More Innocent, and happy') can be interpreted in more than one way.

But the final movement of 'Cooper's Hill' suggests that Denham wants his dual hunts to be read as caution rather than as threat or cyclic history. The caution emerges as a theory of balance between royal power and liberty. History's lesson is that

> Kings, by grasping more than they could hold,
> First made their Subjects by oppression bold:
> And popular sway, by forcing Kings to give
> More than was fit for Subjects to receive,
> Ran to the same extreams.

This leads to Denham's last sustained image, which is a return to the river and again a topographical metaphor. Typically and interestingly the image works with more power than specificity. The force is clear:

> Stronger, and fiercer by restraint he roars,
> And knows no bound, but makes his power his shores.
>
> (ll. 343–7; 357–8)

This is the final couplet, and the concept of power which knows no restraint but itself is a disturbing one. It is also, however, applicable either to 'Fair Liberty' or to kingly power, for both can be seen as operating either with moderation or to excess.

When, early in his poem, Denham introduced Windsor, he did so by way of a contrast between town and country. The former is seen as the locus of 'luxury and wealth', a place where 'they run/Some to undo, and some to be undone', and it is imaged as 'a mist' and 'a darker cloud'. By contrast, the 'happiness of sweet, retir'd content!/To be at once secure, and innocent' (ll. 31–2, 26, 28, 37–8) leads to discussion of the castle and Denham's adjectives are those of the Horatian tradition. Strictly speaking, this has more to do with the modest home of which Horace speaks and which we find also in Herrick, than with the country houses of Jonson and Carew (although Penshurst is relatively modest); and although their poems emphasize similar moral virtues as those inherent in country they are concerned to make it clear that the houses of which they write are centres of civilization. Jonson's Penshurst, in fact, is an exemplum of what a civilized state should be, and the poet sees himself as a visitor to the house. Neither he nor Carew sees himself as representative of the country, and although Herrick is in a position to write as such he rarely escapes from his love of mythologizing and prettifying country. Charles Cotton has a more convincing voice.

In 'To my Friend, Mr John Anderson From the Country' Cotton does not so much argue for the moral superiority of country and its values as seek to counter the claims of the city to a higher quality of life. His poem is basically a listing of comparisons. Town is characterized by 'furious men of War', 'bawling Duns' and 'unwholesome dames', whereas country has 'excelling ale', women who are 'All full and plump without, and warm within', and 'honest Hobinol and Clout'. The values suggested by Cotton's listing are products of generosity (the beer's strength, the women's willingness) and the life style implied is of robust satisfaction of appetite. There is little here of Jonsonian civilization or of the quiet retirement of which Denham speaks. Cotton writes with affection for the life he describes and seems to enjoy the detail:

> . . . many another stiff and sturdy lout
>> That play at wasters,
> Shoe the wild mare, and lick the board.
>> ('To my Friend Mr John Anderson from the County')[28]

But it should be added that the poem is an attractive and friendly transformation of country in clearly literary terms. The comparison between town and country is formally presented and in it the latter is seen in terms of modified pastoral (Hobinol and Clout) with sex having the simplicity of libertine versions of the Golden Age.

What is unusual about Cotton's country poems is that his centre does really seem to be there. He is affectionate about his part of the kingdom and feels little need to make a case for it along moral lines. When, in another epistle, 'A Journey into the Peak. To Sir Aston Cokin', he uses a contrast between the coldness of the Peak and the warmth of Cokayne's house, Pooley Hall in Warwickshire, he produces an interesting version of a theme which had attracted Carew. Carew uses a heat/coldness contrast to stress the moral worth of Wrest, while Cotton similarly uses the 'comfortable heat' of Pooley's setting as locus of the 'honest, free delights' and 'piety . . . peace . . . love' which he associates with Cokayne's house. The

poet–figure is attracted by all this and ends his poem by promising another
visit:

> But once again, dear Sir, I mean to come,
> And thankful be, as well as troublesome.

'A Journey into the Peak' is not a town-and-country poem, but a com-
parison of two types of country, and the fundamental contrast offered be-
tween Derbyshire and Warwickshire could easily have involved a negative
response to the former, 'this frozen clime', 'this our frozen zone'. But
Cotton's affection comes through in his wit and humour. The latter is di-
rected at himself –

> in my veins, did nought but crystal dwell,
> Each hair was frozen to an icicle

– and his mistress:

> My mistress looking back, to bid good night,
> Was metamorphos'd like the Sodomite.
>
> (ll. 5–6; 11–12)

The comedy of Cotton's account both communicates affection for the
Peaks and serves to define the tone of the whole poem, in that it prevents
the praise of Cokayne's way of life from seeming serious in the manner
of Jonson and Carew. That way of life remains satisfying and attractive,
but in Cotton's poem it scarcely seems part of a moral system.

But it is the 'Epistle to John Bradshaw, Esq.' that Cotton's feeling
for his own region is most strongly conveyed. Like 'A Journey into the
Peak' it is a departure poem, or a poem of return home, and it describes
the journey back to the Peaks. In the last paragraph the poet speaks of
himself again at home, using his typical self-mockery:

> And now I'm here set down again in peace,
> After my troubles, business, voyages,
> The same dull Northern clod I was before.
>
> (ll. 79–81)

He goes on to develop the idea of being unchanged:

> Just the same sot I was e'er I remov'd;
> Nor by my travel, nor the Court improv'd;
> The same old-fashion'd Squire, no whit refin'd.
>
> (ll. 85–7)

The self-mockery takes the edge off what could have seemed boorish com-
placency, while the feeling for the permanence of his country life both fur-
ther defines his own unchangingness and pins it down to a specified locale:

My river still though the same channel glides,
Clear from the tumult, salt and dirt of tides,
And my poor Fishing-house, my seat's best grace
Stands firm and faithful in the selfsame place
I left it four months since.

(ll. 98–102)

Cotton is perhaps the only poet of the century who conveys this feeling
for specific rural place. Drayton has something of it, but his response is
more dispersed than Cotton's, and although Cotton has not the same stress
as Jonson upon the values of the particular as representative of what should
be generally possible, he does associate a specific feeling for a particular
country with generosity and friendship. His is a roughened version of the
Horatian ideal and it comes across as a way of life rather than as a code
for living. It involves a turning away from the great affairs of state and the
retreat which is Cotton's Peaks suggests withdrawal from the national con-
cerns of the mid-century, but Cotton's achievement is to prove on the
pulses the possibility of modest satisfaction.

But although Cotton's sense of country feels both genuine and attract-
ive, it remains true that his preference for country can be assimilated, at
least partly, to the literary traditions of the Horatian and the pastoral. The
strength of these traditions in the seventeenth century is not, however,
merely a matter of literary fashion. At times, most notably in Jonson, it
is an aspect of the search for a system of ethics for a whole society, while
it can also be seen as significant in the light of social and political concerns
of the century and as a reflection of the strong rural and provincial tradi-
tions of England. When Jonson locates a sustained discussion of the good
life he is trying to say something about the conditions of living which may
be conducive to social and moral responsibility, and he is, both in 'To
Penshurst' and 'To Sir Robert Wroth', quite clearly aware that this involves
recognition of conditions which are not conducive to such responsibility.
When Cotton locates satisfaction in his Peak home or at Pooley Hall he is
turning away from the idea that such satisfaction can be found in towns
and great affairs. Both men are responding as much to social conditions
as to literary traditions.

Those poems which we have looked at so far that are concerned with
the matter of town and country have all expressed preference for the latter,
and it is axiomatic throughout the century that town life is inferior. But
this is an axiom that should be treated with caution, since it is only part
of the story. There is, for instance, the qualification which Herrick some-
times expresses, while one of the merits of Cotton's version is that his ac-
counts have the detail to suggest the limitations of the rural. Moreover,
poetic accounts of country should not be used in isolation and we should
not assume that attitudes to town and country stay the same throughout
the century.

In 'To Sir Robert Wroth', Ben Jonson provides a powerful embodiment
of the idea of the inferiority of the town. Wroth is admirable because he,
'though so near the city, and the court', is 'ta'en with neither's vice, nor

sport' (ll. 3–4). These are places of extravagance and frenetic activity, of no stability and no innocence, where some 'boast it as his merit,/To blow up orphans, widows, and their states', and where masses 'of wretched wealth' are 'Purchased by rapine' (ll. 78–9, 81–2). Jonson's satire here has the power of his best dramatic writing, but although Jonson is consistently and brilliantly critical of urban life this is not the whole story. Not only does he frequently praise the moral potential and achievements of individuals based at court, but he contemplates the courtly as embodiment of the good life. Of course, it would be absurd to identify court with town, but court none the less is urban rather than rural. Moreover, Jonson's city comedies are double-edged, for the attacks on greed and folly have to be read in the context of his clear enjoyment of the detail of town living and his creative response to the energy and ingenuity which he locates there.

When, therefore, we glance at Jonson's country-house poems in the wider context of his other work, it is clear that these poems provide only one part of his analysis of life styles. Jacobean poems which praise the country are only fully understood when we remember that Jacobean stage comedy draws heavily on the urban for its energy and recall that the social flow of the Jacobean period is away from the country, as legislation on residence makes clear. Poets may stress the virtues of country precisely because there were people who were evidently uncertain about its alleged superiority. And when the theatres reopened after the Commonwealth the theatrical case against the country had become overt, and country is seen as the home of the boor and the naive.

Poetry of place in the first half of the seventeenth century tends to be poetry of the country, but even this is a partial truth. For while it is true of poetry which is specifically topographical, the term 'poetry of place' could be extended, and if it is extended it becomes clear that place in nontopographical verse is often urban. So the focus of love lyric, for example, is often still the court, and satirists are preoccupied with urban vice and follies. As the century goes on, the town becomes increasingly prominent, even though it does not come in for very much praise. In Thomas Durfey's 'Second Dialogue between Crab and Gillian', for instance, town forms a contrast to country, and is to be despised as a centre of drunkenness and debauchery:

> God b'w'e to the Knight,
> Was bubl'd last Night;
> That keeps a Blowze,
> And beats his Spouse.
> (*Restoration Verse*, p. 24)

Such a satirical view of town continues, at times, to be set against the traditional praise of country, but it is a feature of verse in the second half of the century that it finds little real sustenance in ideas of the country. Cotton does, but he is almost alone. Town becomes central partly because towns were becoming more and more important and London more and more the focus of national life (at least as that is defined by Londoners). But arguably this also happens because regionalism took a bad knock in the Civil War and rural myths ceased to have significant relationship to actuality. Town life may be fit only for satire, but it is the best there is. In such poems as Rochester's 'A Letter from Artemisia in the Town to Cloe in the Country' country life has no virtue at all. Innocence here means ignorance; the Horatian peace is tedium and grossness. Town is vicious and exploitative, but at least there is variety and activity. In the same way, place in Dryden's *Absalom and Achitophel* is urban and again it is treated satirically, but Dryden does not offer any rural alternative. However bad town may be that is where life, such as it is, is. Alexander Radcliffe's 'A Call to the Guard by a Drum' indicates that such a view is not only that of the major poets. Town here is a place of 'crack'd Earthen Pispots', of 'snoring and farting, and spewing on Benches', and of 'damn'd fulsom Ale, and more damn'd fulsom Wenches' – but Radcliffe has no alternative to offer. It is interesting that when an alternative is presented by John Oldham it takes the form of an imitation of Juvenal's third satire. Country is a retreat here, but less through its positive values than because town is unbearable. It is fair to add that Oldham's fixation on town as overrun by foreigners ('made the common sewer/where France does all her filth and ordure pour'[29]) means that it cannot be seen as locus for the native character. His protagonist, therefore, proposes retreat. But his expectations are scarcely high:

> What place so desert, and so wild is there,
> Whose inconveniences one would not bear,
> Rather than the alarms of midnight fire,
> The fall of houses, knavery of cits.

In *Poly-Olbion* Drayton surveys Britain in a way which suggests that he felt no important distance between town and country, while the continuities between the values located at Penshurst and those Jonson praises in court-based individuals suggest that he felt unity to be possible. Marvell and Denham have more reason to doubt such unity, and this doubt is as much political as topographical. Restoration poets seem to take division between the two for granted and, moreover, lose any real interest in the country. What they articulate is something which can be related to London's increasing dominance. Country loses its appeal, partly because power is seen to be progressively sited elsewhere, with the development of magnate politics and with the growth of trade during and after the Restoration. The great establishment literature of the eighteenth century will be almost wholly urban.

Notes

1. This view lies behind the doctrine of 'virtual representation' developed in the late seventeenth century to defend absurdities in the franchise.

2. See Stephen Orgel, *The Jonsonian Masque* (Cambridge, Mass., 1967).

3. See Conrad Russell, *The Crisis of Parliaments* (Oxford, 1974), pp. 289–90, 298.

4. See Valerie Pearl, *London and the Outbreak of the Puritan Revolution* (Oxford, 1960).

5. See Robert Ashton, *The English Civil War* (London, 1978), pp. 5–7.

6. 'A proclamation commanding the gentry to keep their residence at their mansions in the country . . .', in J. P. Kenyon, *The Stuart Constitution, 1603–1688* (Cambridge, 1966), p. 502.

7. Most of the standard books on the Civil War and its causes treat of these issues (see General Bibliographies). On the last, see especially J. S. Morrill, *The Revolt of the Provinces* (London, 1976).

8. Russell, especially pp. 357–9.

9. J. H. Plumb, *The Growth of Political Stability in England, 1675–1725,* (London, 1967), *passim.*

10. See on this Raymond Williams, *The Country and the City* (London, 1973), especially Ch. 3–6.

11. See M–S. Røstvig, *The Happy Man* (Oslo, 1962) and S. Stewart, *The Enclosed Garden* (Madison, 1966).

12. Girouard, *Life in the English Country House* (New Haven, 1978), pp. 87–100. See also J. Turner, *The Politics of Landscape* (Oxford, 1979).

13. See May McKisack, *Medieval History in the Tudor Age* (Oxford, 1971) and A. L. Rowse, *The England of Elizabeth* (London, 1964).

14. William Browne, *Britannia's Pastorals* (Menston, 1969), pp. 1–2.

15. 'Tavie is a River, having his head in Dertmore in Devon, some few miles from Marie-Tavy, and fals South-Ward into Tamar.'

16. Again an issue commented on in most standard works. See General Bibliographies.

17. Williams, esp. pp. 40–7.

18. Girouard, p. 82.

19. By Don Wayne of the University of California, in a so far unpublished study, 'Penshurst: The Semiotics of Place and the Poetics of History'.

20. See the *New English Dictionary*, VIII, 'Rapture' (especially pp. 1, 5).

21. Williams, *passim.*

22. Williams argues for complacency, [n. 10 above], pp. 40–7.

23. On 'Upon Appleton House' see J. Wallace, *Destiny His Choice* (London, 1968), pp. 232–57; A. Patterson, *Andrew Marvell and the Civic Crown* (New Jersey, 1978). pp. 101–9; D. Friedman, *Marvell's Pastoral Art* (London, 1970), pp. 213–46.

24. 'B' Text, Draft iv. ll. 189–92. John Denham, *Cooper's Hill, Expans'd Hieroglyphicks*, edited by Brendan O Hehir (Berkeley, 1969), p. 151. O Hehir's edition contains a full critical account of the poem and of various interpretations of it.

25. See *Biographia Literaria*, especially Ch. xii, xiii, for Coleridge on the imagination.

26. See G. Parry, *The Golden Age Restor'd* (Manchester, 1981), pp. 184ff.

27. See O Hehir, pp. 211–12, 223–7, 244–50.

28. Unfortunately most of Cotton's poems are undatable.

29. 'A Satire, in imitation of the third of Juvenal', in *The Poems of John Oldham*, with an introduction by Bonamy Dobrée (London, 1960), p. 188.

Chapter 3
Poems of occasion

Introduction

In Chapter 2 we looked at a number of topographical poems. In a sense, this chapter is concerned with poems and time, that is, poems written in response to some specific event, whether historical or fictional. The poems in question are mainly concerned with people and events in the public eye, and so it was tempting to call the chapter 'Public poetry'. But so much seventeenth-century verse is public rather than private that such a title would have been too loose to be helpful, for even where seventeenth-century poems are ostensibly as intimate as in feigning a lover's address to his mistress, the manner usually assumes an audience of more than one. Most lyrics of the period are public in this sense.

Many poems of the period, however, are public in a more obvious way, in that they are concerned with some particular person or event as related to norms of social behaviour and ethics. Such poems tend to be epitaphs, elegies, or epistles, and very often they work by praising the subject as exemplifying the moral standards by which society operates or should operate. The particular figure is offered as an inspiration to society, or as someone whose death is a social impoverishment. Thus Abraham Cowley writes to John Wilson, Bishop of Lincoln, on his release from prison that

> Your very sufferings did so graceful shew
> That some straight envy'd your Affliction too.
>
> ('To the Bishop of Lincoln', 1641)

– and Edmund Waller's 'Epitaph on Sir George Speke' (1682) stresses Speke's social virtues:

> Sober he was, wise, temperate,
> Contented with an old estate,
> Which no foul avarice did increase,
> Nor wanton luxury make less.

Such poetry is perhaps difficult for us to respond to. It works by presenting the individual in terms of the model or ideal, and, in doing this, it is consistent with the process of the typical love sonnet of the sixteenth century, in which the mistress is praised by being seen as exemplifying erotic ideals. Such attitudes to individuality remain strong through the eighteenth century and are only decisively challenged in the Romantic period. Romantic emphasis on individuality has made it difficult for us to respond positively to art which is more interested in social personality than in individualism.

This type of public poetry can usefully be related both to tradition and to social circumstances of the seventeenth century. Tradition here, as so often with seventeenth-century art, involves the classics. In particular, the poetry of specific persons or events draws upon classical Latin poetry concerned with social ethics; the poetry, above all, of Horace. The basis of such poetry is the view that humans are social beings and that social behaviour is primarily a matter of ethics rather than metaphysics. The sense that the happiness of the individual depends upon moderate and reasonable social behaviour dominates Horace's verse, rather than any feeling that a god or gods enforces socially responsible attitudes and actions. Horace's high prestige in the Renaissance helps to explain his appeal in the seventeenth century (an appeal reinforced by the heavy use made of his verse in school education) but it can be argued that the social ethics which he emphasizes were particularly relevant in the seventeenth century because of the social stresses of that century. So Waller's praise of Speke – the emphasis on temperance, sobriety; and on the absence of avarice and prodigality – can be related to Horatian imperatives, but it is just as relevant to the extravagance and office-grabbing of the seventeenth century itself. In fact, it is a common practice to use a classical model as the basis for an account of some aspect of contemporary life, a clear example being Oldham's imitation of Juvenal mentioned at the end of Chapter 2.

Another general issue arises from all this, the question of how to understand the type of poem to be considered in this chapter. Many examples of the type are addressed to people socially superior to the poet, and it would be naive to assume that they offer simple versions of truth, in precisely the way in which it would be naive to assume that all the mistresses of the love lyrics were, in 'real life', women of remarkable beauty. But it would be equally, if cynically, naive to see all such poems as simple flattery either. Waller clearly presents Speke in a flattering light, partly by excluding from his picture the weaknesses which we assume he, like most people, had, but nevertheless the presentation of Speke as a model of social virtue involves discrimination, whereby Speke becomes the exemplar of some qualities (moderation, contentment, and so on) rather than of others. He thus becomes, in his death, a useful model for those still living in being presented as a mirror of a particular kind, and in so far as Waller's epitaph is flattery it is flattery with a function. This tendency to provide a public, or social, context for praise is so strong in the seventeenth century that, as we shall see, it operates even in poems of occasion which are intimate in mourning a wife or a brother.

Types of praise: Jonson to Cotton

If the history of seventeenth-century love lyric can be said to begin with John Donne, it is equally reasonable to see that of seventeenth-century poetry of occasion as starting with Ben Jonson, for while Jonson did not invent this type of verse it is hard to think of any earlier English poet, with the possible exception of George Gascoigne, whose achievement is so much bound up with such writing. He shares with Gascoigne, and with the Wyatt of the satires, a strong sense of England as place; and his account of England is conducted in terms of a consistent and rigorous ethical view, whereby men and women are evaluated in terms of their relationship with norms of social behaviour which Jonson saw operating in England, or wished to see operating there. The fact that Jonson so often uses classical imitation to articulate his views does not reduce the relevance of these views to the nature and concerns of his contemporary society,[1] and he establishes, at the start of the century, the emphasis of occasional verse upon the representative significance of the people of whom he writes. Here, for instance, are the opening lines of an epigram on Sir Thomas Roe:

> Thou hast begun well, Roe, which stand well too,
> And I know nothing more thou hast to do.
> He that is round within himself, and straight,
> Need seek no other strength, no other height;
> Fortune upon him breaks herself, if ill,
> And what would hurt his virtue makes it still.
>
> ('To Sir Thomas Roe')

The only detail which is at all striking on first reading is the image of Fortune breaking herself, but there is at once the feeling of confidence in the poet's discriminations, and the poet's confidence comes to seem justified, as we come to know the poem better, by the unobtrusive concreteness of the language (stand, round, straight, seek, breaks, hurt). Yet although Roe is praised in concrete language no attempt is made to particularize him. The chosen language is plain and general, while there is a movement between second and third person pronouns which effects a relationship between the named individual, Roe, and the broad category of virtuous men.

The Roe epigram is typical of Jonson's poems of praise, both in its manner (the plain, confident claims and discriminations) and in its terms of praise. So Edward Herbert is praised for 'standing upright to thyself' ('To Sir Edward Herbert'), and the same distinction is made between virtue and fortune in an epigram on the Earl of Salisbury:

Who can consider thy right courses run,
With what thy virtue on the times hath won,
And not thy fortune.
                ('To Robert, Earl of Salisbury')

As a reader comes to know *Epigrams* (1616) better, the poems of praise
in that collection are seen to form a group, not merely because they are
a set of eulogies, but also because the celebrated virtues contribute to a
consistent view of what humans should ethically be, and because Jonson's
stylistic methods of presenting this are as consistent as the views them-
selves. Moreover, the poems of praise are also defined negatively, in that
these poems are contrasted with the satirical epigrams, in which negative
qualities are defined and located within individuals. Thus the experience
of reading *Epigrams* through is one of being asked to make comparisons
and to draw conclusions, involving, for example, the William Camden of
Epigram XIV and the 'Court-worm' of the next poem:

All men are worms: but this no man. In silk
'Twas brought to court first wrapped, and white as milk;
Where, afterwards, it grew a butterfly:
Which was a caterpillar. So 'twill die.

Such contrasts both enhance a reader's sense of there being two dominant
and opposed groups in the collection and work to give the poems of praise
the effect of satire-in-reverse, so that qualities offered as ethically desirable
are seen as utterly distinct from the evils lashed in the satirical epigrams.
But it should be repeated that Jonson consistently presents the admirable
individual as being so because representative of general social categories.
So Sir William Uvedale is 'thou piece of the first times, a man/Made for
what Nature could, or virtue can', and Sir William Jephson is a 'man of
men, to whose loved name/All gentry, yet, owe part of their best flame'
('To Sir William Uvedale', 'To Sir William Jephson')

In *Epigrams*, then, comments on individuals are related to a view of what
is desirable in society at large, and, broadly speaking, individuals are
praised or attacked in terms of their contributions to society. In his longer
poems of occasion Jonson has the space to work out more fully his view
of the relationship between individual and society. The poems in question
cover a great deal of ground, but can be roughly categorized into two
groups, those addressed to the poet's social superiors and those to friends.

When 'To Penshurst' was discussed earlier, the point was made that the
house and the Sidney family were seen there as exceptions to a norm of
pretentious and deracinated houses and house-builders, and it is an important
feature of Jonson's epistles that the addressee is often seen as an isolated
source of hope in a society felt to be desperately in need of such hope. The
Countess of Rutland is seen in the context of a society dominated by 'al-
mighty gold', for which 'life, conscience, yea, souls are given' and which
'buys great grace, and hunts poor fame' ('Epistle to Elizabeth, Countess
of Rutland', ll. 4, 2, 15, *The Forest*, 1616). Lady Aubigny is praised because

> You, madam, young have learned to shun these shelves
> Whereon the most of mankind wrack themselves,
> And, keeping a just course, have early put
> Into your harbour.
>> ('Epistle. To Katherine, Lady Aubigny', ll. 89–92, *The Forest*)

Such epistles present societies in which

> 'Tis grown almost a danger to speak true
> Of any good mind, now: there are so few.
>> (ll. 1–2)

In 'A Speech according to Horace' (*Underwoods*, 1640) the poet's sense of social deterioration is so strong that he cannot even offer there the hope and consolation epitomized by a Rutland or an Aubigny.

Friends are also seen in the light of corrupt societies, most powerfully in 'An Epistle to a Friend, to Persuade Him to the Wars' (*Underwoods*, 1640), in which the poet's feeling for the energetic details of a sordid life produces such images as

> fall upon her back
> In admiration, stretched upon the rack
> Of lust . . .

and

> Planting their purls, and curls spread forth like net,
> And every dressing for a pitfall set
> To catch the flesh in, and to pound a prick.

These go to make the poet's advice to the friend seem inevitable:

> Go quit them all. And take along with thee,
> Thy true friend's wishes, Colby, which shall be,
> That thine be just, and honest, that thy deeds
> Not wound thy conscience.
>> (ll. 49–51, 65–7, 175–8)

Jonson's view of social life, then, clearly is often pessimistic, one of a society where energy is vicious and gold dominates. But although the poet may have visions of worlds where 'prosperity mocks/The fate of things: whilst tottered virtue holds/Her broken arms up, to their empty moulds' ('A Speech according to Horace', ll. 100–2) he is seldom the poet of despair. Against such visions he offers what is represented by the ethically admirable individuals of the epigrams and epistles. So far this has been illustrated mainly in terms of Jonson's praise of socially prominent individuals, but this does not mean that the poems are simply flattery in verse. What we are dealing with is very often a matter of dual function, so that *Epigrams*, LXXVI transforms Lucy, Countess of Bedford, into the ideal object of poetic devotions in a way which is clearly flattering, and at the same time the terms of the transformation ('yet more good than great'; 'Hating that solemn vice of greatness, pride') also make the Countess a model of social greatness.

But Jonson also offers friendship as itself something to set against social degeneracy. So the wishes of a true friend are offered to Colby to help him preserve himself from moral woundings, and the warmth of the splendid 'Inviting a Friend to Supper' (*Epigrams*) is in the offering of full but moderate enjoyment as a refuge in a world of guilt and suspicion. The same kind of warmth is found in the generosity of the Camden epigram and in the prescriptions of the ode 'High-spirited friend':

> I send nor balms, nor corsives to your wound;
>   Your fate hath found
> A gentler, and more agile hand, to tend
> The cure of that, which is but corporal, . . .
> Yet doth some wholesome physic for the mind,
>   Wrapped in this paper lie,
> Which in the taking if you misapply.
>   You are unkind.
>   (ll. 2–5, 9–12, *Underwoods*, 1640)

The pressures of corruption in society are such as to isolate virtue, but friendship operates to reduce isolation, and, in the same way, Jonson sees the poet's role as being to analyse the social situation and to offer the analysis to those people in society who are seen as capable of responding to, and being reassured by, such analysis. The poet's task is to 'draw true lines' and this for Jonson entails both the recounting of vice and the drawing out of virtue: 'I, madam, am become your praiser' ('Epistle. To Katherine, Lady Aubigny', ll. 20, 21).

This drawing out of virtue is one aspect of Jonson's constant concern to make something of experience, to seek out what can be learnt from a person or event. This entails that movement between the particular and the general which is acted out in the pronouns of the Roe epigram discussed earlier, but it is also evident in the way in which moral reflections are used in the epistolary poems. In 'An Epistle to Sir Edward Sackville . . .' (*Underwoods*), for example, such reflections are presented as permanent truths (their permanence underlined by the typical use of classical material Englished). Such a concern to learn and to relate particular cases to general categories appears even in Jonson's most personal poems, in such epitaphs as the wonderful 'On My First Son' (*Epigrams*), in which his grief tests and is tested by the traditional religious consolations, and in the equally fine 'To the Right Honourable, the Lord High Treasurer of England' (1631) where personal hardship is so movingly translated into a plea for the dignity of the poet's art.

Jonson's contribution to the seventeenth-century poem of occasion is most important in that he sets at its centre a serious and sustained ethical analysis. Poems of praise are made more than flattery, through the prominence and consistency of social ethics and through the constant effort to relate praise of the individual to analysis of society at large. But the manner of Jonson's epigrams, epitaphs, and epistles is also very important in the history of the seventeenth-century occasional poem. Most of the poems we are here concerned with are in couplets, and the Jonsonian couplet is flexible, capable both of informality and familiarity and of dignity and precise detail. Moreover, the style is sober yet eloquent, marked more by verbal restraint than by extravagance (though satirical passages may be highly coloured) with the consistency of the terms of praise and the plainness of their presentation being the artistic guarantee of truth. It is a style conducive to discrimination, hostile to hyperbolic effect (even though the praise may be, at root, hyperbolic) and appropriate to material which is viewed as, literally, mundane.

Jonson thus sets the standard for the seventeenth-century occasional poem, both by making claims for its seriousness and by creating a style which is fitted for genuine reflection. Seeing what is made of Jonson's example involves looking at funereal poetry, at the poetry of power and rule, and also at poems of friendship and of moral eulogy.

It is perhaps excessive to say that any person can teach another how to think, but lessons in the appropriate articulation of thought may be possible, and it seems that Thomas Carew learnt from Jonson how to render the sense of thinking in verse. In his 'To Ben. Johnson. Upon occasion of his Ode of defiance annext to his Play of the new Inne' Carew mixes praise and advice with a precise assurance which is itself Jonsonian. *The New Inn* was a failure on production (1629) and Jonson's 'Ode of defiance', a violent exercise in self-justification, clearly disturbed Carew. He sees Jonson as an artist of great achievements, one with a 'just chastizing hand', a writer all of whose 'Eaglets may/Endure the Sunnie tryall' and who has produced a 'tun'd quire of Swans'. Also, Carew constantly supports Jonson against the detraction of lesser men. The age is 'sotted' and can offer only 'empty scribbling' and 'a flock of cackling Geese' to compare with Jonson's achievement. Therefore

Thy labour'd workes shall live, when Time devoures
Th'abortive off-spring of their hastie houres.

In this couplet Carew blends flattery and judgement cleverly, alluding both to Jonson's pride in the care he took with his writing and to the gibes made at him for the care he took.

But, in Jonsonian fashion, Carew is concerned to make something of the occasion, rather than to flatter or blandly soothe the hurt and angry poet–dramatist. 'Truth' is a key word in Jonson, and truth is one of Carew's concerns here:

> and yet 'tis true
> Thy commique Muse from the exalted line
> Toucht by thy Alchymist, doth since decline.
>
> (ll. 4–6)

Respect for truth, together with love of his friend and mentor and generous discrimination, leads Carew on to speak of Jonson's 'immodest rage' and his 'ytch of praise'. The overall blend of advice, praise, and feeling for the importance of art makes the poem a striking piece of criticism and, in its artistic quality, a tribute to Jonson's influence.

'Influence' is also a topic in another of Carew's poems to a fellow poet, 'To my worthy friend Master Geo. Sandys, on his translation of the Psalmes' (1638) where again the quality of Carew's poem is the true compliment to Sandys, implying as it does that the work of his fellow has drawn him to think about himself and his own work. Carew often produces a more decorative texture than Jonson, and his wit shares something with Donne:

> Who knowes, but that her wandring eyes that run,
> Now hunting Glow-wormes, may adore the Sun.

But the sense of determination to respond seriously to the publication of Sandys's translation is Jonsonian, as is the control of the verse paragraphs and the appropriate tentativeness in lines like these:

> Perhaps my restlesse soule, tyr'de with persuit
> Of mortall beauty, seeking without fruit
> Contentment there . . .
> Weary of her vaine search below, Above
> In the first Faire may find th'immortall Love.
>
> ('To my worthy Friend Master Geo. Sandys',
> ll. 15–16, 23–5, 27–8)

These two Carew poems are relatively private poems of occasion, and are particularly impressive for the way in which friendship is communicated through tone, but with Abraham Cowley's 'To the Lord Falkland' we return to the poetry of public occasion, since Cowley is writing about Falkland's return from one of Charles I's slightly absurd expeditions against the Scots. Yet Cowley is not primarily concerned with the politics of the expedition. Falkland was a scholar and thinker by temperament, a man who was only involved with politics with some reluctance and from a sense of social duty. Having been a moderate critic of royal policy, he became a member of the King's party, a Secretary of State; and he died at the Battle of Newbury in 1643. Cowley sees his involvement in the Scottish expedition as a juxtaposition of the active life with the contemplative. Falkland represents the latter and Cowley addresses the North:

> Return him safe: Learning would rather choose
> Her Bodley, or her Vatican to loose.

But Cowley is not concerned to offer an individualized sketch or analysis of Falkland, who is transformed into a model of learning:

> All things that are but writ or printed there,
> In his unbounded Breast engraven are.
> There all the Sciences together meet,
> And every Art does all her Kindred greet,
> Yet jostle not, nor quarrel.

But this 'great Prince of Knowledge is by Fate/Thrust into th' noise and business of a State', whereas

> He is too good for War, and ought to be
> As far from Danger, as from Fear he's free.
> ('To the Lord Falkland', ll. 3–4, 5–9, 19–20, 37–8)

Cowley suggests, in fact, that, as Falkland enacts the proper unity of science and arts, so the state should demonstrate an equivalent unity of functions, and if this happened Falkland would not be drawn into military activity, but would carry out his natural function – 'Let Them the State Defend, and He Adorn'. So Falkland's involvement in the expedition comes to be seen as an instance of malfunction, and in this way Cowley's poem makes the occasion something of a commentary upon the politics of his time, the witty, polished couplets not wholly hiding awareness of something wrong.

Cowley's poem puts the individual into a social context and is concerned with individuality only in relation to society. So far as the poem goes Falkland exists as a social being. His talents may be private, in so far as scholarship is a private activity, but their significance is as adornment of the State. In this sense Cowley's poem is unlike Richard Lovelace's 'Advice to my best Brother . . .', even though they have themes in common; and the difference is reflected in terms of style, this being partly a matter of decorum. Cowley, addressing a member of the aristocracy, uses a formal, moderately elevated style:

> Great is thy Charge, O North; be wise and just,
> England commits her Falkland to thy trust.
> ('To the Lord Falkland', ll. 1–2)

Lovelace, writing to his brother, is appropriately more informal:

> Frank, wil't live handsomely? Trust not too far
> Thy self to waving Seas.
> ('Advice to my best Brother', ll. 1–2)

Lovelace is not concerned with matters of state, even though Francis Lovelace belongs to the public world. His poem deals with the question of how a man should live in relation to the State, but it does not take for granted, as Cowley's does, that private and social functions are finally one. If Cowley's poem can be said to be about how a state should foster its Falklands, Lovelace's is about how the individual should operate in relation to the demands and opportunities of the state, and this puts it in the tradition of Wyatt's third satire. Lovelace offers, as the secret of living 'handsomely', the values Horace presents and Jonson endorses – the ethics of the 'golden mean', peace, steadfastness, calm, 'a breast of proof'. It is a poem about how to cope in an uncertain world, and it attempts to relate philosophy and the individual case by blending general reflections and direct appeal: 'Frank to undo thy self why art at cost?' (ll. 47, 16)

This directness and informality belong to the poetry of friendship, and in such poetry the reader is put in the position of overhearing an intimate address, which may be, as here, serious advice, or, as in Suckling's 'An Epistle' (Sir,/Whether these lines do find you out . . .') relaxed and even, superficially, trivial. Like Jonson's 'Inviting a Friend to Supper', Suckling's poem is an invitation. It is assumed that poet and addressee share a common body of knowledge and similar attitudes. This is communicated not only by such a reference as that to Jack Bond:

> Leave Socinus and the Schoolmen,
> (Which Jack Bond swears do but fool men)

but also by the jaunty way in which the addressee's philosophical concerns are listed:

> (Whether Predestination,
> Or reconciling three in one,
> Or the unriddling how men die,
> And live at once eternally
> Now take you up).
> ('An Epistle', ll. 10–11, 3–7)

Yet Suckling's poem is not intimate in the sense of being private, if by 'private' we mean cultist. Linguistically the lines are widely accessible and the poem is based upon a juxtaposition of ways of life which is widely known. This means that 'An Epistle' finally defines a society. Cowley's poem is addressed, simultaneously, to Falkland and the nation, and Lovelace's is firmly directed to his brother, while relating the latter's way of life to philosophical categories. Suckling, however, mediates between the particular occasion and the broad accessibility of his style by defining a society which is neither a narrow élite nor the whole nation. It is a society of the educated and sophisticated, those who will understand references to Socinus and the 'Colledge Steed' and will respond to the cosmopolitanism of

> News in one day as much w'have here
> As serves all Windsor for a year.
> (ll. 8, 27–8)

The style itself suggests that this witty society carries its convictions and commitments lightly, so that 'The sweat of learned Johnsons brain,/And gentle Shakespear's eas'er strain' becomes part of the entertainment which London offers. But the easy informality of the manner also suggests that what matters is friendship itself.

Lovelace's epistle gives advice and Suckling's invites a friend to come to London. Charles Cotton's 'Epistle to Sir Clifford Clifton' takes as its occasion the effort to reply to a letter from Clifton. The informality of Suckling's couplets is broadened here, at times to the point of burlesque:

> Faith, in an old drawer, I late had not been in,
> 'Twixt a coarse pair of sheets of the housewife's own spinning.
>
> (ll. 31–2)

Also, the characteristic directness of the poetry of friendship is taken further than in Suckling:

> I kissed her, and hugg'd her, I clapt her, and chuck't her,
> I push'd her down backward, and offer'd to have (fuck't her).
>
> (ll. 65–6)

Cotton's poem, in fact, undercuts everything it deals with. His muse is a 'Jade' and a 'poor slut', the poet himself is seen as an impoverished *bon viveur*, and even Clifton has a 'little fat buttock'.

But although the mode of friendship poetry is formally debased here, the effect is thoroughly pleasant and Cotton conveys the feeling that he and Clifton really are friends, that Clifton's letter was 'a kind and good one', and that the poet is concerned to produce an entertaining reply. Although this epistle is stylistically quite unlike Lovelace's famous 'The Grassehopper' (which is addressed to Cotton's father) both poems present friendship as something which sustains both writer and addressee in uncertain worlds. In Cotton's poem there is little of the ethical confidence of Lovelace's epistle to his brother or of Suckling's confidence in the existence of a society of like livers. But friendship itself endures, and has value in and for itself.

Funereal verse for private figures: to Milton and Dryden

Friendship and love, obviously enough, may be vital things to hold to and value in the face of the uncertainties of experience; and death is one of the great uncertainties. In the seventeenth century, with infant mortality high,

disease commonplace, and life expectancy low, death has a presence which
is lacking in a modern Western society, and so it is not surprising that fu-
nereal poetry is an important part of occasional verse. Death is a con-
clusion, even if to believers in a deity no more than the completion of an
inferior state; and one of the chief concerns of funereal poetry in the sev-
enteenth century is the issue of what has been completed by the death.
Another is where the death leaves the living.

Milton's 'Lycidas' (1638) is the most famous funereal poem of the cen-
tury, and its fame is justified. But although its use of classical and Christian
allusion has been often analysed, accounts of the poem have tended to ig-
nore the extent to which 'Lycidas' belongs very clearly to the tradition of
funereal poetry in its century. Its concerns are not peculiar to Milton, and
so I want, in this section, to approach his poem by way of an account of
some other attempts to face and cope with issues similar to those which
the death of Edward King confronted Milton with. And here, as elsewhere,
the starting-point has to be Ben Jonson.

Jonson wrote fine epitaphs on the deaths of two of his children. A
daughter, Mary, died after only six months (a very small completion) and
in 'On My First Daughter' (*Epigrams*) the poet is able to see the death only
negatively, as something which preserved 'her innocence'. The epi-
taph is quiet, its grief indicated rather than dramatized. Yet the pain is au-
thenticated by the placing of 'less' in the second couplet:

> Yet, all heaven's gifts, being heaven's due,
> It makes the father, less, to rue.

– and by the tenderness of the ending:

> This grave partakes the fleshly birth.
> Which cover lightly, gentle earth.
>
> (ll. 21–5)

The loss is registered, but it is placed and understood in the context of
Christian ideas about God lending children to parents and of the Queen
of heaven's retinue of virgins. The poet seems able to reconcile himself to
the loss (whereas the matching 'On My First Son' is much tenser, at times
bitter *Epigrams*) and concentrates upon creating a decorous memorial for
the infant.

In both epitaphs Jonson's achievement anticipates aspects of later sev-
enteenth-century poetry on the deaths of people close to the poet. One fea-
ture is restraint and another is precision of craftsmanship – the placing of
'less' noted above, and the proper word play of 'say here doth lie/Ben Jon-
son his best piece of poetry' in 'On My First Son'. There is also the plain-
ness of style in both poems, allowing both emotion and reflection to
emerge with what seems little rhetorical elaboration. Further, the individual
death is related to traditional themes of consolation, so that the particular
is made to test the general, but can also be understood, and perhaps ac-

cepted, in terms of it. The poet pays tribute to the dead by shaping his material into reflections for the living.

Such ways of writing about death are again evident in Henry King's great poem on the death of his wife, 'The Exequy' (*Poems*, 1657), which is, incidentally, one of the most successful examples of the reconciliation of the influences of Donne and Jonson in the period. King's determination to make his poem a fitting tribute is clear from the careful control of his octosyllabic couplets:

> Nor wonder if my time goe thus
> Backward and most preposterous;
> Thou hast Benighted mee. Thy sett
> This Eve of blackness did begett,
> Who wast my Day.
>   ('The Exequy')

Similarly, the poet is concerned to do more than simply to record his grief, and what he produces is an appropriate demonstration of it. So he adapts motifs of love poetry to funereal purposes:

> By thy cleere Sunne
> My Love and Fortune first did run;
> But Thou wilt never more appeare
> Folded within my Hemispheare.
>   (ll. 29–32)

And he projects pictures of himself in his life after his wife's death:

> But hark! My Pulse, like a soft Drum
> Beates my Approach, Tells Thee I come.
>   (ll. 111–12)

King's ability to find clear, emotionally exact, and lucid images makes his poem a public one, while its precision makes its conclusion both a moving tribute to his wife and an appropriate enactment of Christian acceptance of death:

> I am content to live
> Divided, with but half a Heart,
> Till we shall Meet and Never part.
>   (ll. 118–20)

The organization 'The Exequy' is of a very high order, allowing the poet the degree of objectivity necessary for the proper wit of this couplet addressed to the grave:

With a most free and bounteous grief,
I give thee what I could not keep.

(ll. 67–8)

Here, as in Jonson's epitaphs, there is a careful balance of attention be-
tween the dead person and concern with the responses of the still living,
with King (in this respect rather like George Herbert) placing the particular
circumstances and individual emotions in contexts of theme and language
which demonstrate connections with widely known processes of nature,
offering parallels between his daily risings and the movement of the sun,
and between his wife's body ('My Little World') and the earth to dem-
onstrate hope through belief in unity. Neither King nor Jonson seems
mainly interested in dramatizing grief itself, and the same is true of Cot-
ton's 'To the Memory of my worthy Friend, Colonel Richard Lovelace'
(?1658). But Cotton is more obviously concerned than the other two poets
to commemorate his subject by making him a model of virtue. This model
is, in the first paragraph, a general one, where Lovelace's youth is 'an ab-
stract of the World's best parts', during which period of his life his training
in arms and arts leads to a maturity in which he provides standards of hon-
our and truth. But in the second paragraph rather more detail is offered.
Here the sweetness of temper so influences senses and affections that these
are 'smooth'd'

to a calm, which still withstood
The ruffling passions of untamed blood,
Without a wrinkle in thy face to show
Thy stable breast could a disturbance know.

In addition, Lovelace is seen as 'In fortune humble, constant in mischance'.
Cotton is explicit about Lovelace's function as model. His example pro-
vides 'Two glorious lights' and an instance of 'What a Man should in his
full perfection be', but the poet does not try to convince the reader through
hyperbole, but writes conversationally, even plainly, with a Jonsonian con-
cern to make valid distinctions:

Valiant to envy of the bravest men,
And learned to an undisputed pen,
Good as the best in both, and great; but yet
No dangerous courage; nor offensive wit.

('To the Memory of my worthy Friend')

Cotton is less concerned, it seems, with the communication of grief than
with the definition and presentation of worth, the latter being seen mainly
in terms of the Jonsonian ethic of constancy and moderation. Lovelace,
poet and Civil War activist, is seen, appropriately, as combining arts and
arms, which, as in Cowley's poem on Falkland, represent unity and define

'What Man should in his full perfection be'. Lovelace died (probably) in 1658 and his record during the Civil War seems to have been one of stead-fast and committed support of the King, while his 'To a Grasse-hopper' indicates that, in defeat, he valued the same qualities as those for which Cotton praises him. One royalist, Cotton, commemorates another, Lov-elace, as a model of constancy at a time of hardship, but it should be added that this is done with a quiet dignity and good sense which make 'Cavalier' more than a description of casual hedonism.

In any worthwhile poet who uses established genres, the result is likely to involve some sort of debate between individuality and tradition. So it is not surprising that Cotton's ethical model is Jonsonian (and, beyond that, classical) and closely related to the Cavalier experience following the defeat of Charles I. Nor is it surprising that when Henry Vaughan writes poetry of grief he marks it with the emphases of his other verse. Vaughan, being a poet preoccupied with the search for union with God, is perhaps inevi-tably concerned with death, most obviously in a group of lyrics which are found at intervals in the first half of *Silex Scintillans* (1650), and in which he focuses upon the death of his brother.

But it is not wholly accurate to say that these poems focus upon the death of his brother. Vaughan is not really equipped to describe grief at the death of another person, because the whole set of his mind is to see the experience of this world as itself a loss, the sublunary state being seen as a fall, a loss of paradise and heaven. So for Vaughan to lose this life is, in fact, a gain, the shedding of the dross which is the material world and the gaining of the pure light of God and eternity. And so, although he may speak of mourning and tears at the start of 'Thou that know'st for whom I mourne' and may refer, at the end of the same poem, to the 'white' soul and 'pure and steddy' faith of the deceased, his real interest is not either in recording grief or in presenting his brother as an ethical model for the still living, but in using the specific occasion to exemplify his usual view of human and divine life. So in 'Thou that know'st . . .' he presents his brother's death as designed to prompt the poet himself to reflect upon his own state:

> But 'twas my sinne that forc'd thy hand
>> To cull this Prim-rose out,
> That by thy early choice forewarn'd
>> My soule might looke about.
>> ('Thou that know'st . . .', ll. 9–12)

As his soul looks about, it gleans lessons which are pure Vaughan, even while being religious commonplaces:

> O what a vanity is man!
>> How like the Eyes quick winke
> His Cottage failes.
>> (ll. 13–15)

Such reflections lead the poet to the conclusion that 'my gaine is great,/My losse but little to it'.

Vaughan's main weakness is perhaps glibness. His consistent and seemingly firm convictions about the worthlessness of the material world and the desirability of union with his God reduce the likelihood of any real tension in his poems. The predictability of such poems as 'Thou that know'st . . .' is not necessarily a weakness, but poetry in which there is no tension can easily become tedious, as it does whenever Vaughan fails to make his verse enact what he is saying, as here:

> Come, come, what doe I here?
>> Since he is gone
> Each day is grown a dozen year,
>> And each houre, one.
>>>> ('Come, come, what doe I here?', ll. 1–4)

On the whole, Vaughan's poems of grief lack the tension between loss and faith which makes Jonson's epitaphs outstanding, and that humane directness combined with faith which makes King's 'Exeqy' so moving. Vaughan neither individualizes the dead person nor makes a socio-ethical model of him, but instead uses his brother's death in a typical demonstration of the uselessness of material life and the desirability of escaping from it as soon as possible into union with God. He can, nevertheless, write quite effectively about loss:

> Silence, and stealth of dayes! 'tis now
>> Since thou art gone,
> Twelve hundred houres, and not a brow
>> But Clouds hang on.
>>>> ('Silence, and stealth of dayes')

Here, and in 'Sure, there's a tye of Bodyes', Vaughan is impressive, but it is noticeable that what strikes him most strongly in the death of his brother is the confirmation of what he already knows. Since it is only 'flatterers' who consider the sublunary to be true life, there can be no real reason for grief in the death even of a brother, and so Vaughan's poems of grief are, paradoxically, finally poems of celebration.

So far, we have been concerned with poems which treat of the deaths of people close to the poet, and the poets concerned have sought to use the fact of death in different ways, while having in common the determination to make something of the death and the avoidance of emotional extremes. But seventeenth-century poets also had occasion to write about the deaths of persons who were not close in blood or friendship and who were also not major public figures, and such circumstances cause, at least for poets of taste and talent, problems of tact and tactics. Perhaps the most famous instance of this occurs with Donne's two long poems on Elizabeth Drury (1611–12), 'An Anatomie of the World' ('The first Anniversary') and 'Of the Progresse of the Soule' ('The second Anniversarie').

Drummond says that Jonson told him that 'Donne's *Anniversary* was profane and full of blasphemies: that he told Mr Donne, if it had been written of the Virgin Mary it had been something; to which he answered, that he described the idea of a woman, and not as she was'. Jonson's unease has been shared by modern critics, although John Carey has recently argued[2] that there is no good reason to regard the poems as about anything other than what they purport to be about – Elizabeth Drury. But there remains the problem of in what sense these two poems are about the dead young woman. Both the reply which Jonson quoted to Drummond and the full titles of the poems themselves offer clues to Donne's approach to his problem, which is basically that he did not know Elizabeth Drury and hence could hardly have written about her 'as she was'. To take her as 'the idea of a woman' offers a way out of this situation, especially as the kind of idealization suggested is an expected part of the formal funeral elegy.

But the full titles take us further. 'The first Anniversary' has as its full title 'An Anatomie of the World. Wherein, By occasion of the untimely death of Mistris Elizabeth Drury, the frailty and the decay of this whole World is represented'. What this suggests is that a poem on a large subject has been occasioned by a particular event. That event, the death of Elizabeth, provides the situation which exemplifies 'the frailty and the decay of the whole World', and there is an obvious difference between the poem being about someone and being about something 'occasioned' by someone. Donne, moreover, uses the same formula in the title of the second of these poems – 'Of the Progresse of the soule. Wherein, By occasion of the Religious death of Mistris Elizabeth Drury, the incommodities of the Soule in this life, and her exaltation in the next, are contemplated'. Donne's formula provides a way of masking his ignorance of Elizabeth and of maintaining decorum. The poet memorializes her by taking her death and alleged virtue as data, so that the bodies of the two poems are reflections upon human existence seen as prompted by her death. In itself, this formula is hardly extraordinary, since, as we have seen, exemplification is a common tactic even when poets are writing of people they knew intimately. The compliment to, and memorialization of, Elizabeth Drury is the poems themselves: her death has led the poet to these reflections, and there are frequent enough reminders of Elizabeth and her death in the poems to keep a reader aware of their inspiration, reminders like the repetition of the pattern 'Shee, shee is dead: shee's dead'. And, of course, once the poems themselves, as objects, are seen as the memorialization, the brilliant discursiveness of Donne's style can be seen as part of the compliment.

In his 'Obsequies to the Lady Anne Hay' (1629) Thomas Carew faced a somewhat similar problem, and found a somewhat similar solution. Anne Hay was a distant cousin and Carew admits that he knew little of her:

> But who shall guide my artlesse Pen, to draw
> Those blooming beauties, which I never saw?
>
> (ll. 19–20)

Typically, Carew deals with his problem partly by exploiting his considerable feeling for texture, by which he creates in the poem's first para-

graph a convincing sense of general grief at Anne's death. The precision
of the opening lines gives some idea of the technical triumph:

> I heard the Virgins sigh, I saw the sleeke
> And polisht Courtier, channell his fresh cheeke
> With reall teares.
>
> ('Obsequies to the Lady Anne Hay', ll. 1–3)

Having created this sense of grief at the death, Carew then considers the
problems which his ignorance of Anne Hay presents: how will 'posteritie
beleeve my story' if Anne's 'crowded graces, and the glory/Due to her riper
vertues' are related by a poet who is 'Without the knowledge of her mortall
state'? (ll. 21–4). This leads to a critique of what are seen as conventional
strategies in this type of situation – appeals to legend, to 'the Worthies of
her sex' and to 'Morall, and Divine Exactest lawes' (ll. 30, 33–4), all of which
the dead person is conventionally held to exemplify. This is criticism, in
fact, of the model we have seen several poets using earlier in this chapter.
But even while criticizing this device, Carew is praising Anne Hay by say-
ing that she is worth something better than this. The final paragraph offers
this something better.

Carew, in fact, neatly solves his problem by evading it, wittily and
decorously writing a poem about the problem itself. So the final paragraph
begins by summarizing what he will not do:

> We will not bathe thy corps with a forc'd teare,
> Nor shall thy traine borrow the blacks they weare.

Anne is too good for this, or indeed for verse:

> Thou art the Theame of Truth, not Poetrie.

Therefore,

> Thou shalt endure a tryall by thy Peeres,
> Virgins of equall birth, of equall yeares . . .
> Shall draw thy picture, and record thy life.
>
> (ll. 43–4, 46, 47–8, 50)

The use of the future tense throughout this last paragraph neatly exonerates
the poet from attempting the task itself, even while it allows him to assert
that Anne is the summary of all beauty and that she contained 'all the
seeds/Of every Vertue' (ll. 60–1). Once again the poem itself is the tribute,
a witty yet tactful memorial to the deceased, in which the poet's sensitivity
to the problems caused by Anne's youthfulness and his ignorance of her
is part of the tribute.

Like Donne and Carew, John Milton has, in 'Lycidas', the problem of
dealing with the death of someone he did not know well. There is no evi-

dence to suggest that Milton knew Edward King, the formal subject of 'Lycidas', particularly well, although Christ's, the college at Cambridge where they were both students, was not very large. 'Lycidas' was, in fact, first published in *Justa Eduardo King*, a collection of poems in Latin, Greek, and English produced in commemoration of King's accidental death. As such, the poem is part of a semi-public tribute. But if Milton did not know King particularly well, he clearly knew enough to be aware of parallels between himself and the dead man, and this allows a different strategy for commemorating King's death by drowning, a strategy which makes 'Lycidas' a peculiarly intimate elegy.

'Intimate' may seem, at first, an odd word to use, since perhaps the most famous feature of the poem is pastoralism and since another obvious element is the adaptation of allusions and motifs from classical poetry and from the Scriptures. If we think of 'intimate' as suggesting detailed personal reference and/or the articulation of an evidently highly individual viewpoint, and if we approach 'Lycidas' with such expectations, we shall be disappointed, for instead of such things we find Milton engaged in fitting both King's death and the poet-figure's response to this into traditions, seemingly concerned to depersonalize both subject and writer.

Pastoral and classical and biblical references work to distance the formal occasion of the poem, and this could be seen as a sensible approach to the problem of writing about someone not close to the poet and also as a way of generalizing the material, with a view to stressing the 'lessons' of King's life and death, the latter being an approach seen in other funereal poems of the century. But it is important to note how, from the opening lines, the poet-figure is an active part of the pastoral theme:

> Yet once more, O ye laurels, and once more
> Ye myrtles brown, with ivy never sere,
> I come to pluck your berries harsh and crude.[3]

The reason given for the enforced plucking and shattering of leaves is that 'Lycidas is dead, dead ere his prime', and this opening immediately establishes a link between poet and subject, the latter's youth being matched by the immaturity of the poetic fruits, while there is also the suggestion that the violence of the plucking comes about because the life of Lycidas is not itself ripe. Also, this opening, through its imagery, immediately indicates that the material of the poem is to be seen in the context of heroic achievement, and particularly of artistic achievement. But this generalizing tendency is checked, so that although the poem goes on to treat of the basic 'public' facts of King's life and death (his poetry, his religious vocation, his drowning) and although the effect of his death is, conventionally enough, stressed:

> Thee, Shepherd, thee the Woods and desert caves,
> With wild thyme and the gadding vine o'ergrown,
> And all their echoes mourn –

> (ll. 39–41)

Milton is also concerned with the implications of King's life and death for himself. In 'On My First Son' Jonson had tried to answer his own question 'why/Will man lament the state he should envy?', and 'Lycidas' shares this concern, which Milton expands so that his poem becomes an examination of the purpose or purposelessness of life. This produces, simultaneously, a discussion of faith and a therapeutic exercise: the fact and implications of King's life need to be felt out as much as thought out, and the ultimate tribute to King is that the final act of his life (his drowning) comes to be that which allows the poet to reassert his faith, a faith which he shares with King. Moreover, the use of tradition works to give the poem's discussion a context: the events are not to be seen as unique.

But such a tribute can only seem true if the poet can make it feel heart-felt, and Milton achieves this impression by concentrating on points where he seems to have identified with King. So there is anger that Lycidas was not protected when he most needed protection ('Where were ye Nymphs . . .', l. 50) but also the feeling that protection would have been in vain against forces equivalent to those which in legend destroyed Orpheus, and here the reference to legend works to link Lycidas and poet-figure with the idea of all poets. The forces which destroyed Orpheus were the Maenads, and at this stage in the poem the poet is clearly projecting his resentment at all those forces which are beyond human control and comprehension, and such egocentricity is part of what the poem needs to displace if there is to be consolation and renewed faith. But before there is any possibility of this, there are more particular sources of anger and resentment which need to be expressed. Like the poet-figure, Lycidas was a poet, and this gives a special poignancy to the opening, where one young poet is con-strained to write a premature elegy for another. It is this which leads to the questioning of the vocation itself:

> Alas! What boots it with uncessant care
> To tend the homely slighted shepherd's trade,
> And strictly meditate the thankless Muse?
>
> (ll. 64–6)

The poet knows the stock answer ('Fame is the spur . . .', l. 70) but this is not, at this stage, sufficiently active in him to be adequate consolation, and the sense of outraged doubt dominates the orthodox consolation. Simi-lar disproportion is more marked in the famous passage about unworthy shepherds, where the shared concern of Lycidas and the poet-figure with the religious life joins with the latter's anger about the complacent neglect of sheep by the shepherd to produce the most powerful lines in the poem. At this stage, the fury can only be expressed, not contained or resolved, although there is grim satisfaction in contemplating the 'two-handed engine at the door', and the poet copes with his problem by turning away from it:

> Return, Alphéus, the dread voice is past
> That shrunk thy streams.
>
> (ll. 132–3)

The pattern of the rest of the poem is clear and well known, with the poet-figure working his way, via the partial explanations and the outbursts which make up the body of the poem, to the point where he can accept the Christian view of death:

> Weep no more, woeful shepherds, weep no more,
> For Lycidas, your sorrow, is not dead,
> Sunk though he be beneath the wat'ry floor.
>
> (ll. 165–7)

When the poet can feel this, as well as knowing it, it is possible for the death of Lycidas to be sufficiently placed to allow a turning to 'fresh woods, and pastures new' (l. 193). Achieving this psychological state allows the surviving poet to continue to 'strictly meditate' the muse. The vocation can continue, even despite the death of a devotee, and that is the real tribute to King – his death has taught that 'lesson'. But it is very important that we understand that the poem has not taken its pastoral and allusive form for decorative reasons. King's death can only signify beyond the merely personal because Milton has drawn the parallels. In 'Lycidas' the drawing together of the particular occasion and analogues from classical legend and the Scriptures honours Lycidas/King by typifying him.

Perhaps the only elegiac poem of the century which can match 'Lycidas' for range and richness, aptness, and mastery of material and manner, is John Dryden's 'To the Pious Memory of the Accomplisht Young Lady Mrs. Anne Killigrew',[4] which, like 'Lycidas', is one poet's tribute to another. Like Milton, Dryden incorporates basic information about his subject, with references to her activities as poet and painter, allusion to her father and brother, reference to her slow death, but whereas Milton develops parallels between poet and subject Dryden concentrates more upon direct praise. This is tactful in itself, because by 1686 Dryden had over forty-five years of writing behind him, while Anne Killigrew was still in the apprentice stage at her death. Comparisons like those in 'Lycidas' could hardly, therefore, have been other than embarrassing. What Dryden does is to make Killigrew, through his transforming art, a representative of art and its value.

This device is most brilliantly evident in the sixth and seventh stanzas. In the sixth Dryden praises Killigrew as a poet who invades the painter's territory:

> To the next Realm she stretcht her Sway, . . .
> And the whole Fief, in right of Poetry she claim'd.
>
> ('To the Pious Memory', ll. 92, 98)

Dryden himself had an interest in painting and in the relationship between the arts,[5] and in the second part of this stanza he describes Killigrew's achievements as poet-painter:

The Sylvan Scenes of Herds and Flocks,
And fruitful Plains and barren Rocks,
Of shallow Brooks that flow'd so clear,
The Bottom did the Top appear.

(ll. 108–11)

The wit of this is that Dryden is using his art to duplicate Anne Killigrew's own achievement and thereby to compliment it.

The same kind of witty aptness appears again in the following stanza. There the fact that Anne had done royal portraits allows Dryden to praise the King and Queen, but praise of them is also praise of Anne, for it is her art which has realized their qualities and thus, formally, led to the poet's praise of them. In both stanzas, Anne's achievements are seen in public terms, with her painting – whether pastoral or portraiture – presenting the inner life of the subject by concentrating on externals; and in both stanzas Anne's example is seen as a demonstration of the active and beneficial function of art.

Unlike Milton, Dryden does nothing to suggest that the death of Anne Killigrew led to any crisis for his own vocation or faith. It is only at the end of 'Lycidas' that Milton's poet-figure can turn away from his topic, having only then come to terms with its implications for himself. The death of Lycidas/King is the poem's central fact, and the idea that, through death, Lycidas has been born into a higher life (something which Vaughan can accept with ease) is only available to the poet-figure when grief and anger have been worked through and thus relieved. Dryden, however, feels able to begin his ode with Anne Killigrew already at home in heaven after her death:

Thou Youngest Virgin-Daughter of the Skies,
    Made in the last Promotion of the Blest.

(ll. 1–2)

Anne's promotion does not surprise or distress the poet, as Milton's poet-figure is distressed or as the man in the medieval *Pearl* is confused and upset. Instead, the translation of Anne in her youth is made the mark of her quality, and her example is what matters, as in the fourth stanza, where the 'Arethusian Stream' of her poetry stands as a rebuke to those who have 'Made prostitute and profligate the Muse'. Anne has been promoted to heaven, but from the earthly viewpoint she is a

Harbinger of Heav'n, the Way to show,
The Way which thou so well hast learn'd below.

(ll. 194–5)

'To the Pious Memory . . .' is a poem of great rhythmical richness and a masterpiece of architectonics. Like the other poems discussed in this section, it is a strategy for dealing with the problems of writing well of material which is neither familiar nor of obvious public concern. Like the other poets discussed, Dryden makes the quality of the poem the real tribute.

Funereal verse for public figures: to Cotton and Dryden

Poetry with a public face will inevitably be concerned at times with the deaths of great public figures, and the seventeenth century saw the production of a great deal of such verse. Much of this appears in collections produced to mark the relevant death, and to read such tributes is to be reminded of how conventional and routine the tributes can be. But seventeenth-century memorial poetry is at times more than just conventional, although success in this form has less to do with originality than with the skilful deployment of conventional themes.

One major occasion for the publication of memorial verse was the death of Prince Henry, son of James I, in 1612. Henry seems to have been a person of real promise and attractiveness, and he became the focus of hopes for the future as the limitations of James became more and more apparent.[6] Promising youth is an obvious focus for anyone who feels disappointment at the present state of affairs and the idea of a new beginning is a seductive one, especially when that new beginning is, paradoxically, seen as the return to an imagined purer past state. The hopes centred upon Henry and the distress at his death can thus be associated with, for example, the idea of Elizabeth as Astraea (Justice returning to earth) and with the joy which greeted the accession of James after the uncertainty of the last years of Elizabeth.

Edward Herbert was one of the poets who responded in verse to Henry's death and his 'Elegy for the Prince' is an interesting treatment of the problem of writing about a national figure. Edward Herbert, brother of George, is more talented than the neglect of his verse might suggest. He has a largely unjustified reputation for being difficult and his verse (which seems to have been no more than an occasional occupation) has a definite if sometimes awkward individuality which, in 'Elegy for the Prince', leads to a public poem of real intelligence and force. Decorum means that critical analysis of the personality and achievements of the dead person can hardly be expected, while an expanded list of stock idealizing attributes would have only limited interest. Herbert deals with these problems, rather as Donne did with Elizabeth Drury, by taking Henry as the focus for speculations about the nature of human life, and he is helped in this by himself being a philosopher.[7] Such a focus is appropriate in this case since, as heir to a throne, Henry could be seen in the light of the idea of monarchy as head of the body politic and thus as representing the essential life of the State, while the fact that he was a person of real ability gives such ideas more than conventional weight. Herbert begins with a series of questions, which themselves represent the impact of the death:

Must he be ever dead? Cannot we add
Another life unto that Prince that had
Our souls laid up in him? Could not our love,
Now when he left us, make that body move,
After his death one Age?

And he goes on to construct his poem around the issues of the helplessness
of man and the nature of existence which these questions introduce. The
witty discussion is clearly hyperbolic, but Herbert's strongly philosophical
bent leads to verse which, at its best, has some persuasive weight:

> Nor shall we question more,
> Whether the Soul of man be memory,
> As Plato thought: We and posterity
> Shall celebrate his name, and vertuous grow,
> Only in memory that he was so.
> (ll. 42–6)

The elegy gives little idea of Henry's personality, and it would be rash to
read it as a literal account of the poet's true emotions. Herbert, it seems,
is not concerned to offer Henry as a model of virtue or virtues, but he
praises him as one whose death leads to examination of the nature of life.
The quality of lines like those just quoted makes this less extravagant than
it may sound.

Edward Herbert was a diplomat and thinker, a man of a distinguished
family with a record of service to the State. William Drummond, another
of Henry's elegists, is remembered as 'Drummond of Hawthornden' and
his centre is Scotland rather than England, while his verse seems resolutely
slightly out of date and his gifts are unlike Herbert's. His tribute to Henry,
'Teares on the Death of Moeliades' (1613), has a clear basic pattern, which
leads a reader from the questioning of death to a lament that Henry was
not allowed to die heroically, to exposition of the effect of his death on the
natural world, to consideration of Moeliades's life after death and thence
to consolation. But this pattern is articulated through amplification rather
than, as it would have been with Herbert, argument, and the effect Drum-
mond achieves is appropriately grave and dignified, if often rather pedes-
trian. At times Drummond seems to strain rather too hard for effect:

> In gloomie Gownes the Starres about deplore,
> The Sea with murmuring Mountaines beates the Shore,
> Blacke Darknesse reeles o're all, in thousand Showres
> The weeping Aire, on Earth her Sorrow powres,
> That (in a Palsey) quakes to finde so soone
> Her Lover set, and Night burst foorth ere Noone.
> ('Tears on the Death of Moeliades', ll. 29–34)

Drummond's Henry is not a figure with any definition, either as individual or as a model. The importance of his loss is asserted, and the poet tries to present this through his handling of rhetoric, but his control is shaky (as in the lines above and in phrases like 'warme encrimson'd Swords' and 'Townes raz'd, and rais'd', ll. 41, 53) while his substitution of amplification for thought leads to sprawling. But Drummond, derivative and mediocre though he often is, has the technique and imagination to respond to the idea of temporal life as futile, so that the long closing section of the elegy has an impressive movement and some striking phrasing:

> Thou wondrest Earth to see hang like a Ball,
> Clos'd in the gastly Cloyster of this All:
> And that poore Men should prove so madly fond,
> To tosse themselves for a small Foot of Ground.
> Nay, that they even dare brave the Powers above,
> From this base Stage of Change, that cannot move.
> All worldly Pompe and Pride thou seest arise
> Like Smoake, that scattreth in the emptie Skies
>
> (ll. 163–70)

The death of a public figure does not in itself necessarily offer rich possibilities for poets, particularly since decorum limits analysis and restricts choice of detail. It is also worth remembering that great public figures are often mediocre or downright unattractive. On the whole it is the imaginative quality of the poet, rather than the nature of the subject, which will produce success or failure. So far as Prince Henry was concerned, the fact of his youth allowed for emphasis on lost potential, but, by the same token, meant that there could be little achievement to discuss. Herbert deals with the situation by working outwards from the particular death to reflections derived legitimately from it, and stylistically he uses a plain manner which presents extravagance in sober language. Drummond, through the elaboration of stock funereal motifs and an ornate, allusive style, seeks to transform the individual, Henry, into the typical. Despite the metaphysical element in Herbert's style, it can be argued that his elegy and Drummond's provide two models for the public elegy in the seventeenth century. Poems by Charles Cotton and John Dryden give some idea of how such models could be used.

Cotton's short poem 'On the Lord Derby' (?1651) is in decasyllabic couplets and is about James Stanley, seventh Earl of Derby, a royalist who was captured and executed after the Battle of Worcester in 1651. The context of Derby's death provides Cotton with an obvious focus for his elegy – to set Derby's life and death in the wider situation of the nation after the second defeat of the royalist cause. But Cotton does not concern himself primarily with the dramatic possibilities of the situation and has nothing like the pictorial impact of Marvell's cameo of Charles on the scaffold in his 'Horatian Ode', even though Derby's execution could easily be set in a martyr tradition, as Charles's was done by royalists. Nor does Cotton have much to say about the individuality of James Stanley. Instead, Derby is a model, most particularly of loyalty:

> 'twas thy nobler sense to die
> A constant lover of thy loyalty.

And

> Amongst which throng of Martyrs none could boast
> Of more fidelity, than the world has lost
> In losing thee.

Derby manifests 'steady faith' and is 'Great, and good Derby'. He is a Jonsonian figure, used to make both a political point about monarchy and rebellion and a philosophical point about virtue and reason; while the guarantee of Cotton's right to see Derby in this way lies in the control, discrimination, and intelligence of the style. These features are present in the opening lines:

> To what a formidable greatness grown
> Is this prodigious beast Rebellion.

They are developed in the second paragraph:

> In this great ruin, Derby, lay thy Fate,
> (Derby, unfortunately fortunate)
> Unhappy thus to fall a sacrifice
> To such an irreligious power as this;
> And blest, as 'twas thy nobler sense to die
> A constant lover of thy loyalty.

The sense of Cotton's intelligence is heightened by the imaginative quality of his response to Derby's execution and what that represents to the poet. This is most marked at the end, where Cotton is addressing the rebels:

> When you have finish'd there, fall on the rest,
> Mix your sham'd slaughters with the worst, and best;
> And, to perpetuate your murthering fame,
> Cut your own throats, despair, and die, and damn.

What is striking here is how the emotion is directed and controlled, with the punning 'murthering fame' and the scornful alliteration of the last words.

Cotton's is a fine elegy, in which the death of Derby is appropriately used to reassert values important to the poet himself. He makes Derby significant by linking him with the cause for which he died and he has the imaginative tact to allow the weight of the case to make its own impact, the power of the final lines being increased by the restraint in the body of the poem. So 'On the Lord Derby' is a good example of what the plain-style poem of praise can achieve. By contrast, Dryden's 'Threnodia Augustalis'[8] (1685) demonstrates a loftier style in the hands of a master of the elaborate public poem.

'Threnodia Augustalis' is a long poem (517 lines) and is offered as a full-scale tribute to Charles II, its Latin motto indicating its pretensions and the subtitle – 'A Funeral-Pindarique' – claiming a genealogy reaching back to the Greek ode-writer Pindar, the celebrant of heroes. Dryden is attempting a laureate poem, in which the poet-figure is the voice of the nation, a point which is made in the poem by the movement between singular and plural pronouns. A personal response is suggested by the opening – 'Thus long my Grief has kept me dumb' – but is quickly modulated into the general:

> Like Niobe we Marble grow;
> And Petrifie with Grief.

This blending of the singular and the plural is typical of Dryden's method, the poem being a complex mixture of historical, mythological, biographical, and personal elements. Moreover, these elements are clearly transformed, so that what we are given is evidently an idealized version of Charles's reign and death. This is what the Niobe reference suggests, where the event is raised to the height of classical myth, and is made clear in the lines which immediately follow:

> Our British Heav'n was all Serene,
> No threatning Cloud was nigh,
> Not the least wrinkle to deform the Sky;
> We liv'd as unconcern'd and happily
> As the first Age in Natures golden Scene.
>
> (ll. 9–13)

Historically speaking, this is an astonishing claim to make of the last part of the reign. The year 1683 saw the Rye House Plot and the executions of Sidney and Russell, while Titus Oates was arrested in 1684 and the following year saw the Monmouth Rebellion. But Dryden is not really interested in history. He is concerned more with drama, with a striking contrast which he builds up to emphasize the suddenness of the King's illness and death:

> We slept securely, and we dream't of more:
> When suddenly the Thunder-clap was heard.
>
> (ll. 15–16)

It should be added, however, that Dryden is less unresponsive to historical actuality than may at first seem to be the case, for the idea of a sleeping nation, 'Supine amidst our flowing Store', a nation taken 'unprepar'd and out of guard' (ll. 14, 17) by the King's collapse suggests the same kind of 'lethargy' which Jonson had attacked in his 'An Epistle to a Friend, to persuade him to the Wars', and this view receives some support from Pepys's Diary. In Dryden's fiction Charles is separated from responsibility for this lethargy, and his qualities are seen as creating a new Golden Age, but the King's death points to the fragility of things and the poet's lines hint that the nation should have been more alert.

Dryden is clearly concerned to present the country as both virtually destroyed by Charles's death and heartened by the accession of his brother: 'Our Atlas fell indeed; But Hercules was near' (l. 35). Dryden's James is seen as 'Pious Brother, sure the best/Who ever bore that Name' (ll. 36–7). He is utterly loyal and 'Guiltless of Greatness', but his time having come he is to be seen as 'Martial Ancus' to Charles's Numa (ll. 45, 465–6). James does seem to have been loyal to his brother, but Dryden's version of what his reign might be is almost ludicrous in the light of the facts. Yet here again there is a sense in which this scarcely matters, for what Dryden is doing is to develop another dramatic contrast, between pacific Charles and warlike James, and to offer a model of what he sees as politically desirable, a more aggressive foreign policy, as a result of which 'Gaul and Batavia' (France and the United Provinces) 'lick the dust, and Crouch beneath their fatal Foe' (ll. 478–80). History may say that to see James as 'A Prince on whom . . . The Welfare of the World it safely might repose' (ll. 237–8) was wildly optimistic even in 1685, but Dryden is more interested in what should be than in what is.

The account of Charles's moral nature shows a similar mixture of truth and idealization. Here Dryden makes use of listings of descriptive adjectives: 'Intrepid, pious, merciful, and brave'; 'Kind, good and gracious' (ll. 206, 220). Such adjectives are fleshed out by an account of Charles's exile and restoration, in which the King is seen as

> That all forgiving King,
> The type of him above,
> That inexhausted spring
> Of clemency and Love.
>   (ll. 257–60)

Charles's grace is such that he takes on Christ's role, for as Christ assumed the sins of mankind, though guiltless himself, so Charles

> . . . ask'd that Pardon which he ne'er refus'd:
> For faults not his, for guilt and Crimes
> Of Godless men, and of Rebellious times.
>   (ll. 262–4)

This is clearly a partial account. It omits Charles's faults and involves some pious lying (the evidence suggests, for example, that the King was hardly a pious man) but, for whatever reason, Charles was genuinely merciful at the Restoration and does seem to have been courageous.

'Threnodia Augustalis', then, is an idealized version of the history it commemorates, and it is more than merely another public elegy because of the quality of Dryden's writing. The thought in the poem is unremarkable, even where the style is witty, as with the conceit of fish as a 'wat'ry Herd' and with the analogy between medicine and war:

> But, like a fortress on a Rock,
> Th'impregnable Disease their vain attempts did mock;
> They min'd it near, they batter'd from a far
> With all the Cannon of the Med'cinal War.
>
> (ll. 141, 167–70)

But the thought in such a poem as this should be unremarkable, since it is meant as the expression of general views. What makes the commonplace memorable is the poet's ability to be confidently simple, as in the monosyllabic antithesis here:

> Calm was his life, and quiet was his death.
>
> (l. 285)

And there is the assured handling of rhetorical patterns:

> For all those Joys thy Restauration brought,
> For all the Miracles it wrought,
> For all the healing Balm thy Mercy pour'd
> Into the Nations bleeding Wound.
>
> (ll. 292–5)

The combination of this level of technical ability with serious general intelligence makes the poem a substantial achievement. Its material and polish may at first produce no more than a sense of generalized competence, but the quality lies in the artfulness of the structure and style.

Types of praise: Daniel to Marvell

There is considerable overlap between poems about the deaths of great public figures and poems about such people still alive, and seventeenth-century verse about the virtues and achievements of the living makes a contrast with the negatives of public satire, which will be looked at in Chapter 4. As with public elegies, it is unlikely that such verse will have much criticism of its subjects to offer, but the best is more than mere flattery.

Samuel Daniel's 'A Panegyrike Congratulatory' (1603) is an explicitly public poem, as the rest of the title makes clear – 'Delivered to the Kings most excellent majesty at Burleigh Harrington in Rutlandshire'. Indeed, the word 'Panegyrike' itself indicates a poem which is both laudatory and public,[9] while the length (nearly 600 lines) and stanza form (ABABABCC) both suggest a large-scale formal presentation. By comparison with, say, Dryden's major eulogies, Daniel seems stylistically plain, but he achieves an impressively controlled sense of stylistic continuity and reasonableness, and this reduces the feeling of hyperbole. James I is, of course, praised, but the praise is thoughtful and the context for the praise seems more than just decorative.

Daniel persistently sees Britain in terms of natural metaphors:

> What a returne of comfort dost thou bring
> Now at this fresh returning of our blood,
> Thus meeting with th'opening of the Spring,
> To make our spirits likewise to imbudde?
> What a new season of incouraging
> Beginnes t'inlength the dayes dispos'd to good.
>
> (st. 17)

By making such links with nature Daniel is indicating both harmony and unity, the latter tying up with his stress on the Union of Scotland and England under James. Within the states such unity and harmony are seen as the gifts of the new monarch, who is both divinely appointed and humanly chosen:

> God makes thee King of our estates, but we
> Do make thee King of our affection.
>
> (st. 5)

But Daniel is concerned to do more than assert that James is a great and a good thing, and this involves him in setting the King in a temporal context. James exists both in relation to the nation's past and to the future, the beginning of his reign being a drawing together of history ready for the movement to what is to come. And although Daniel's predictions are not very accurate, his optimism catches the real hope which was widely expressed at James's accession and is a presentation of a view of a harmoniously unified society which the poet wishes the King to aspire towards. In fact, Daniel's predictions are more accurately seen as admonitions, as the tenses here suggest:

> There great exemplare prototipe of Kings,
> We finde the Good shal dwell within thy Court;
> Plaine zeale and truth free from base flatterings,
> Shall there be entertain'd and have resorte.
>
> (st. 23)

Daniel recalls the 'ancient stubbornnesse' (st. 7) of the people and his account of what the court of James should be is sharpened by his awareness of what courts often are. Such details give 'A Panegyrike' a critical dimension, and this also occurs in Jonson's 'A Panegyre, on the Happy Entrance of James, Our Sovereign, to His First High Session of Parliament in This Kingdom, the 19 of March, 1603'.

Like Daniel, Jonson sees the King and State in terms of the natural

world. James is associated with the sun (one of the commonest metaphors
for kingship) and his beams are healing. But Jonson sees these kingly beams
as also 'searching' and he renders the nature of what needs to be searched
with theatrical power:

> But these his searching beams are cast, to pry
> Into those dark and deep concealéd vaults,
> Where men commit black incest with their faults;
> And snore supinely in the stall of sin,
> Where murder, rapine, lust do sit within.

This is a vision of 'damps' which would '(if not dispersed) infect the
crown,/And in their vapour her bright metal drown' ('A Panegyre . . .'
ll. 8–12, 16–18).

Jonson presents these 'damps' to create a contrast with the united joy
which, he says, greets the King on his way to Parliament:

> No age, nor sex, so weak, or strongly dull,
> That did not bear a part in this consent
> Of hearts and voices.
> (ll. 58–60)

He goes on to make it clear that the rejoicing involves social harmony –
'This was the people's love, with which did strive/ The nobles' zeal' – but
the image he uses to reinforce the point is interesting in its delicacy:

> yet either kept alive
> The other's flame, as doth the wick and wax,
> That friendly tempered, one pure taper makes.
> (ll. 70–72)

The image captures the interdependence of orthodox social theory, but it
is also an image of something fragile and unstable.

'A Panegyre' is a poem of celebration and hope, but Jonson's awareness
of dark forces and his taper image suggest a steady sense of uncertainties
which make the future problematic. This ties up with the placing of James,
as in Daniel's poem, at a point of balance between past and future. Jonson
uses the figure of Themis to advise the new King, and Themis offers firm
reminders of kingship gone wrong, of a past where 'laws were made to
serve the tyrant will' and 'acts gave licence to impetuous lust' (ll. 99, 101).
Moreover, the advice which Themis offers is direct and clear:

> kings, by their example, more do sway
> Than by their power; and men do more obey
> When they are led than when they are compelled.
> (ll. 125–7)

The poem's final lines offer a nation united in conviction that James will
profit from such advice and act upon it:

> With a twice louder shout again they cried,
> 'Yet, let blessed Britain ask (without your wrong)
> Still to have such a king, and this king long'.
>
> (ll. 160–2)

'A Panegyre' offers an imaginative heightening of the joy which did greet James, but it also offers the poet's awareness of the difficulty of sustaining such a level of harmony. Sadly, the advice and vision of Jonson's poem were not to be reflected in reality.

Such poetry as this uses known verbal codes (king as sun, etc.) to praise a public figure in a public manner, and what is done that goes beyond simple eulogy is done obliquely: adverse criticism can hardly be direct, given the mode. But the rise of Oliver Cromwell created a problem for poets who wrote about great men and women. Cromwell came to a position comparable to that of a monarch, and was in fact offered the throne, but he was neither of royal blood nor did he assume the throne. The problem, therefore, for poets who wished to celebrate Cromwell was to find or create a public vocabulary for doing so. On the whole the poets concerned either evaded the problem or failed to solve it, and that is a revealing aspect of political thought in the mid-century.

In his 'A Panegyric to my Lord Protector' (c. 1655), Edmund Waller tries to handle the issue of Cromwell by assimilating him to traditional language and ideas. Waller is well aware that Cromwell is a *de facto* equivalent to a monarch and he seeks to normalize the situation in various ways. Thus Cromwell is given a pedigree, as it were, by being placed in a line established by allusion to Neptune, Julius Caesar and Augustus; to David and Joseph (ll. 9, 149, 170, 136, 188). This pedigree, establishing Cromwell as heroic in both classical and biblical myth, bypasses questions of his relationship with the native tradition of rulers, but Waller is also concerned to place Cromwell in that tradition and does so by implicitly making a monarch of him. So Waller presents Cromwell in traditional monarchic images, as the sun which 'night's vulgar light destroys' and as a lion (ll. 144, 165); and he links Cromwell's victorious foreign policy with Edward III and Edward the Black Prince. Moreover, Waller defines Cromwell's function in the State in monarchic terms. In the poem's first stanza the function is 'to bridle faction, and our hearts command', while towards its end the Protector is seen as parent – 'So England now does, with like toil oppressed,/Her weary head upon your bosom rest'. Waller also normalizes the abnormal by linking Cromwell with such traditional relationships as that of the microcosm and macrocosm ('Our little world, the image of the great', l. 49) while the whole effort to make the situation seem at one with tradition is mimed by the style, most notably by the calm pairings and antitheses – 'The greatest leader and the greatest isle!'; 'Justice to crave, and succour, at your court'; 'us, embraced by the sea and you' (ll. 24, 30, 40). In Waller's poem everything slots into place, is balanced and harmonious. The poet seems uninterested in trying to find new categories for this unique ruler, and little effort is made to deal with the special circumstances of Cromwell's rule. Andrew Marvell, however, shows something of the strain of really trying to think about what Cromwell represents, and seems to have been genuinely interested in the man, writing three English and two Latin poems about him.

The most famous and most debated of these is 'An Horatian Ode'(1650)[10] and a great deal of paper has been used in trying to convince readers that the poem is simply for Cromwell or for Charles. But any serious study of loyalties in the England of Charles and Cromwell indicates that such simplicity was not always possible. There were, of course, many for whom loyalty was clear cut and absolute. Cleveland and Lovelace, for example, seem to have had no doubt at all about their support for the King, while Milton remained firmly committed to the Good Old Cause until his death, but there were many for whom choice at the outbreak of war was far from easy and many whose loyalties were painfully defined through the developing pattern of events, while others were mainly concerned to remain as neutral as possible. We, in a secular age, should not be too easily cynical about providential readings of events in a religious age, and we should be well able to respond to pragmatism where we find it.

'An Horatian Ode' is remarkable in being a highly intelligent poem written while events were still unstable. By June/July 1650, when the poem was written, Charles had been executed, monarchy and the House of Lords abolished (February 1649), the Commonwealth had been declared (May 1649), and Cromwell had campaigned successfully in Ireland. But the future Charles II was a threat, while the implications of a commonwealth, the challenge of Levellers and Diggers, and the question of Cromwell's own role were all live issues. Marvell's poems often suggest that he found commitment difficult, but if this seems psychologically revealing it should be added that 'An Horatian Ode' can also be read in terms of social psychology. Marvell here sees Cromwell primarily as a force, an 'active star' which marks out a 'fiery way' (ll. 12, 16) and which acts by rending and burning. Formulae like '''Tis madness to resist or blame/The force of angry heaven's flame' (ll. 25–6) suggest a providential view of history, but other couplets indicate that Marvell is also aware of *realpolitik*:

> Though justice against fate complain,
>   And plead the ancient rights in vain:
>   But those do hold or break
>   As men are strong or weak.
>
>   (ll. 37–40)

What seem to be inconsistencies in the poem are ways of representing the complexities of the situation, and so the famously enigmatic ending is a tense representation of a problematic condition of the State.

When Marvell came to write 'The First Anniversary of the Government under His Highness the Lord Protector, 1655' he had, as the title indicates, five more years of experience to draw upon, and the poem is interestingly less tentative than the earlier ode had been. Marvell quickly and firmly establishes Cromwell not just as a greater spirit than Charles had been in the quasi-physics of 'An Horatian Ode', but as a figure in the monarchic tradition. Cromwell is 'Sun-like', he 'doth with new lustre spring', he 'shines the jewel of the yearly ring' (ll. 8, 11–12). He is seen as the rebuilder of the State, the imagery being that of Daniel's panegyric to James, and as builder-musician Cromwell is equivalent to Amphion, a figure with whom James was often compared.[11]

In this poem, however, Marvell goes beyond just assimilating Cromwell to a monarchic tradition, and suggests that he transcends that tradition. Monarchic succession is wittily seen as necessary because 'one thing never was by one king done' (l. 22). Kings are satirized:

> Thus (image-like) an useless time they tell,
> And with vain sceptre strike the hourly bell,
> Nor more contribute to the state of things,
> Than wooden heads unto the viol's strings.
>
> (ll. 41–4)

Cromwell is immediately offered as contrast:

> While indefatigable Cromwell hies,
> And cuts his way still nearer to the skies.
>
> (ll. 45–6)

This is not to say that 'The First Anniversary' is a simple poem. Marvell's manner remains thoughtful and he is aware of factors which threaten the stability which is given as Cromwell's achievement, as is clear in the fine tensions of the great building image, in the account of the attempted assassination, and in the conditional language of 'Hence oft I think if in some happy hour/High grace should meet in one with highest power' (ll. 131–2). But although Marvell is properly responsive to the uncertainties of the situation, he does seem relatively at ease with the actualities of Cromwellian power.

The assimilation of Cromwell by adapting to him the images and functions of monarchy is taken further in the 'Poem upon the Death of His Late Highness the Lord Protector' (1658) when the poet turns from considering Oliver's death to the transfer of power to his son, Richard:

> He, as his father, long was kept from sight
> In private, to be viewed by better light;
> But opened once, what splendour does he throw?
> A Cromwell in an hour a prince will grow.
>
> (ll. 309–12)

The attempt to fit Richard to Oliver's pattern was to be faulted by time, but what is interesting is that Marvell sees Oliver as having established a dynasty. The revolution has become little more than a squabble about which kingly line shall rule – a seventeenth-century Wars of the Roses.

Marvell's elegy is less convincing than either of his other English poems on Cromwell. It seems to lack focus, to be going through the motions, perhaps because Marvell felt he had already had his say about Cromwell, perhaps because the constitutional difficulties of the last years of the Protectorate (culminating in the offer of the crown in 1657) had worn down even supporters of the revolution. After all, if crowns were again to be worn, did it not make sense to offer them to traditional rulers?

Something of the same lack of drive marks Dryden's 'Heroique Stanza's, Consecrated to the Glorious Memory of his most Serene and Renowned Highnesse OLIVER Late LORD PROTECTOR of this Common-Wealth etc.' (1659). As the title makes tediously clear, Dryden is not sparing of praise, but the heavy end-stopping in the poem creates the effect of a list, when compared with Waller's smooth flow or with the careful argument of 'The First Anniversary'. But Dryden also works by assimilating Cromwell to old traditions. Questions of rights are avoided by dwelling on Cromwell's successful foreign policy, which hints at Edward III and Henry V; by seeing Cromwell as princely in function ('But to our Crown he did fresh Jewells bring'; 'Such was our Prince', ll. 26, 125) and as a force both natural and supernatural ('Swift and resistlesse through the Land he past'; 'naturally all souls to his did bow': 'When such Heroique Vertue Heav'n set out,/The Starrs like Commons sullenly obey', ll. 49, 74, 105–6). This is reminiscent of the greater spirit of 'An Horatian Ode', but Dryden's poem has little of Marvell's tense balance. Perhaps one reason for the passing of the revolution was that it proved easier to read new events in the language of old ones.

Notes

1. G. A. E. Parfitt, 'Ben Jonson's Classicism', in *Studies in English Literature*, ed. Carroll Camden (Texas, 1971). For criticism of Jonson's *Epigrams* see particularly R. Dutton, *Ben Jonson: to the First Folio* (Cambridge, 1983), pp. 75–92 and J. Gardiner, *Craftsmanship in Context* (The Hague, 1975), especially pp. 12–53.

2. John Carey, *John Donne, Life, Mind and Art* (London, 1981), pp. 101–3

3. For critical accounts of 'Lycidas' see especially A. S. P. Woodhouse, *The Heavenly Muse* (Toronto, 1972), pp. 83–98 and J. A. Wittreich Jr, *Visionary Poetics* (San Marino, 1979), Ch. 2.

4. On the Killigrew ode see E. Miner, *Dryden's Poetry* (Bloomington, 1967), pp. 253–67 and M. Van Doren, *John Dryden* (Bloomington, 1920), *passim*.

5. Shown, for instance, in his *A Parallel Betwixt Poetry and Painting* (1695).

6. See D. H. Willson, *King James VI and I* (London 1956), *passim*.

7. Author of *De Veritate* and *De Religione Gentilium*.

8. On 'Threnodia Augustalis' see Miner, *passim* and Van Doren, *passim*.

9. See J. D. Garrison, *Dryden and the Tradition of Panegyric* (Berkeley, 1975), pp. 3–19.

10. On 'An Horatian Ode' see particularly J. Wallace, *Destiny His Choice* (London, 1968), pp. 69–105; A. Patterson, *Andrew Marvell and the Civic Crown* (New Jersey, 1978), pp. 60–9; R. Colie, '*My Ecchoing Song*' (New Jersey, 1970), pp. 62–71. On 'The First Anniversary' see Wallace, pp. 106–44, and Patterson, pp. 68–90.

11. See G. Parry, *The Golden Age Restor'd* (Manchester, 1981), p. 232. Amphion, son of Zeus and Antiope, was a musician who built the walls of Thebes.

Chapter 4
Satire

Introduction

Satirists work on the assumption that experience can be sorted into black and white. This assumption may correspond to a genuine belief that experience does take such form, or it may be a guise adopted by the satirist for analytic purposes, but in either case the satirist's concern is mainly with the black in experience, with, that is, vice, folly, blind ignorance, and stupidity. The satirist predicates that such darkness is socially dominant and focuses chiefly on the contemporary. He may have any of several starting-points: the ethico-theological (for example, a belief in Fallen Man), the psychological (poet as depressive) or the social (belief that the society he is concerned with is degenerate). But whatever his departure point and basis for analysis the satirist presents himself as concerned to indicate those social evils which should be extirpated. His role, then, is opposite to that of the poet of praise, who, as we have seen, creates models of goodness, transforming persons into examples of what a society can and should aspire to. The satirist concentrates upon that in society which corrupts it and creates models of what should not exist in any healthy society.

But while it is possible and necessary to draw such clear distinctions, it should be added that the distinctions often break down in practice, or at least need modifying. Satire plays a part in much literature which is not formally satire, and it is the case that a lot of English literature is satirical without being satire. In fact, formal satire only becomes established in England in the 1590s, when it emerges as a self-conscious, classically based alternative poetry, notably through Hall, Marston, and Donne. This formal satire draws particularly on Persius and Juvenal, develops the figure of an aggressive, analytic persona both fascinated and disgusted by the vice and folly of contemporary society, and packs the lines (usually decasyllabic couplets) with detail which concentrates upon surface observation of dress, appearance, and action. Such Elizabethan satire is preoccupied with urban settings, often that of court, and it is a type of poetry which challenges Spenserianism and the sonnet-boom at their roots.[1]

Such poetry appears, at first sight, to be no more than a brief fashion, its chief landmarks being Hall's *Virgidimarium, I–III* (1597) and Marston's

Scourge of Villainy (1598), for after 1600 it is not until the Civil War that verse satire is again prominent. Indeed such satire was banned in 1599 (which perhaps suggests that it was near to some sensitive truths). But in fact satire is very important in early seventeenth-century literature, in prose, in verse which avoided the ban, and – above all – in drama. The plays of Shakespeare, Jonson, Marston, and Middleton contain some of the best satirical writing in English, the tradition of Hall and Marston finding its immediate descendants in *Troilus and Cressida*, the *Antonio* plays, *Poetaster*, and *Revenger's Tragedy*. But it remains true, none the less, that satire is a central preoccupation among poets of the early seventeenth century only for Ben Jonson. Donne's poems (leaving aside the early *Satyres*) often have satirical detail and George Herbert is capable of satirical moments, but in Jonson's poetry satirical analysis is often fundamental.

Jonson never calls a poem of his a satire ('A Satirical Shrub' being the nearest he comes) and he has little interest in working the satirical vein of the 1590s (at least in his poems, for his early comedies do use the surgical and sadistic imagery of that satire). His ideal is Horatian rather than Juvenalian,[2] although this is less a matter of style – since Jonson's satirical detail is often packed and dynamic in Juvenal's manner – than that Jonson follows Horace in making satire part of the analysis, rather than the whole story. He does analyse in terms of black and white, and individual poems may suggest that vice, stupidity, and ignorance are almost all that there is to experience, but Jonson, even more than most poets, needs to be read whole, and knowledge of his work indicates a struggle between his response to social weakness and his belief that mankind is also capable of humane and honourable behaviour. In this context *Epigrams* is an epitome of Jonson's way of seeing and presenting experience, for, if we read that collection through, we find that, for instance, the moving assertion of William Camden's human worth is sandwiched between an attack on the danger of quack doctors (xiii) and another on the vacuity of a courtling (xv). As a collection, *Epigrams* juxtaposes the vicious and the virtuous, presenting an analysis of experience in terms of moral extremes, the tension and conflict lying between the poems.

The satirist works to present a negative mirror. When a reader looks in this mirror he/she sees little except deformity and the bestial: Man looking at Yahoo. What is unusual about Jonson is that he offers two mirrors, the satirical and the celebratory, his art being a dialogue between the two. Thus Jonson's satirical poems do not merely *imply* an alternative set of moral positives, for his art *presents* these in his poems of praise. His constant interest in society and social values means that he works most commonly with surface detail, but his details consistently refer to the absolute moral values in which he believes. In 'An Epistle to a Friend, to Persuade Him to the Wars', he writes of those who

> leap mad on a neat pickardil,
> As if a brise were gotten in their tail,
> And firk, and jerk, and for the coachman rail,
> And jealous of each other, yet think long

To be abroad chanting some bawdy song,
And laugh, and measure thighs, then squeak, spring, itch,
Do all the tricks of a saut lady bitch.

(ll. 70–6)

The violently erratic activity and the concern with the superficial could be contrasted with the self-knowledge and stability of those whom Jonson celebrates elsewhere, but both the satire and the praise belong to a consistent account of society in terms of ethical absolutes.

For Jonson, then, satire is far more than a literary fashion. It is one way of analysing society, or – perhaps more accurately – one response to that scrutiny of society and the individual which is Jonson's main concern. He tends to extremes of optimism and pessimism and the poems show various combinations of these impulses, from the conditioned optimism of 'To Penshurst', to the more sombre discussion of 'Epistle. To Katherine, Lady Aubigny', to the distress of 'A speech according to Horace'. A satirical element in the account of society and the individual is as inevitable, it seems, in Jonson's verse as in the work of William Langland, but it is important to add that the specifically Christian sanctions of Langland and of the whole 'complaint'[3] tradition are largely missing in Jonson. The moral values with which Jonson works are assimilable to Christianity but not exclusive to it, and Jonson makes little effort to give his analysis any metaphysical dimension. His perspective is essentially secular and he relates details to a comprehensive account of society seen in the light of ethical tradition. Jonson followed Horace in showing that satire can be part of a serious and sustained account of society based upon a sense of what is possible for man as secular being. Far from being either a fashion or a self-contained genre, satire is in Jonson part of the poet's total armoury and this incorporation of satire is perhaps Jonson's chief contribution to the history of satire in the seventeenth century and after. Arguably, *Absalom and Achitophel* and *The Dunciad* are such great satirical poems because they are not only satires. Both owe a lot to Jonson.

Cleveland, *Rump*, and 'Painter' poems

Jonson died in 1637, the year of 'Lycidas' and of Descartes's *Discourse*; of the case of *Rex* v. *Hampden* and of the punishments of Burton, Bastwick, and Prynne.[4] Chapman, Webster, Marston, George Herbert, Donne, and Shakespeare were already dead, while Dryden and the future Charles II were young children. Jonson's last years seem to have been sad ones, and part of the sadness may have been bewilderment at a changing world. I have argued elsewhere that Jonson's feeling for tradition made it difficult for him to respond to the tensions of the years before the Civil War except with a mixture of foreboding and assertions of the urgency of reanimating traditional values.[5] In this he resembles the neutralists of J. S. Morrill's *The Revolt of the Provinces* (see Gen. Biblio., sect. (i)), and his impulses are similar to the view of the Civil War as essentially conservative in intention which is presented in Robert Ashton's *The English Civil War* (see Gen. Biblio., sect. (i)). Jonson can see little but disaster in innovation and for him, as for most of his contemporaries, this means that the only acceptable social model is that of monarchy and its concomitant hierarchies. In poem, play, and masque Jonson shows awareness of social restlessness below the gentry and doubts about the sense of responsibility among the upper classes. Typically, he feels that both the restlessness and the irresponsibility are dangerous. Since the only acceptable model is the traditional one, any pressures inimical to it must be suppressed, rechannelled, or reformed if chaos is to be averted.

The Civil War and the Commonwealth, by one account, demonstrate the accuracy of this view. The unthinkable becomes fact; monarchy is abolished and the King beheaded. This is a seventeenth-century version of fears of nuclear war becoming fact. In this period of intense activity satire plays a part and is violently partisan. But although the satire of the period involves ideological differences and variations of social models, it is best seen as part of the debate about how to reclaim a past felt to be better than the degenerate present. Satire tends to measure the present by the standards of the past (a past which is often more myth than actual) and is, in this sense, conservative. The satire of the Civil War and Commonwealth is no exception.

It has been suggested that Civil War satire is too close to its material to be of much permanent value, and the royalist John Cleveland is often cited not only as the most talented of these writers but also as the most obscure. But although Cleveland is a difficult poet, he is also a misunderstood one.

Cleveland is at times strongly reminiscent of the Elizabethan satirists, especially when he uses their imagery, as here:

> Come keen Iambicks, with your Badgers feet,
> And Badger-like, bite till your teeth do meet.
> Help ye tart Satyrists, to imp my rage,
> With all the Scorpions that should whip this age.
>
> ('The Rebell Scot' ll. 27–30)

Earlier in the same poem he presents the poet-figure similarly enraged:

> I am all on fire,
> Not all the buckets in a Countrey Quire
> Shall quench my rage.
>
> (ll. 5–7)

– and goes on to claim that 'A Poet should be fear'd/When angry, like a Comets flaming beard' (ll. 7–8).

The idea of the poet as a fearful figure can be linked with Cleveland's stress elsewhere upon the poet as magician:

> See, they obey the Magick of my words.
> Presto; they're gone.
>
> ('The Mixt Assembly', ll. 63–4)

In 'Smectymnuus' there is a similar suggestion of the power of the poet:

> My task is done; all my hee-Goats are milkt;
> So many Cards i'th stock, and yet be bilkt?
> I could by Letters now untwist the rable;
> Whip Smec from Constable to Constable.
>
> (ll. 91–4)

Obviously, the language of biting and whipping suggests an aggressive and impatient poet, and 'The Rebell Scot', like most of Cleveland's poems, has a single dominant tone. The poem begins abruptly:

> How? Providence? and yet a Scottish crew?
> Then Madam Nature wears black patches too

– and goes on as a high-pitched attempt to find language which will adequately express the poet's rage. So 'Had Cain been Scot, God would have chang'd his doome'; 'Scotland's a Nation Epidemicall'; it is 'a race/Able to bring the Gibbet in disgrace' (ll. 63, 70, 113–14). He ends:

> A Scot, when from the Gallow-Tree got loose,
> Drops into Styx, and turnes a Soland-Goose.

Cleveland's poetic rage is clearly destructively intended, an attempt to annihilate that which he attacks through a bombardment by synonym. But his rage also works by tranformation of what he attacks into the unnatural. The compressed and unharmonious style creates the impression of the grotesque, but Cleveland is also fascinated by monstrous unities, as in 'The Mixt Assembly', with its 'discolour'd Mates', 'strange Grottesco' and 'speckled and ringstreaked lambs' (ll. 5, 6, 14). To Cleveland this is a mad world:

> A Jig, a Jig: And in this Antick dance
> Fielding and doxy Marshall first advance.
>
> ('The Mixt Assembly', ll. 67–8)

Fielding is the second Earl of Denbigh, while Marshall is the preacher Stephen Marshall. What outrages Cleveland is both the union of secular and religious and that between the aristocrat and the man of humble origin:

> Thus Moses Law is violated now,
> And Ox and Asse go yok'd in the same plough
>
> (ll. 93–4)

There is the same sense of outrage at the unnatural in 'Smectymnuus', the title itself providing the poet with his main theme:

> Smectymnuus? The Goblin makes me start:
> I 'th 'Name of Rabbi Abraham, what art?
>
> (ll. 1–2)

Both this poem and 'The Rebell Scot' begin with a volley of questions, while 'The Kings Disguise' opens with a single fundamental enquiry:

> And why so coffin'd in this vile disguise,
> Which who but sees blasphemes thee with his eyes?

Moreover, as is probably already clear, Cleveland asks his questions and elaborates upon them in considerable detail. He seems fascinated, in 'A Dialogue between Two Zealots ...' by details of puritan activities and attitudes, while in 'The Mixt Assembly' he elaborates the pairing of Fielding and Marshall into a considerable list.

The idea of the poet as magician works two ways and these offer a clue as to the peculiar nature of Cleveland's satire. He speaks of 'the Magick of my words', and clearly the poet, as poet, has the power to transform the objects of his verse into whatever he chooses. His art can create and destroy as it wishes, and in that sense 'Presto; they're gone' is an accurate formula for how art can operate. But there is also a sense in which the poet is claiming more than he can perform, for the fury and obsessiveness of his style indicate that he cannot dismiss his subjects from his mind, and so the claim that 'My task is done' is a lie. He can create monsters but, like Frankenstein, cannot guarantee their destruction.

The linking of Fielding and Marshall creates one of Cleveland's monsters, and in 'The Mixt Assembly' the Earl of Denbigh is only one of several aristocrats seen in this way, for Cleveland also refers to Lord Saye and Sele, Baron Montague of Kimbolton, and Baron Wharton. In Cleveland's terms they contribute to the unnatural by yoking themselves to people like Marshall, Cornelius Burgess, and Oliver Bowles in the Assembly, thus breaching hierarchy and departing from traditional loyalties to the monarchy. This suggests an unnatural unity to be set against a natural social unity of a traditional kind, and it is this which lies beneath much of Cleveland's violent rage.

A strongly hostile reaction to the aspirations and actions of parliamentarians is, of course, to be expected from a royalist poet, and it suggests that Cleveland's use of the techniques of Elizabethan satire is more than literary imitation, since the abrupt rhythms and violent imagery of Marston are clearly appropriate to the emotions which Cleveland wishes to vent.

But what makes him a poet of particular interest is the evidence that his anger and distress go beyond just outrage at the presumption of parliamentarians. Here the key poem is 'The King's Disguise'.

Charles left Oxford on 27 April, 1646, and gave himself up to the Scots at Southwell on 5 May. Although his motives were consistent with his aim to regain power without serious concessions, and presumably, therefore, would have met with Cleveland's approval, this action by the King clearly distressed the poet. What is interesting, however, is not so much the distress itself but that Cleveland sees Charles's action as a betrayal of himself and of his office:

> Oh for a State-distinction to arraigne
> Charles of high Treason 'gainst my Soveraigne.
>
> ('The King's Disguise', ll. 5–6)

Behind this lies the idea of the King's two bodies, the distinction being between the King as individual and the King as office-holder[6]. Ideally, the two bodies become one in harmonious unity, but Charles has violated that harmony:

> What an usurper to his Prince is wont,
> Cloyster and shave him, he himselfe hath don't. . . .
> The Sun hath mew'd his beames from off his lamp,
> And Majesty defac'd the Royall stamp.
>
> (ll. 7–8, 11–12)

The unnaturalness of this is such, the poem's opening lines tell us, that it is blasphemy for anyone to see the King disguised in this way and the poet's eyes 'hold it their Allegeance to winke' (l. 4). The poet-figure can scarcely bear what it sees and the latter part of the poem is a pathetic search for hope and consolation:

> A Prince most seen, is least: What Scriptures call
> The Revelation, is most mysticall.
>   Mount then thou shadow royall, and with haste
> Advance thy morning star, Charles's overcast.
> May thy strange journey contradictions twist,
> And force faire weather from a Scottish mist.
>
> (ll. 113–18)

But the poet's hurt incredulity cannot be dispersed and the last couplet enacts this:

> But oh! he goes to Gibeon, and renewes
> A league with mouldy bread, and clouted shooes.

This league provides an exact parallel with the union of Denbigh and Marshall, Kimbolton, and Burgess.

Cleveland shows no sign of having considered the parliamentary case or of any awareness of the defects in Charles himself. His loyalty seems unquestioning, but he renders, as no other poet of the period does, both the strength of traditional models of obedience and social hierarchies and the anguish of seeing these fail. He attempts to deal with the new situation by making opponents into monsters but his obsessive attempts at demolition suggest that, for him, no accommodation is possible. A reader is, therefore, left with the impression that for Cleveland the King was the only source of security, and when defeat and self-betrayal take that source away the poet has nothing to fall back upon. Lacking Marvell's fascination with power itself, Milton's conviction in the cause even when that is betrayed, and Lovelace's stoicism, Cleveland can only express hurt bewilderment through violent creation.

Cleveland is the best example of the 'biting' satirist among Civil War poets, while John Denham exemplifies a more jocular satirical manner. In his major poem, 'Cooper's Hill', he shows himself capable of serious and extended contemplation of ideas of power and rule, but his satirical verse works through song forms and has, in general, a light tone. Thus in 'News from Colchester' he uses the persona of a puritan and writes a defence of bestiality:

> Help Woodcock, Fox and Naylor,
> For Brother Green's a stallion,
>   Now alas what hope
>   Of·converting the pope
> When a quaker turns Italian?[7]

This involves satire of puritan ethics, defined by opponents as hypocrisy:

> No surely, quoth John Naylor,
> 'Twas but an insurrection
>   Of the carnal part,
>   For a quaker in heart
> Can never lose perfection.
>   (ll. 56–60)

Sexual deviance was often alleged against puritans, and Cleveland would see this as symbolically typical, but Denham seems to find it unsurprising and even amusing. Similarly, in 'A Western Wonder' and 'A Second Western Wonder' he mocks parliamentary reaction to military engagements in the West Country:

> Do you not know, not a fortnight ago,
>   How they bragged of a Western wonder,
> When a hundred and ten slew four thousand men
>   With the help of lightning and thunder?
> There Hopton was slain, again and again,
>   Or else my author did lie.
>   ('A Western Wonder', ll. 1–6)

Here again, Denham's satirical manner is indirect, it being the internal rhymes and exaggeration which make the point. Rather than seeking to flay the opposition, Denham works with a mockery which feels fundamentally good-humoured:

> O what a damp it struck through the camp!
> But as for honest Sir Ralph,
> It blew him to the Vies, without beard or eyes,
> But at least three heads and a half.
>
> ('A Second Western Wonder', ll. 5–8)

If Denham were to be characterized solely on poems like these, it would be easy to see him as a lightweight, rather careless figure, who refused to take even the war seriously. But such a view is countered not only by 'Cooper's Hill' but also by other poems, like 'The Progress of Learning' and 'Natura Naturata', and Denham's satirical verse is best seen as a strategy for coping with the crisis of the war. To the uncompromising Cleveland, opponents are so vile that the only way to social health is through their extermination. Denham, however, concentrates upon the absurdity of those on the other side and his good humour suggests that he does not see opponents as of another species. 'Verses on the Cavaliers Imprisoned in 1655' indicates that such an approach need not hide awareness of the harshness of conflict:

> Then Marshall draw near, let the prisoners appear
> And read us their treasons at large,
> For men think it hard to lie under a guard
> Without any probable charge.
>
> (ll. 5–8)

The last two lines quoted show a firm grip on the frustration and grimness of the situation. Yet this poem also shows that Denham was aware that it was not only the parliamentarians who might seem absurd:

> Ned Prodgers looks pale, but what does he ail?
> (For he diets with that fat droll)
> He must dwindle at length that spends all his strength
> At the grill and the little hole.
>
> (ll. 41–4)

Basically, Denham deals with the Civil War and Commonwealth by underlining the absurdity of humans. By refusing to be wholly committed to personalities and issues he improves his chances of psychological survival.

Several of Denham's satires appear in the anthology called *The Rump* ('or an Exact Collection of the Choycest Poems and Songs Relating to the Late Times') which was first published in 1662, two years after the Restoration. Obviously, a miscellany 'By the most Eminent Wits, from Anno

1639 to Anno 1661'[8] is likely to offer a variety of styles and tones, but it is striking, granted the bitterness of the war and what was at stake, that so many of the *Rump* poems have more in common with Denham's manner than with Cleveland's. A number of them use the same device as that of Denham's 'News from Colchester', of presenting the poem as from the mouth of the enemy (the fiction being that the opponent is so corrupt that the folly and wrongheadedness of his position are revealed through his own voice). There is, for example, 'The Parliaments Hymnes', in which the effects are made obliquely:

> Put down the King and Hartford, Lord,
>   And keep them down for aye;
> Thy chosen Pym set up on high,
>   And eke the good Lord Say.
>
> (*The Rump*, I, p. 65)

There is no satirical vocabulary here, the author relying on the signals sent out by the names used and by the idea (blasphemous from the poet's viewpoint) that Pym is the chosen of God. Pym becomes a version of monarchy, and in poem upon poem he is 'king Pym'. This relates to the great theme of disturbed hierarchies:

> The name of Lords shall be abhorr'd,
>   For every man's a Brother,
> No reason why in Church and State
>   One man should rule another.

Such an egalitarian outlook was, in fact, held only among extremists, as the Putney Debates, for instance, made very clear, but the opportunities which the Civil War offered for men of relatively humble background to participate in national affairs were enough to frighten royalists (and many parliamentarians as well) and the poets of *The Rump* were right to see the challenge to the King as potentially subversive of hierarchy. But it is interesting that the author of 'A Song. To the Tune of Cuckolds all a-row' links subversion with promiscuity, as the second half of the stanza just quoted makes clear:

> But when the Change of Government
>   Shall set out fingers free,
> Wee'l make the wanton Sisters stoop,
>   And hey then up go we.
>
> (I, p. 16)

The idea of sexual licence and the associated idea of greater freedom for women were both commonplace accusations against puritans. To royalists, such ideas represent variations of that opposition to tradition which they insisted on attributing to parliamentarians, and although this involves considerable distortion of the outlook of the main stream of parliamentarian opinion it has enough validity in relation to extremists to make an effective smear. So the blending of anti-hierarchy politics with sexual promiscuity is a frequent *Rump* theme. Thus in 'The Character of a Roundhead, 1641' a Roundhead is one 'that doth the Bishops hate,/And count their Calling reprobate', one that 'doth high Treason say,/As often as his yea and nay', but also one who 'goes five miles to preach and pray,/And lyes with's Sister by the way' (I, p. 42).

At times this feeling that opposition equals sedition leads to a sense of real outrage, expressed in class terms. So there seems to be genuine bewilderment in 'To whom it concerns':

> What would you have? can Reformation border
> On Sacriledge? or Truth upon Disorder?
> Can Rifeling and Religion dwell together?

– and almost at once the poet indicates that for him such anarchy has arisen through breaches in hierarchy:

> Go, ply your Trades, Mechanicks, and begin
> To deal uprightly, and Reform within.
>
> (I, p. 113)

If opposition is seen in terms of transgression of hierarchy, it is necessarily being seen in class terms and is necessarily unnatural. This is reminiscent of Cleveland's presentation of the enemy as grotesque, and such imagery is a way of making the point that the enemy is distorting the natural harmony and unity of the State as traditionally conceived. The idea of the enemy as monstrous is common in *The Rump*, in, for example, 'A Monster to be seen at Westminster', in the opening lines of 'The Publike Faith' ('Some talk of Africk Monsters, which of old,/Vain superstition did for Godheads hold') and in 'The Monster' (I, pp. 85, 97, 118).

On the whole the poems of *The Rump* are not sophisticated analyses of the Civil War and Commonwealth, nor are they satirically incisive in Dryden's manner. The poets see little or no need for analysis, since the enemy is self-evidently wrong, and their manner ranges from the satirical adaptation of song and ballad (so 'Pyms Anarchy' is a version of Carew's 'Aske me no more where Jove bestows', *Rump*, I, p. 68) to the decasyllabics of 'To the City' (I, p. 114).

The *Rump* poems provide a good example of how satire may grow from particular socio-political circumstances rather than primarily literary ones. The impulse to write is provided by events and personalities in the non-literary world, and literary tradition is used in the articulation of the impulse. In this respect these poems may be contrasted with the work of the satirists of the 1590s, who seem more interested in imitating classical Latin satire than in the social conditions which they write about. But it is possible for satire to arise from a combination of literary and social responses and this is the case with a series of poems which is produced between 1665 and 1667. These poems are the so-called 'Painter' satires, which are particularly associated with Marvell and which form part of the large, rather neglected body of Restoration political satire.[9]

According to Lord,[10] the device of a poet pretending to be giving advice to a painter was introduced to England by Busoni's poem about a Venetian naval victory over the Turks off Crete in 1655. The appeal of a device which links poetry with painting is obviously connected with the interest in the relationship of the two arts in the seventeenth century,[11] but the 'Painter' satires spring directly from reaction to Edmund Waller's 'Instructions to a Painter', a poem which, like Busoni's, is laudatory rather than satirical.

Waller's poem celebrates what he chooses to regard as an English naval victory over the Dutch off Lowestoft on 3 June 1665, and what it offers is a highly artistic version of fact, a version marked particularly by antithesis and elevation. The antitheses, for instance, calmly define the loyalty and patriotism of the Lord High Admiral, James, Duke of York:

> His bright sword now a dearer interest draws,
> His brother's glory and his country's cause.

Or they mark out James's fortitude:

> where such a prince is by,
> Resolved to conquer or resolved to die.[12]

Such writing suggests reason and order, a definable and controllable world. But it it simultaneously an idealized one, wherein the specific details are related to general and heroic categories, So Dutch–English conflicts are seen in classical terms. York transcends Achilles and Opdam's fall is compared with Phaeton's, this thread of allusion culminating in the complimentary comparison between Charles II and Augustus Caesar:

> Like young Augustus let his image be,
> Triumphing for that victory at sea.
>
> (ll. 301–2; Lord, p. 29)

Metaphor is similarly used to elevate the English at large. The Dutch are 'hungry wolves' which, however, 'Stop when they find a lion in their way' (where the plural 'wolves' is contrasted, with artful flattery, with the singular 'lion') and the Dutch fleet are 'fowl which scatter to avoid the shock' of English falcons (ll. 23–4, 57–8).

Waller, clearly, is presenting a heroic and triumphant England, one which is identified with its restored monarchy to such an extent that James's brother's glory' and his 'country's cause' are seen as synonymous. The author of 'The Second Advice to a Painter' (1666) – probably but not certainly Marvell – reacts to this version of England by, as Lord says, mimicking 'the structure, style, attitudes, and substance' of Waller's poem (p. 31). In doing so, the poet offers an alternative account of England.

In 'The Second Advice' this account is defined by reaction from

Waller's, and the reaction is quite specific. Thus, for instance, where Waller had presented the visit of the Duchess of York to the fleet at Harwich in May 1665 as 'Like Thetis with her nymphs' (l. 82) 'The Second Advice' offers a degrading comparison:

> So the land crabs, at Nature's kindly call,
> Down to engender at the sea do crawl.
>
> (ll. 57–8; Lord p. 34)

And where Waller offers James as a lion, the satirist has Prince Rupert 'armed in a whole lion cap-a-chin', but in a context which indicates ludicrous pretension (ll. 95–6).

Waller had calmly identified peace, glory, and trade as the King's concerns:

> ˙ that care
> Which keeps you waking to secure our peace,
> The nation's glory, and our trade's increase.
>
> (ll. 318–20; Lord p. 29)

The poet of 'The Second Advice', however, sees the motives for the conflict with the Dutch in a way which separates glory from trade and roots the conflict in the venal:

> Coventry sells the whole fleet away.
>
> (l. 40)

Ideals do not operate – 'Thus having fought we know not why, as yet,/We've done we know not what nor what we get' (ll. 317–18) – but specific gains can be discerned:

> But for triumphant checkstones, if, and shell
> For duchess' closet,'t has succeeded well.
>
> (ll. 325–6)

Waller had used heroic metonymy, whereby the nation and its interests were identified with and seen as synomymous with the monarchy. 'The Second Advice' satirically perverts this by seeing selfish exploitation of the nation by its great men as the characteristic feature of the conflict with Holland. In the world of Waller's poem there is order and contentment; in 'The Second Advice' corruption, cowardice, and hypocrisy.

The typical stance of the satirist of the 1590s is that of the witty pessimist, a persona which regards man as inherently corrupt. Cleveland's is a similar stance and it is, for him, validated by the progress of the Civil War. But the outlook of the poet of the second and third 'Advices' is less negative and more specific. Following Waller's pattern, both satires end with 'envoys' to the King and these are careful to establish a distinction between Charles and the great personages under attack. In the envoy to

'The Second Advice' the King is 'Dear object of our joys' and he is presented through the traditional image of light which both Jonson and Daniel had used in panegyrics for James I:

> thy light does gild our days
> And we lie basking in thy milder rays.
>
> (ll. 347–48)

The King's influence is benign but his effect is weakened

> While swarms of insects, from thy warmth begun,
> Our land devour and intercept our sun.
>
> (ll. 349–50)

Waller's lions and falcons have here become insects, and the poet-figure of 'The Second Advice' is a Jonsonian satirist-adviser. This figure is more explicitly presented at the end of 'The Third Advice':

> What servants will conceal and couns'lers spare
> To tell, the painter and the poet dare.
>
> (ll. 439–40; Lord, p. 58)

The advice the poet dares is simple enough ('Only let vice be damn'd and justice flow' – l. 444) but it is seen as urgent:

> Hark to Cassandra's song ere Fate destroy,
> By thy own navy's wooden horse, thy Troy.
>
> (ll. 447–8)

The King is in danger from those around him (a theme of Elizabethan and Jacobean history plays) and Art, as with Jonson, has a loyalist political function to fulfil.

But satire is volatile stuff. The poet of the second and third 'Advices' presents himself as the fearless but loyal adviser to the King. Yet to the author of 'The Answer of Mr. Waller's Painter to his Many New Advisers' (1667) such satirical help is no help at all. He sees the stance of poems like 'The Second Advice' as hypocritical, and distances himself:

> I have no mixtures to paint Treason's face
> So fair, for Loyalty to make it pass.
>
> (ll. 31–2; Lord, p. 61)

To him the satirists 'blemish princes on report' in order 'to make the rabble sport' (ll. 33–4), and what they consider sanative criticism is, to him, simply slander.

There is some reason to feel that the author of 'The Answer . . .' is genuinely and thoughtfully disturbed by the attacks on the Restoration government. He does not deny weaknesses among governors ('who allows (princes) men does therewithal/Allow 'em possibility to fall' (ll. 43–4) and claims that he himself 'could find colours to expose/Faulty grandees',

> But this checks me, that whatsoe'er is aimed,
> Few such are mended by being proclaimed.
>
> (ll. 70, 71–2)

In his view there is some agreement of aim, but a difference about procedure:

> You would have all amended. So would I,
> Yet not deface each piece where faults I spy.
>
> (ll. 67–8)

The poet of 'The Answer . . .' does not tell us what he would do, and seems, in fact, to accept Art's impotence in affairs of state:

> My colors will not alter forms of state
> After the whimsies of each crowning pate.
>
> (ll. 49–50)

His position has something in common with that of the 'Advices' in so far as it accepts that power in Restoration England inheres in princes and grandees. But the 'Advices' add that such power is self-interested and thoroughly corrupt. So the Duchess of Albermarle, in 'The Third Advice', admonishes her husband to

> Find out the cheats of the four millioneer.
> Out of the very beer they steal the malt,
> Powder of powder, from powdered beef the salt.
>
> (ll. 328–30)

Jobbery seems to have become institutionalized in the Restoration, and to read Pepys is to feel that the second and third 'Advices' were closer to the truth than Waller had been and that the trust and charity of 'The Answer . . .' were misplaced. At the same time, however, there is no reason to believe that the loyal advice of the poems attacked in 'The Answer . . .' was efficacious in the slightest, except in so far as these poems, with other political satire, helped to define the socio-political atmosphere out of which came the Glorious Revolution of 1688.

The most ambitious attempt to convey the political atmosphere of the 1660s is 'The Last Instructions to a Painter' (1667), a poem which sees itself as completing the series:

> After two sittings, now, our Lady State,
> To end her picture, does the third time wait.
>
> (ll. 1–2; Lord, p. 68)

Although 'The Second Advice' had used naval affairs to suggest the state of the nation, that poem had followed Waller in concentrating mainly on the engagement with the Dutch off Lowestoft, whereas 'Last Instructions' offers itself as explicitly concerned with 'Lady State' as a whole. It is almost 1,000 lines long and, as we shall see, uses a variety of styles, but there is a controlling purpose and a coherent vision.

'Last Instructions' does not directly concern itself with the attack made in 'The Answer . . .', but its envoy reaffirms the position taken in the earlier 'Advices', that the satire of these poems is sanative, not destructive, and the reaffirmation is both confident and impressive. The poet makes a clear, if conventional, distinction between ruler and advisers:

> So his bold tube man to the sun applied
> And spots unknown to the bright sun descried,
> Showed they obscure him while too near they prease,
> And seem his courtiers, are but his disease.
>
> ('Last Instructions', ll. 949–52)

The mention of courtiers here can be linked with the distinction between court and country which is basic to the poem, and the telescope image draws out the analytic function of the satirist while refreshing the stock ruler/sun image.

The telescope-poet has an important function to perform in exposing the sins of those who, for wholly selfish reasons, would isolate king from people:

> Bold and accursed are they that all this while
> Have strove to isle our monarch from his isle,
> And to improve themselves, on false pretense,
> About the common prince have raised a fence;
> The kingdom from the crown distinct would see
> And peel the bark to burn at last the tree.
>
> (ll. 967–72)

Both the enclosure image and the burning tree suggest a monarchic ideal close to Waller's, and they link with the analysis of antagonism between court and Parliament which occupies much of the body of the poem. What is needed is the activity of those who 'serve the king with their estates and care' and who 'in love on parliaments can stare' (ll. 987–8). If this can be achieved, the kingdom can be truly common:

> Give us this court and rule without a guard.
>
> (l. 990)

Although 'Last Instructions' is powerfully satirical it is not wholly pessimistic. Its satire is rooted in a specific socio-political context rather than in a despairing view of human nature, and the poem provides important positives to set beside its negative. There is, of course, the King himself, innocent of what is wrong, yet seen as perceptive and careworn (ll. 885–90), and there is the poet-figure, fearlessly presenting 'those spots to sight' (l. 957). But there are also conscientious Members of Parliament and such heroic figures as Archibald Douglas (ll. 649–96) to indicate reason for hope. In fact, one of the most impressive features of the poem is the tense balance between opposing forces, while another is the range of style used to communicate this balance.

There is, for instance, the energetic precision of a couplet like this:

> Paint then St. Albans full of soup and gold,
> The new court's pattern, stallion of the old.
>
> (ll. 29–30)

There is also the brutality of the attack on the excise auditor, John Birch, who 'of his brat enamour'd, as't increased,/Buggered in incest with the mongrel beast' (ll. 145–6). The metaphor is unpleasant, but it is a fine example of satire finding concrete expression for the general (fiscal) vice. Further, more generally, the controlling device of giving instructions to a painter stresses the visual, and 'Last Instructions' conveys not only precise details but elaborate satirical portraits (notably that of Lady Castlemaine) and energetic scenes of self-interest and venality. The active, viciously energetic satirical world threatens the virtuous and the unprotected, and the poet has the range to give moving expression to the latter. One good example takes us back to the Dutch Wars.

Waller's version of the 1665 conflict had presented England as unified and victorious, and a telling comment on such complacency is provided by the humiliating Dutch raid in the Thames and the Medway in the summer of 1667. When this is treated in 'Last Instructions' the humiliation is a major concern, but the poet is less interested in the rights and wrongs of the Dutch action than in what the raid's success indicates about 'our Lady State'. England is imaged in terms of 'bashful nymphs' and 'beauties ere this never naked seen', ripe for violation by a De Ruyter reanimated by tempting beauty. The concern, however, is primarily with those responsible for leaving 'bashful' England exposed, and that concern is conveyed with wit and sensitivity (ll. 523–34)

But the finest example of how the poet ranges in style comes with the passages of Charles's vision, a passage which lifts the poem to real illumination of the state of the State. The vision reinforces the England/naked woman parallel, and does so both movingly and with anger:

> Naked as born, and her round arms behind
> With her own tresses interwove and twined;
> Her mouth locked up, a blind bfore her eyes,
> Yet from beneath the veil her blushes rise,
> And silent tears her secret anguish speak.
>
> (ll. 893–7)

The Restoration: Oldham and Rochester

The 'Advice to a Painter' poems have been largely forgotten, except among specialists, partly because they are very intimately involved with the details of their material and partly because of uncertainties of authorship (post-Romantic fixations on the figure of the author make many uneasy when dealing with anonymous works and those of uncertain authorship). One effect of this neglect has been to isolate Dryden from his proper context, and another has been to ignore an important aspect of the development of the decasyllabic couplet as the dominant form for satire.

John Oldham has also been largely forgotten, but the neglect of his verse does not spring from obscurity or awkwardness. On the contrary, an immediate impression is likely to be of clarity and control, as here, in the opening lines of 'A satyr upon a woman who by her falsehood and scorn was the death of my friend' (1678)[13]:

> No! she shall ne'er escape, if Gods there be,
> Unless they perjured grow, and false as she;
> Though no strange judgment yet the murdress seize
> To punish her, and quit the partial skies;
> Though no revenging lightning yet has flashed
> From thence, that might her criminal beauties blast;
> Though they in their old lustre still prevail,
> Guilt, which, should blackest Moors themselves but own,
> Would make through all their night new blushes dawn.

The stages of the argument are clearly marked and the language used is direct, even rather bare. In the same paragraph Oldham shows neat use of the triplet:

> Though she from justice of all these go free,
> And boasts perhaps in her success, and cry:
> 'Twas but a little harmless perjury;
>
> (Robinson, p. 42)

– and effective use of listing (which was to become a favourite Augustan device):

> I rise in judgment, am to be to her
> Both witness, judge, and executioner.
>
> (Robinson, p. 42)

A reader is also likely to be impressed by the control of large structural units. In the poem under discussion, for instance, there is the use of the repeated 'Though' to build up to the introduction of the poet-figure as the instrument of revenge, and the consequent feeling that the first paragraph is a genuinely significant structural unit.

The clarity of Oldham's satirical style (a feature even when he is concerned with details which are now markedly dated) is matched by the simplicity of his basic satirical strategies, and in particular by his fondness for the device of attacking a person, or category of person, by using what is presented as that person's own voice. We have seen this device in some of the *Rump* poems, and Oldham uses it without discernible increase in sophistication. Thus the first of the *Satires upon the Jesuits* (1681) presents 'Garnet's ghost addressing to the Jesuits, met in private cabal just after the murder of Godfrey' (Dobree, p. 85). As in the *Rump* examples, the idea is that the objects to be attacked will condemn themselves from their own mouths, but this is not done by indirect and gradual revelation but by presenting the malice and evil as overt and relished:

> By hell 'twas bravely done! what less than this,
> What sacrifice of meaner worth, and price
> Could we have offered up for our success?
>
> (Dobrée, p. 85)

Oldham's liking for this type of satirical strategy is also shown in his imitation of Juvenal's famous third satire (1682) and in 'A satyr concerning poetry' (?1682), both of which include poet-figures which are only framing devices for the attacks made by, respectively, Timon and Spenser. Even where Oldham uses the poet-figure as spokesperson, rather than an inset satirist (like Timon) or a self-revealing target (like Garnet) his method is to work through a single dominant figure, and thus a single dominant viewpoint emerges. The resultant unanimity is reinforced by the simplicity of his characterization. His Garnet, the Loyola of the fourth satire against the Jesuits (strictly, Loyola's 'image') and the poet-figure of 'A satyr, addressed to a friend' (?1682) are all uncomplicated figures, expressing an attitude rather than a set of attitudes.

Such simplicity, together with the clarity and control of Oldham's manner, might suggest a calm and confident satirist. But this does not seem to be what Oldham is seeking to convey, and, in fact, his view of satire is a violent, engaged one. So, in 'A satyr upon a woman . . .' he speaks of being 'Armed with dire satyr, and resentful spite' and asks for 'spiteful powers' to 'help me rhyme her dead' (Robinson, pp. 42–3), while the prologue to the 'Satires upon the Jesuits' talks of evils which produce responses that

> urge on my rank envonomed spleen,
> And with keen satire edge my stabbing pen,
> That its each home-set thrust their blood may draw,
> Each drop of ink like aquafortis gnaw.
>
> (Dobrée, p. 84)

This is Cleveland's voice, and behind it there is that of John Marston. Moreover, the style which such violence indicates is one which Oldham actually uses at times:

> Like Delphic hag of old, by fiend possessed,
> He swells; wild frenzy heaves his panting breast,
> His bristling hairs stick up, his eyeballs glow,
> And from his mouth long streaks of drivel flow.
>
> ('Satires upon the Jesuits, III'; Dobrée, p. 104)

Or again:

> Some base, unnamed disease her carcase foul,
> And make her body ugly as her soul:
> Cankers, and ulcers eat her, till she be
> Shunned like infection, loathed like infamy.
>
> ('A satyr upon a woman . . .'; Robinson, p. 44)

Such imagery of disease may be reinforced by the savage scatology of

> Within a gaudy case, a nasty soul,
> Like turd of quality in a gilt close-stool.
>
> (Robinson, p. 43)

or the brutal bathos of

> Tell how blessed Virgin to come down was seen,
> Like playhouse punk descending in machine.
>
> ('Satires upon the Jesuits, III'; Dobrée p. 112)

Such violence, however, seldom leads in Oldham to the incoherence found in Cleveland: control usually remains, as in the careful balance of 'Shunned like infection, loathed like infamy', and one of Oldham's limitations as a satirist is connected with this feature of his writing: his rages often seem literary rather than lived.

At the end of 'Astraea Redux' (1660) Dryden writes:

> Oh Happy Age! Oh times like those alone
> By Fate reserv'd for Great Augustus Throne!
> When the joint growth of Armes and Arts foreshew
> The World a Monarch, and that Monarch You.
>
> (ll. 320–3)

This piece of literary typology has its counterpart in the development of classical imitation in Restoration and Augustan satire. Samuel Johnson was to regard imitation as most fully developed by Pope[14], and his own satires are explicit imitations. In imitating both Juvenal's third satire and Horace, Satires, I. ix Oldham helps to establish imitation as a type of satire in English and asserts that classical Latin patterns are applicable to his contemporary circumstances. To assert analogies between Augustan Rome and Restoration England, however, is not so much to claim coincidence as to suggest that patterns of folly and corruption are perennial. At its simplest this is no more than to claim that there are bores in all societies, and Oldham has no particular difficulty in taking over Horace's pattern to re-establish it in a contemporary setting. But there is more of a challenge when Oldham imitates Juvenal.

Juvenal's third satire is concerned with disgust at urban living and a decision to retreat to the country; and in rendering this in English terms Oldham can draw on a native tradition which reaches back at least as far as Wyatt's first satire. But it is precisely in the strength of the tradition that danger lies, for the existence of a strong tradition facilitates glib application of it to contemporary circumstances. To avoid the facile the poet needs to ensure that his version has the weight of detail of, say, the opening and closing passages of Jonson's 'To Sir Robert Wroth' or the philosophical assurance of Samuel Johnson's 'Vanity of Human Wishes'.

Oldham achieves partial success when he imitates Juvenal. His writing comes alive when he is attacking French influence upon Restoration society:

> Thy gaudy fluttering race of English now,
> Their tawdry clothes, pulvilios, essences;
> Their Chedreux perruques, and those vanities,
> Which thou, and they of old did so despise.
>
> ('A Satire, in imitation of the Third of Juvenal', Dobrée, p. 191)

And he can suggest the dangers of London streets quite effectively:

> twenty to one you meet
> Some of the drunken scourers of the street,
> Flushed with success of warlike deeds performed,
> Of constables subdued, and brothels stormed.
>
> (Dobrée, p. 201)

But he is less successful in providing an alternative to the town. Both Wyatt and Jonson communicate some real feeling for country as a reasonable alternative, while Samuel Johnson, although he conveys little faith in the rural, does demonstrate that there is sustenance in stoicism. Oldham, however, gestures rather helplessly towards 'true English rage' and his country is only a vague sketch. Also, the best passages of his poem work as local satire and largely lack a sense of being rooted in ethical beliefs. Patriotism may be a belief, but in Oldham's poem it works only as John Bullish chauvinism, or racial cliché.

There is, more generally, the sense in Oldham's satirical poems that satire is easy for the poet. He relies upon stark contrasts, so that 'A satyr, addressed to a friend' fails to examine its own premiss of 'a college life, and learned ease', merely using it as a starting-point for another attack on the corruption of public life, while 'A satyr concerning poetry' is content to exemplify 'the dang'rous rocks of poetry' at a general and superficial level (Robinson, pp. 70, 76).

The style of Oldham's satires is at times convincingly indignant, most strikingly in the 'Satires upon the Jesuits', in which the crudeness of the antipathy to the Jesuits, the brutal extravagance of the analysis, and the exclusion of any sense of doubt and balance come over as felt hatred and genuine fear. Here, in a sense, the clarity of Oldham's mind pays off, at least if we take 'clarity' to include 'simplicity', for the harsh narrowness of these poems reflects very accurately the fearful simplicities shown by Restoration society in face of the Titus Oates revelations and associated matters.[15]

Thus the seeming tension between clarity and control, on the one hand, and violence and rage, on the other, is just that – *seeming* tension. The violence and rage may feel genuine enough, but they do not really threaten the clarity and control. Rather than acting as a challenge to the possibility of control in a world seen as dangerously near to moral and social dissolution, they justify a control which is maintained by being confidently simple-minded. This, perhaps, is what truly marks representative art. What Oldham lacks is the radical doubt which will later lead to the closing paragraph of the final book of Pope's *The Dunciad*, in which all the local satire of contemporary society is made to embody a threat to civilization itself.

Paradoxically, then, even Oldham's most engaged satires, those on the Jesuits, in which there is both acute observation and strong feeling, are finally both local and complacent. Perhaps the best way of reinforcing this point is to compare Oldham's Garnet with Dryden's Shaftesbury/Achitophel. Garnet is rendered by Oldham into a powerfully evil figure, which is finally theatrical. The menace is felt, certainly, but it remains confined within the fiction of the poem, whereby human nature is simplified into a stock figure of evil. Dryden's Shaftesbury is also evil, but Dryden has more sense of how the figure came to be what it is, a feeling for motivation and psychological complexity which includes feeling for the figure as well as hatred of it. Because of this, Shaftesbury/Achitophel is not confined, as Oldham's Garnet is, but constantly operates across the lines between art and life.

Another point can be made about Oldham by thinking about *Absalom and Achitophel*. That poem (which will be discussed in more detail below) is a fine example of how tradition can be used. Dryden draws together his awareness of epic, the habit of biblical typology, and the formal literary 'character' to make a contemporary satire in which the local situation is illuminated by analogy. Oldham's view of satire as biting and stabbing includes Cleveland and, behind him, Elizabethan satire, but whereas Cleveland's persona relates the literary stance with the fear and doubt of his own royalism under stress, Oldham's use of a similar persona seems literary rather than the response to contemporary social conditions: Dryden uses tradition, Oldham imitates it.

In contrast to the sense of Oldham as a self-conscious literary satirist, carefully shaping his effects, John Wilmot, Earl of Rochester, although a poised and often ironic poet[16], creates an impression of informality which

might be linked with the insouciance associated (sometimes wrongly) with
Cavalier verse:

> Were I (who to my cost already am
> One of those strange, prodigious creatures, man)
> A spirit free to choose, for my own share,
> What case of flesh and blood I pleased to wear,
> I'd be a dog, a monkey, or a bear,
> Or anything but that vain animal
> Who is so proud of being rational.
>
> ('A Satyr against Reason', ll. 1–7, 1675)

The standard edition of Rochester's poems contains several 'impromptus',
and whether these are genuinely informal or not they may be linked with
the sense of Rochester's voice being halfway between conversation and art:

> Son of a whore, God damn you! can you tell
> A peerless peer the readiest way to Hell?
>
> ('To the Postboy', ll. 1–2, 1676)

And although Rochester is clearly an educated writer, capable both of con-
siderable range of allusions and of formal imitation, his verse is almost
always clear (sometimes even plain) and idiomatic, less dense than Cleve-
land's, less polished than Dryden's.

Rochester's structures reinforce this impression of informality. Often he
seems content with simple listings, or with the linear structure of poems
like 'Tunbridge Wells' and 'A Ramble in St. James' Park' (1672, 1674). In
the former, particularly, he uses the common satirical device of the poet-
figure observing, as a detached and sceptical observer, a series of characters
designed to reinforce and justify the scepticism of the poet-figure and to
convey his satirical acumen. The series seems of arbitrary length and the
poem is self-confirming. Surveys of this kind can, as in 'A Letter from
Artemisia in the Town to Chloe in the Country' (?1675), convey the feeling
of ubiquitous folly, but sometimes all that is communicated is the im-
pression that Rochester's wit can reduce almost any material to his initial
premiss. Thus a poem like 'Signior Dildo' (1673) seems simply to stop
when the poet gets tired of listing examples of female perversion.

This repetition of examples, a typical satiric technique, can be linked
with Rochester's second main type of structure, that of argument. So in
such poems as 'Upon Nothing' (1678) and 'Against Reason' structure is a
philosophical proposition, and the tactic is to make argument work to en-
force the given proposition and to undermine opposition to it. In 'Upon
Nothing', in particular, Rochester shows his ability to write lucidly even
while dealing with abstractions:

> Ere Time and Place were, Time and Place were not,
> When primitive Nothing Something straight begot;
> Then all proceeded from the great united What.
>
> (ll. 4–6)

Satire is based on the conviction or pretence that society is degenerate, and the satirist's mask necessarily, then, includes a sense of disillusionment. This may communicate itself, where the poet is not only a satirist, as the extreme presentation of the darker side of experience, seen as one part of the poet's total response to experience as a whole. Or the satiric mask may seem no more than a fashionable disguise or a costume worn for the fun of trying out a line of approach. But in Rochester's case satire seems the necessary consequence of his response to living, and thus more than a literary attitude, even where it is clearly aware of literary contexts. Restoration poetry is so conscious of its own wit and attitudes that 'sincerity' is even more difficult to define than usual, but Rochester's emphases have a near-obsessive quality which (without suggesting a simple autobiographical link) indicates anchorage in experience.

Obsessiveness in Rochester suggests two features above all else, obscenity and the reduction of the human to the animal. Both features are common in satire and should not be seen in simple psychological terms. But Rochester writes some of the most determinedly obscene verse in the language, and it is important to make the point that he chooses to do so. He can write non-obscene satire ('Upon Nothing', 'A Letter from Artemisia . . .') and it is therefore proper to argue that his obscenity has a purpose – it is not *only* obsessive. There is, at times, a daringness, as if the poet is amused that he dares to write obscenely about named people, secure in his own social standing or reputation or anonymity. So the satirical lyric 'On Mrs Willis' reduces her brutally to elementals:

> Bawdy in thoughts, precise in words,
>   Ill-natured though a whore,
> Her belly is a bag of turds,
>   And her cunt a common shore.
>
> (?1680, ll. 17–20)

There is also an element of braggadoccio, which can seem strikingly immature in its self-consciousness:

> I've outswilled Bacchus, sworn of my own make
> Oaths would fright Furies, and make Pluto quake;
> I've swived more whores more ways than Sodom's walls
> E'er knew, or the College of Rome's Cardinals.
>
> ('To the Postboy', ll. 3–6)

The daring and the seeming immaturity are, however, parts of the overall point, being reflexes of an empty world. Rochester can write convincing love lyrics of a traditional kind, but he does so decreasingly as the years pass. Yet he does not abandon lyric. Rather, as in 'On Mrs Willis', he keeps lyric forms but substitutes obscenity for love. This tendency is already present in the song 'Fair Chloris in a Pigsty lay' (?1680), but there the contrasts between pastoralism and 'reality' are not so much extreme as amused, even slightly tender:

Frighted she wakes, and waking frigs.
　　Nature thus kindly eased
In dreams raised by her murmuring pigs
And her own thumb between her legs,
　　She's innocent and pleased.
　　　　　　　　　　　　　(ll. 36–40)

But the contrast is there, and on other occasions is neither amused nor
tender. Even in 'Fair Chloris in a pigsty lay' Chloris's dream is of rape,
and Rochester is an aggressively male poet. Thus he responds readily to
the tradition used in 'The Imperfect Enjoyment' (?1680) and boasts the
ubiquity of the rampant penis:

Stiffy resolved, 'twould carelessly invade
Woman or man, nor ought its fury stayed:
Where'er it pierced, a cunt it found or made.

There is also the fantasy of endless violation:

This dart of love, whose piercing point, oft tried,
With virgin blood ten thousand maids have dyed.
　　　　　　　　　　　　　(ll. 41–3, 37–8)

But the suggested dependence upon potency fails in 'The Imperfect En-
joyment', and when it does there is nothing left. In Rochester, at times,
the penis is a metonymy for the male. But he produces equivalent substi-
tutions for women, and if 'The Imperfect Enjoyment' presents the bitter
self-contempt of male failure to satisfy the female, 'A Ramble in St. James's
Park' brutally registers male fear of female insatiability, and thus the im-
possibility of satisfaction for either sex.

From failure of confidence in orthodox sexuality comes the attention to
deviation in Rochester's verse. If Chloris's masturbation is seen as a mix-
ture of innocence and pleasure, the displacement of orthodox sex is else-
where fantasised and empty, a restless search to fill unoccupied orifices.
Moreover, Rochester is fascinated, it seems, by the merging of fantasy and
actuality, whereby his obscenity plays across figures imagined or masked
by literary names and others who are specified by name as live figures in
his Restoration landscape. Not only are his Chloris and Corinna reduced
to their sexual parts, but so are the real women listed in 'Signior Dildo'.
Beneath the trappings of pastoral lyric Chloris's thumb is active; while
beneath the titles of such as Barbara Palmer the dildo operates.

Seen in this way, the Rochester world is dominated by a sexual itch
which inflames even as it mollifies, becoming a hell of unsatisfiable desires
reminiscent of *The Revenger's Tragedy*. In this hell humans become animal,
but Rochester knows that humanity has reason, and therefore that when
humans become animal they fall below the animal. But he is boxed in, so
that when, in 'A Satyr against Reason and Mankind', he asserts belief in
'right Reason' he not only questions the operation of such reason in human
behaviour but defines it as dependent upon the senses:

I own right reason, which I would obey:
That reason which distinguishes by sense
And gives us rules of good and ill from thence,
That bounds desires with a reforming will
To keep'em more in vigor, not to kill.
Your reason hinders, mine helps to enjoy,
Renewing appetites yours would destroy.

(ll. 99–105)

The problem with this, of course, is that over and again Rochester demonstrates that 'vigor' is finally void.

When Rochester writes lines like these:

When your lewd cunt came spewing home
Drenched with the seed of half the town,
My dram of sperm was supped up after
For the digestive surfeit water.

('A Ramble in St. James's Park', ll. 113–16)

it is tempting to see him as simply obsessive, dirty-minded, and anti-feminine. He is at times reminiscent of De Sade[17] (though usually without the sadism) but, like De Sade, there is an analytic precision which suggests that 'obsession' is not a sufficient word, particularly since it denies the evidence that obscenity is something which Rochester chooses at times, while avoiding at others. On the other hand, the detail and frequency of Rochester's obscenity make it difficult to believe that this is merely analytic, the chosen vehicle of a satirical account of a society. As with Swift's scatology, there is the dual feeling that the stressed detail is both chosen and symptomatic of a fixation. By this account the product is not merely psychologically revealing, nor is it best seen as the consequence of a disordered personality.

Rochester's verse belongs to a period from about 1665 to 1680, and is thus conterminous with the bulk of the reign of Charles II. That reign is a curious one. There are in it factors which can be seen as encouraging relaxation and hedonism: the relief for many non-royalists of finding that the King was not vindictive; the excitement, for the court at least, of translating French culture to England; the general relief that, in some sense, the strains of several decades were past. But there are, equally, factors which point the other way, towards tension and uncertainty: the anxiety about Roman Catholicism; fears of absolutism; fears about surviving puritan extremism. There is also the evidence that the reign of Charles II was one of potentialities and, simultaneously, of dangers in the nature and running of the State. So Pepys's *Diary* reveals both a pride in the possibilities of mercantile efficiency and an awareness of the ubiquity of corruption. At the same time this dual response involves a class element, with middle-class virtues of hard work and sound economy rubbing against evidence of grandee ostentation and aristocratic incompetence. Restoration society is uneasily poised between the bloody revolution against the government of

Charles I (which led, almost by accident, to regicide) and the bloodless revolution against James II (one which effectively established a mixed constitution and the rule of the grandees).

Rochester's poetry shows almost no direct interest in politics. His emphasis on sexual preoccupations and intrigues clearly hints at negligence of other concerns, and 'A Satyr on Charles II' (1673) explicitly presents the idea of the King as dominated by his own sexual urges:

> Though safety, law, religion, life lay on't,
> 'Twould break through all to make its way to cunt.
>
> (ll. 19–20)

But, by the standards of the 'Painter' satires, Rochester is clearly a social rather than a political satirist, and this suggests that to him the proper concerns of the poet do not include involvement in the way a state is governed; and here it is instructive to recall Donne and Jonson.

Unease plays its part in the work of both of these great poets of the early part of the seventeenth century. Donne, the more introspective of the two, can feel the potential of love (whether secular or divine) but persistently doubts the accessibility of it. Jonson, more directly concerned with the social and ethical, has a vision of what humans should be capable of achieving in this life, but also a fear that the race will betray its potential. In Jonson's case the social and the political are conterminous, the one involving the other. When we turn back from these men to Rochester, we become aware of continuities, but also of marked differences. For him, the social seems largely apart from the political, and the teasing sense that optimism and pessimism are close together, which is found in both Jonson and Donne, has passed in Rochester's case into extremism, whereby the gap between aspiration and actuality has reached a point at which the latter scarcely any longer exists. So, in the 'Satyr against Reason and Mankind', the idea of an exemplar of 'right Reason' survives, but the chances of that idea being exemplified seem remote. Jonson found such exemplars, even while also indicating drifting from the standards they set. As for Donne, he can imagine a world made one by two lovers and has an apprehension of what this could mean, while for Rochester rapacious lovers tear at each other or the poet-figure asks the reader to watch the activity of Chloris's thumb.

It may, then, even be slightly misleading to call Rochester a social satirist, if we mean by that a writer who is concerned with patterns of social behaviour and their application to ideas of what society should be. In Rochester's world 'society' means chiefly the privileged, who are presented as living in a world largely independent of other classes. As in Restoration comedy, we are not usually asked to consider how privilege comes about or how it is financed, nor is it suggested that 'society' exemplifies society at large. In Rochester's verse, even this limited sense of society tends to give way to a vision of individuals essentially alone, even within their class. Partnership has declined to the point where Donne's ideal of two people has given way to the sense of persons as autonomous instruments, which, moreover, take pleasure rather than give it. In effect, the penis not only dominates in the male, but becomes the dildo; while the vagina is merely any hole. Here there is a double sort of depersonalization. The human whole is displaced by the dominant part and that is, in turn, made inhuman. At the same time, the individual is made general, and it is hardly metaphoric for the poet-figure in 'The Imperfect Enjoyment' to speak of his penis reaching 'every heart' 'through every cunt' (l. 40).

The clarity, control, and precision of detail which mark Rochester's best verse, and which are perhaps most fully exemplified in 'A Letter from Artemisia . . . ', indicate a considerable intelligence at work, and they mean that Rochester can only be representative of Restoration culture in so far as he sees its essences more clearly than others (thus ceasing to be representative in the usual sense). The view of Rochester as a penitent in his last days may have some truth in it, although the view depends heavily upon a mixture of Bishop Burnet[18] and sanctimonious wish-fulfilment, but it can only be seen as a collapse. What makes Rochester valuable is the sense of his intelligence as both trapped and honest. By this account what Vieth calls 'These strange half-boastful, half-penitential verses' of 'To the Postboy' render this very precisely, especially at their end:

> I have blasphemed my God, and libeled Kings!
> The readiest way to Hell – come quick!
> Boy   Ne'er stir:
> The readiest way, my Lord,'s by Rochester.

As with Thomas Carew, though more tragically, there is the impression of a sensibility which senses that there should be more than what its context presents, but which can find no satisfying way of finding that more. Lacking this, the sensibility turns back to the frenzied mess it has discerned.

The Restoration: Butler and Dryden

To turn from the distressed and divided world of Rochester's verse satires to Samuel Butler's *Hudibras* is to move from satirical analysis of Restoration society to a burlesque account of the Civil War. It also involves moving from satire which is seemingly informal to satire which, while informal in style, is presented on epic scale and involves extended parody of literary romance. The title-page of the first part of Butler's poem[19] tells us that this part was 'written in the time of the late Wars', and the opening lines indicate both the general context and an attitude to it:

> When civil Fury first grew high,
> And men fell out they knew not why;
> When hard words, Jealousies and Fears,

> Set Folks together by the ears,
> And made them fight, like mad or drunk,
> For Dame Religion as for Punk,
> Whose honesty they all durst swear for,
> Though not a man of them knew wherefor.

The war sets 'Folk together by the ears' even though they do not know what it is about. It seems that religion is the problem's root but this is seen as equivalent to a quarrel about a whore.

In *Hudibras* the war is absurd. More specifically, the opposition to the King is ludicrous, and over and over Butler uses the traditional satiric device of seeing the target as animal:

> When he was falling off his Steed,
> (As Rats do from a falling house;)

> But laying fast hold on the mane,
> Preserv'd his seat: And as a Goose
> In death contracts his talents close;
> So did the knight . . . ;

> Which made him hang the head, and scoul,
> And wink, and goggle like an Owl.
>
> (I. ll. 938–9; I. lll. 524–7; II. l. 119–20)

In *Hudibras* this kind of reduction of human beings through imagery is consistently emphasized by the belittling colloquialisms, as with the word 'squelch' here:

> He tore the Earth, which he had sav'd
> From squelch of Knight, and storm'd and rav'd,
>
> (I. ll. 885–6)

and as with the tweaking here:

> This said, He gently rais'd the Knight,
> And set him on his Bum upright:
> To rouze him from Lethargick dump,
> He tweak'd his Nose with gentle thump.
>
> (I. ll. 971–4)

Furthermore, Butler's famous use of the ludicrous and the bathetic in the treatment of rhyme and rhythm also adds to the reduction of the human:

> Is it forbid my Pulse to move,
> My Beard to grow, my Ears to prick up,
> Or (when I'm in a fit) to hickup;

or

Insconc'd himself as formidable,
As could be, underneath a Table.
                    (II. l. 344–6; III. l. 1115–6)

But Butler's methods do not lead either to the bitter satire of Cleveland
or to the more elegant textures of Dryden, in which irony dominates. Of
all the main satirists of the seventeenth century, Butler is the most directly
humorous, and it is the comic invention which is most striking. Like
Cleveland, Butler mocks the verbal obfuscation of puritan discourse:

I'le force you by right ratiocination
To leave your Vitilitigation,
And make you keep to th' question close,
And argue Dialecticos.
                    (I. lll. 1261–4)

But whereas in Cleveland this is made part of enraged bafflement about
the opposition, Butler is more interested in the absurdity of the issue to
which the language is directed:

The Question then, to state it first,
Is which is better, or which worst,
Synods or Bears.
                    (I. lll. 1265–7)

The central absurdity, of course, is that Hudibras is a knight errant of
the Protestant cause, and casting his satire in the context of knightly ro-
mance provides Butler with his chief mock-heroic device. Cervantes[20] had
already established the possibilities of a ludicrous version of knighthood
(as Chaucer had earlier in the tale of Sir Thopas). Butler takes over the basic
idea and also the picaresque structure. Thus, whenever Hudibras shows his
usual incompetence, whether it is in riding, fighting, or discussion, we are
asked to see the incompetence in the light of genuine, efficient heroic be-
haviour; and the gap between Hudibras and the genuine relates both to the
actual performance and to the beliefs which underlie the performance. We
are to see Hudibras as ludicrous in action and in attitude.

Structure plays its part here. The picaresque pattern soon establishes that
wherever Hudibras goes there will be adventures which will allow Butler
to demonstrate his hero's inability to perform adequately. Milton's Satan
is a rebel against the alleged goodness of God, but he is allowed at times
to act out his rebellion with heroic courage and determination (see Ch. 5,
pp. 185–86). Butler's Hudibras is also a rebel but his rebellion is only comic,
lacking even the pathos which is part of Don Quixote. However, the pic-
aresque does allow Butler a topography of the absurd, and it should be
added that this extends the scale of the satire, for it is not only Hudibras
who is absurd, but the world in which he operates so badly. The opening
lines of the first part speak of men falling out 'they knew not why', and
although Butler's satire is chiefly directed at the pretentious aspirations of

the puritans it, in effect, also reduces the royalist cause. The *world* of *Hudibras* is absurd (by contrast, say, with that of *Absalom and Achitophel*, in which the heroic and the mock-heroic coexist).

But picaresque has its potential weaknesses. The episodic basis of the manner can easily become self-indulgent, a licence to be careless about shape, whereby an indeterminate number of incidents are loosely attached to the central figure's journeyings. Butler's poem was published in three parts, between 1663 and 1678, and it is weak on significant shape. Individual cantos may have shape (although the discursive manner and fondness for developing the local at the expense of the overall reduce the shapeliness even of separate cantos), but there is little sense of any governing principle. This might be seen as finally mimetic, in that the ramblings of Hudibras (both in words and deeds) are incoherent, but the price of this is that the comic epic lacks the drive and cumulative force of a work seriously conceived on the epic scale (an obvious contrast is with the *Iliad*, where Homer makes repetition work together with the development of detail towards crisis). Butler's manner damages that which he attacks, but there is an evenness of structure which means that the impact of the satire does not increase as we read on. Indeed, it tends to diminish with familiarity, particularly since, as with Sterne's *Tristram Shandy*, the chosen comic style rapidly becomes predictable.

The idea of the heroic in Butler's mock-heroic is a general one. It consists in setting the nature and aspirations of Hudibras in a context which reminds a reader of the genuinely heroic world of chivalric romance. But even this is a dubious way of invoking the heroic in the second half of the century. Chivalric romance itself had been mocked with some consistency since the century's start, and Cervantes had made it difficult to take such romance seriously, at least for the sophisticated. Misdirected heroism could be better presented by using the Bible (as Milton did) or by using classical epic as the standard by which false heroism is exposed (as in Dryden). Butler, in fact, makes little effort to measure Hudibras by knightly standards explicitly presented: he is ludicrous in a ludicrous world. Of course, Butler does suggest what a non-ludicrous world might be like. It would be one in which heroic behaviour was possible and would make sense, and it would be one where sense would be a norm, rather than nonsense. The world of Hudibras is one in which the relationship between things, and between word and thing, has become nonsensical. So it is that Hudibras can address himself to 'Synods and Bears' and can misapply the methods of mathematics:

> Resolve by Sines and Tangents straight,
> If Bread or Butter wanted weight;
> And wisely tell what hour o' th' day
> The Clock does strike, by Algebra.
>
> (I. 1. 123–6)

But Butler's is a fallen world, and it is only the comic voice of the poet which reminds us of an alternative, one which is not embodied within the fiction, but comments upon it. So long as the absurd is seen as such, there is hope that it might pass away, but Butler gives us little but the comic voice on which to depend, while the manner of that voice also works to call in doubt whether the absurdity matters. What we enjoy in *Hudibras* is the invention. Since Hudibras himself is immediately presented as ludicrous, and since the world in which he operates is also ludicrous, we have little feeling that Hudibras is a threat to anything which matters. The world has already fallen and Hudibras exemplifies its fall. Whatever paradise there may have been has been lost when the poem opens and there is little sign that it might be regained: as a result, we are left free to enjoy the comedy consequent upon the fall. Further, Butler's style, with its absurd rhymes, ridiculous rhythms, its bathos and parody, works to encourage enjoyment of the spectacle, without the guilt of simultaneously feeling that we are collaborating in our own degeneration.

The achievement of *Hudibras*, finally, bears an interesting relationship to the period to which it belongs. What I have just been describing suggests that the comedy becomes almost autonomous, something to be enjoyed for itself, without attendant feelings of guilty implication on the reader's part. Thus, in a sense, Butler, in the 1660s, and 1670s deals with the rebellion against Charles I by banishing it from history into romance. The idea might be that a reader experiences the rebellion as massive folly, and returns from Butler's world of mock-romance to the reality of the Restoration with some feeling of relief. Alternatively, it is possible to take the sane voice of the poet-figure as indicator of what sane reality has, in the past, been, with the ubiquity of folly in the poem being seen as evidence of a sane world irretrievably lost. Here it may be significant that the episodic *Hudibras* ends with its anti-hero still in full spate, happily in correspondence with his lady. Butler, of course, had no good personal reason to see the Restoration as paradise regained.[21]

As we saw in Chapter 3, John Dryden on occasion writes as if the reign of Charles II is to be seen as the return to paradise, but Dryden also wrote the finest verse satire of the period, his verse representing at its most impressive the Restoration tendency to treat experience as *either* heroic or mock-heroic. Mock-heroic is obviously designed to present its material as itself unworthy of heroic treatment, but it simultaneously suggests that the heroic, as a literary mode, is inappropriate for such material. It involves the critical view that the heroic may be, in some circumstances, untruth: for a corrupt society the 'answering style' must be mock-heroic, a manner which presents its material by the device of marking the gap between what the heroic alleges about experience and experience itself. In mock-heroic the gods have left and only false gods remain, with the style itself reminding a reader of what has been and that it no longer exists. But while mock-heroic is basically designed to point to the falsity of aspiration among the corrupt, it is a paradoxical form of art in that the better articulated it is the more creative it is. Even as pretensions are being destroyed creation is taking place. Dryden's satire is a fine example.

Dryden calls *The Medal* (1682) 'A Satyre against Sedition', whereas *Absalom and Achitophel* (1681) and *The Hind and the Panther* (1687) are only described as 'poems'. But in the prefatory 'To the Reader' for the former Dryden speaks of 'rebating the Satyre . . . from carrying too sharp an Edge' and refers to 'this Satyre' in the corresponding epistle before *The Hind and the Panther*. In both poems Dryden shows his ability at writing in a mixed mode while keeping the heroic and mock-heroic extremes separate.

It might, however, be more accurate to say that in *Absalom and Achitophel* Dryden works his way from mock-heroic to heroic, and that the poem is finally an assertion that the latter remains possible in a poetic world dominated for most of its length by the former. Thus, the centre of energy in the poem is Achitophel, possessed of 'A fiery Soul',

> which working out its way,
> Fretted the Pigmy Body to decay:
> And o'r inform'd the Tenement of Clay.
>
> (ll. 156–8)

Achitophel is 'Sagacious', 'Bold', 'Restless', 'daring' in the first lines of Dryden's portrait (ll. 153–9), and as a judge

> In Israels Courts ne'er sat an Abbethdin
> With more discerning Eyes, or Hands more clean:
> Unbrib'd, unsought, the Wretched to redress;
> Swift of Dispatch, and easie of Access.
>
> (ll. 188–91)

But the energy and virtues of Achitophel are misdirected through 'wilde Ambition' (l. 198) because of which he is 'unfixt in Principles and Place' and his 'fiery Soul' operates to his own destruction (ll. 154, 156). Achitophel is, in fact, doubly destructive, in that he consumes himself and works to the downfall of the nation by shaping Absalom into a rebel. But Achitophel is not really seen in mock-heroic terms, the mixture of qualities and the perception of something 'driven' or fated in him having more in common with tragedy than with the cool demolition and exposures of mock-heroic proper. Achitophel is Dryden's version of Milton's Satan, and the verse, even while defining the evil, creates a figure which is deluded but not absurd.

Achitophel's energy is destructive, in Dryden's terms, because it is directed to overturning the order represented by David, and one of the most impressive features of *Absalom and Achitophel* is how Dryden renders the fragility of the Restoration settlement, while reasserting his faith in the King's ability to control the situation. This involves, among other things, a tactical success in the presentation of David.

Dryden has a major problem in this poem, one which is the direct result of the circumstances in which it was written. Titus Oates had introduced his plot in 1678, while in 1679 Monmouth's army had defeated the Scots at Bothwell Brig and in the following year the House of Lords had rejected the Exclusion Bill after it had passed the Commons. The Bill was reintroduced in 1681, the year of Dryden's poem, and in that same year Shaftes-

bury (Achitophel) was tried. But the problems of succession and Roman
Catholicism had not been solved when Dryden wrote. There was the Rye
House Plot to come, as well as the executions of Sidney and Russell, the
arrest of Oates (1684), and the Monmouth Rebellion. Dryden's problem
was how, as a supporter of Charles II and the Duke of York, to write about
the crisis intelligently, while it was going on, and, if possible, to help to-
wards a resolution of the crisis which would match success with his own
'party' position.

No service would be done to the royalist cause by making Achito-
phel/Shaftesbury a derisory figure, while Dryden also had to find a way
of presenting Absalom/Monmouth which respected Charles's love for his
bastard son. Making Achitophel a figure of force and energy misapplied
both allows for heroic action by David/Charles and takes the main blame
away from Absalom, who is seen in the poem as a dupe rather than a vi-
cious and ungrateful rebel. But there remained the problem of treating
David/Charles, and Dryden's solution is a triumph of creative intelligence.

Because of good advice or native intelligence Charles had acted wisely
when he came to the throne in avoiding vindictiveness. By 1681 he had
sat on that throne for more than twenty years without allowing the tensions
of the Restoration period to become acute crisis, and he had achieved this,
it might be said, by masterly inertia, relying on memories of the past and
his own moderation to prevent the forcing of crisis. The image of a 'merry
monarch' hunting and wenching was perhaps the wisest image for the
period, even if it delayed crisis rather than disarming it. But it could
scarcely be pretended that the period between 1660 and 1681 had been one
of heroic actions by the King or of epic achievements by the State. James,
Duke of York, could be seen as having acted heroically in the Great Fire
and Monmouth's victory at Bothwell Brig could also be given a heroic
gloss, but the manner of Waller's heroic verse was generally less appro-
priate than the satires of the 'Painter' series.

Dryden has the good sense not to offer David/Charles as a simple heroic
character at the start of *Absalom and Achitophel*. What he does instead is
disarming. The strongest case against the King was that he neglected state
affairs for love affairs; so Dryden deals with this by accepting and then
transforming it. His David is promiscuous, but generously so:

> Israel's Monarch, after Heaven's own heart,
> His vigorous warmth did, variously, impart
> To Wives and Slaves: And, wide as his Command,
> Scatter'd his Maker's Image through the Land.
>
> (ll. 7–10)

Given the generosity and scale of David's procreative activities it becomes
mean-minded, so the poetry tells us, to attack him on moral grounds, and
Dryden subtly uses myths of better times to suggest that David/Charles
is associated with antique simplicity. Even while David is scattering his
maker's image he is representing principles of warmth and creativity which
are to be contrasted with the sterile energy of Achitophel/Shaftesbury,

who can father only 'a shapeless Lump' (l. 172). Yet this David is not her-oic: his indulgence is seen as dangerous, and the crisis formulated by Ach-itophel calls for action. Here again Dryden is intelligent. At the start of the poem, David is very clearly a king in the tradition of divine right, directly associated with God and enacting literally the image of king as father to his people of which James I had been so fond. But when Dryden calls the King 'Godlike' in the penultimate line of the poem he is not merely repeating the epithet from its beginning (l. 14). David is godlike at the end because, in Dryden's fiction, he has seen the need to act heroically and has done so.

It might be objected that David/Charles has actually done nothing, and Samuel Johnson felt that the end of the poem was faked.[22] But what David has done is to reassert his kingliness through speech, and the fiction is that nothing more is needed. If Charles will be himself/king, the satirized world of plot and disaffection will dissolve. Seen in this way, Dryden's brief final paragraph is wishful mimesis, the poetic enactment of what should follow the proper assertion of kingship at a time of crisis.

The paradox of *Absalom and Achitophel* is that its most memorable as-sertions are the figure of Achitophel and the opening version of David, and that, therefore, the poem's 'truth' is not so much in its fictitious account of the years after 1681 –

> Henceforth a Series of new time began,
> The mighty Years in long Procession ran:
> Once more the Godlike David was Restor'd,
> And willing Nations knew their Lawfull Lord
>
> (ll. 1028–31)

– as in its awareness of the danger associated with disloyal energy, the fissile nature of the elements of the State, and the King's self-indulgence. We can understand 1688 in the light of Dryden's creation here, even though his version of time after 1681 is woefully inaccurate.

It was suggested earlier that the figure of Achitophel is not strictly mock-heroic, but that David at the beginning of Dryden's poem is a fine example of how mock-heroic can be used with superb delicacy. The ded-ication of David to imparting his 'vigorous warmth' is of heroic dimen-sions, and the writing gives the activity the expansiveness and generosity of heroic action. But David is acting in beds rather than on battlefields or in duels, and even when lust is 'diviner' (l. 19) it remains lust. A truly heroic David will only be seen at the poem's climax.

What Dryden has done, in effect, is to transform the historical Charles into a version of David, a type of generosity and warmth which fills up the space which would have been occupied by true heroism had Charles been truly heroic. Such displacement, working in a more obvious manner, is also the achievement of *MacFlecknoe* (1682), in which the mock-heroic ability to create even as it destroys is very clearly shown.

The destructive potential of mock-heroic has never been better illus-trated that in *MacFlecknoe*. Its obliteration of Richard Flecknoe himself is perhaps gratuitous, given the self-obliteration of the untalented, but *Mac-Flecknoe* has effectively substituted its eponymous hero for the historical

Thomas Shadwell[23] so firmly that the latter's genuine achievements stand
for virtually nothing. How this is done is a perfect example of how mock-
heroic can work. What is involved is exploitation of the heroic manner
itself, seen brilliantly exemplified in the opening lines:

> All humane things are subject to decay,
> And, when Fate summons, Monarchs must obey:
> This Fleckno found, who, like Augustus, young
> Was call'd to Empire, and had govern'd long.

The only detail here which might indicate the mock-heroic is the setting
of Flecknoe's name beside that of Augustus. Suspicions about the poet's
attitude grow when Flecknoe's kingdom is defined as one of 'Verse and
Prose', but the telling undercutting of his realm is held back until the sixth
line:

> Through all the Realms of Non-sense, absolute.
> Complete and undisputed power – over a realm of nonsense.

From this beginning Dryden goes on to define Shadwell with merciless
precision, calling upon the language of epic and deftly transforming it into
the anti-world of mock-heroic:

> Some Beams of Wit on other souls may fall,
> Strike through and make a lucid intervall;
> But Sh — 's genuine night admits no ray,
> His rising Fogs prevail upon the Day:
> Besides his goodly Fabrick fills the eye,
> And seems design'd for thoughtless Majesty:
> Thoughtless as Monarch Oakes, that shade the plain,
> And, spread in solemn state, supinely reign.
>
> (ll. 21–8)

As *MacFlecknoe* proceeds, its effects are more coarsely achieved, and its
ending (a brilliantly contrived parody of the Ascension which is also mock-
ery of Shadwell's own plays) does not have the resonance of the ending
of the final book of *The Dunciad*, but Dryden has made a Mac Flecknoe
which is a tribute to dullness. In the poem Flecknoe is finally dropped
through the trapdoor to the 'hell' beneath:

> down they sent the yet declaiming Bard.
> Sinking he left his Drugget robe behind,
> Born upwards by a subterranean wind.
> The Mantle fell to the young Prophet's part,
> With double portion of his Father's Art.
>
> (ll. 213–7)

As the mantle passes from Flecknoe to Mac Flecknoe, so the historical fig-
ures behind the poem give way to Dryden's fictions, which have had more
life since their creation than their historical counterparts.

MacFlecknoe makes use of the heroic to demonstrate the extent of the perverse, even sublime, dullness of his victims, while in *Absalom and Achitophel* Dryden incorporates heroic possibilities into a commentary upon a political crisis as a way of rendering the scale of that crisis and of the need for genuinely heroic action to deal with it. The case of *Absalom and Achitophel* makes the point that mock-heroic is not for Dryden simply a way of pointing to gaps between the degenerate present and a heroic past, for the present of that poem includes the possibility of heroic qualities operating in the present, as well as ubiquitous mock-heroic ones. It is the intelligence which this indicates which makes Dryden's poem such an impressive commentary, not only upon the Britain of 1681, but also upon the history of the decades which lead up to, and thus create, that year. And it is the same intelligence which makes *The Hind and the Panther* such a fine poem.

Although, as mentioned above, Dryden calls the poem a 'Satyre' in his address to the reader, he subtitles it simply 'A Poem, In Three Parts', and it is, in fact, satirical overall in the broad Horatian sense of a poem which makes use of satire while having an outlook which is ironic rather than wholly satirical. *The Hind and the Panther* exemplifies Dryden's ability to mix modes, its range covering killing satire –

> The bristl'd Baptist Boar, impure as He,
> (But whitn'd with the foam of sanctity)
>
> (I. 43–4)

as well as economical lucidity –

> No written laws can be so plain, so pure,
> But wit may gloss, and malice may obscure,
>
> (II. 318–9)

and panegyric –

> So JAMES, if great with less we may compare,
> Arrests his rowling thunder-bolts in air;
> And grants ungratefull friends a lengthn'd space,
> T'implore the remnants of long suff'ring grace.
>
> (III.273–6)

And beyond this, although there is no space to demonstrate it here, Dryden uses satire constructively in this poem, the varying degrees of severity defining the complexity of the religio-social issues. Critical disagreement about where exactly Dryden's sympathies lie seems to me to demonstrate his achievement even while misunderstanding it, for what is so impressive is how well Dryden has caught the slipperiness of the religious problem at the time when he is writing. To want to penetrate the text and to emerge with a single reading of Dryden's religious position is tempting (if author-centred) but has the same disadvantages as seeking a single reading of the conclusions of *Sir Gawain and the Green Knight* or Chaucer's *Troilus and Criseyde*. It is precisely in the delicate evasiveness of the presentation of hind and panther that the poem's brilliance lies, and this is again a triumph of Dryden's poetic intelligence. His version of Roman Catholicism is wonderfully plausible, and may, at first, look like a proffered solution, but the plausibility is, in fact, part of the poem's point. The smoothness of the hind's account is such an accurate version of Catholic propaganda that it may as reasonably be seen as contributing to the idea of a Catholic threat as dispelling such an idea. And if this seems some way from mock-heroic as usually understood, it should be added that it can be viewed as the apotheosis of mock-heroic, in that it tantalizingly presents a gap that might not even be there. If the hind is right, there is, at the poem's end, the possibility that the heroic suffering of Catholicism in Britain may be rewarded in the fulfilment of the 'glorious Visions of her future state' (*The Hind and the Panther* III. 1298). But if the hind is a deceiver, then the gap between fiction and reality, for which the panther argues, is the truth, and a victory for Catholicism would be a triumph in the mock-heroic vein, so that deceit would rule.

Satire requires fallen worlds. It depicts such worlds and often involves the invocation of prelapsarian alternatives, most obviously in mock-heroic. It is thus the obverse of the type of celebratory verse discussed in Chapters 2 and 3, but it also offers an alternative to the epic account of experience. The literature of seventeenth-century England has more good satire than good epic, but Milton's achievement in epic is perhaps the finest of the century. Moreover, although epic and satire may be usefully contrasted, there is an overlap between the two, for Dryden's *Absalom and Achitophel* has epic elements and Milton was, among other things, a great satirist.

Notes

1. On English satire before 1600 see John Peter, *Complaint and Satire in Early English Literature* (Oxford, 1956) and O. Campbell, *Comiccall Satire . . .* (California, 1938). On seventeenth-century satire see R. Selden, *English Verse Satire, 1590–1765* (London, 1978).

2. The satirical poetry of Horace (65 BC–8 BC) is urbane, reasonable in tone, and contains a strong sense of the ethics of moderation, whereas the satires of Juvenal (AD c. 55 – c. 140) are violent, bitter, and highly compressed.

3. See Peter, *passim*.

4. Charles I took John Hampden to court for non-payment of Ship Money. The King won the case but Hampden became a symbol of resistance to monarchic 'tyranny'. Burton, Bastwick, and Prynne were tried for attacking the bishops and sentenced to lose their ears. They also became heroes of the opposition.

5. See George Parfitt, *Ben Jonson: Public Poet and Private Man* (London, 1976), pp. 142–61.

6. See E. H. Kantorowicz, *The King's Two Bodies* (New Jersey, 1957).

7. 'A Western Wonder' and 'A Second Western Wonder' both appear in print for the first time in 1662, while 'Verses on the Cavaliers . . . ' was apparently first printed in 1655. Like the 'Western Wonder' poems 'News from Colchester' appears in print in 1662, but all three were probably written some years before.

8. *The Rump*, 2 vols (London, 1662).

9. Collected in *Poems on Affairs of State*, edited by G. de F. Lord, 7 vols (New Haven, 1963–75). There is a convenient selection by Lord, *Anthology of Poems on Affairs of State* (New Haven, 1975).

10. Lord, *Anthology, p. 19.*

11. See Lucy Gent, *Picture and Poetry 1560–1620* (Leamington Spa, 1981).

12. ll. 13–14, 17–18, Lord, *Anthology*, p. 21. Lord attributes the two 'advices' and 'Last Instructions' to Marvell (p. 31) but accepts that the attribution is less than certain.

13. In the absence of a standard complete Oldham, my references are to either *The Poems of John Oldham*, edited by Bonamy Dobrée (London, 1960) or *John Oldham: Selected Poems*, edited by Ken Robinson (Newcastle upon Tyne, 1980). 'A Satyr upon a woman . . . ' is in Robinson, p. 42.

14. *Pope: Lives of the Poets*, edited by G. Birkbeck Hill (1905), III, esp. p. 246.

15. See J. P. Kenyon, *The Popish Plot* (London, 1972).

16. There has not been much good criticism of Rochester's satire, but see D. Farley Hills, *Rochester: The Critical Heritage* (London, 1972).

17. The Marquis de Sade (1740–1814), porno-philosopher. His name and sexual tendencies are preserved in the term 'sadism'.

18. Gilbert Burnet (1643–1715), Bishop of Salisbury, claimed to have converted Rochester (*Passages of the Life and Death of John, Earl of Rochester*, 1680).

19. See the Scolar Press facsimile (Menston, 1970). Quotations from *Hudibras*, edited by John Wilders (Oxford, 1967). See Wilders's Introduction and E. Richards, *Hudibras in the Burlesque Tradition* (New York, 1972).

20. Miguel de Cervantes (1547–1616), best remembered for *Don Quixote* (1605, 1615), translated into English, 1612–20.

21. Butler (Wilders edn), pp. xx, xxi

22. *Dryden: Lives of the Poets*, (1905), I, 437.

23. Richard Flecknoe (d. 1678), a Roman Catholic wit and playwright; possibly Irish, perhaps a priest. Thomas Shadwell (*c.* 1642–92), author of thirteen comedies which show him to have been a writer of some talent.

Chapter 5
The epic

Introduction

At the beginning of the seventeenth century there was no such thing as a native epic tradition, at least if the term is taken to signify more that simply a long poem. By the end of the century, however, it could be claimed that there was such a tradition, even though the claim rests heavily on Milton's achievement and on the establishment of mock-epic as a by-product of the real thing. The history of English epic in the seventeenth century is, in fact, more one of attempts to work out a native tradition than of actually establishing one, and to that extent the story may be seen as the continuation of the native tradition of the long poem, modified by some increase in awareness of the demands of classical epic.

A number of features are commonly considered proper to epic, or part of its definition. Structurally, epic should have what could be called 'shaped scale' – that is, both considerable length and length organized in relation to a defined theme and with reference to a central hero or heroes. It is also expected that the epic theme will be one of fundamental importance to mankind's history or that of a particular race. This often emerges as the account of how something like the fall of Troy or the founding of Rome came to pass, which in turn suggests epic's concern with crisis, often crisis in the relation between Man and God (or the gods). It follows that we expect a fitting style, one which renders the seriousness and gravity of the theme and which stresses the permanent rather than the quotidian, while, as epic develops, specific set pieces and stylistic features emerge, such as the arming of the hero and the use of extended simile. It should be added that epic is a way of reading experience. Epic presupposes that Man has stature and that his experiences have significance. Human history, so epic suggests, means something worth recording and presenting on a heroic scale. If an absurdist view of experience is taken epic becomes impossible and thus mock-epic is, among other things, a critical account of the assumptions of epic. Beyond this general point there is what is involved in the term 'heroic', because epic's way of reading experience is to see its significance as lying in heroic man and his adventures, and this predicates that some values and types of experience are more valuable than others. The values of epic include courage and loyalty to the social ideal and the social leader; and the typical categories of epic include war and the testing of physical and moral virtue by absolute rather than pragmatic standards. The world of epic is one of adventures on a public stage, and this world is a predominantly male one, women being confined to roles of support, seduction, and succour.

In terms of such an outline, it can be suggested that by 1600 English poets had produced a number of works which partake of epic without fully qualifying as such. *Beowulf*, *The Battle of Maldon* and *Sir Gawain and the Green Knight* are hero-centred, have elevated style, and concentrate upon large issues of social codes and behaviour, but none of these has the length of true epic, the scale of event or the range of characters. Chaucer's *Troilus and Criseyde* has such scale, but the poem is more intensely concentrated upon a single erotic issue than we expect in epic; while *Piers Plowman* has epic length and a topic of the greatest significance ('What must I do to be saved?'), but it lacks significant shape and its style and immediate objects of concern are often mock-epic rather than epic. By 1600 the only English poem which could really be said to have become part of the European epic tradition was Spenser's *Faerie Queene*, a poem which, incomplete as it is, managed to mix conformity with epic traditions with the matter of Britain and the native (or naturalized) tradition of personification and allegory to create the possibility of a distinctively English way of writing epic. One of the interests of looking at seventeenth-century versions of epic, therefore, is to see how far Spenser's example was followed.

History and epic: Drayton and Daniel

A major theme of seventeenth-century English epic and near-epic is that of rebellion. Both Samuel Daniel and Michael Drayton deal with this theme as it manifests itself in native history. Both men are therefore concerned with loyalty and disloyalty, with power, rule, and responsibility as exemplified in history in ways familiar to anyone who has seen or read historical drama of the period, while it is scarcely necessary to add that these are major concerns of sixteenth-and seventeenth-century politics. Daniel and Drayton, as we shall see, both make use of features from epic in their presentation of history, but both also draw on the tradition of historical chronicle and neither writes pure epic. Later in the century Abraham Cowley, in his aborted *The Civil War* (? 1643), tries to deal with contemporary history as full-scale epic, only to be defeated by events, and Milton continues to treat the themes mentioned above, while removing them from direct embodiment in history and locating them in what might be called pre-history.

In the third canto of *The Barons' Wars* (1603) Drayton speaks of his style as being 'transparent, neat, and cleare', (II. 39),[1] a description which is wholly accurate. A reader is struck by the consistent lucidity of manner, its clarity and moderate tone, as here:

> This chance of Warre, that suddenly had swept
> So large a share from their selected store,
> Which for their helpe they carefully had kept,
> That to their aid might still have added more;
> By this ill-lucke into their Armie crept,
> Made them much weaker then they were before;
>   So that the Barons reinforc'd their Bands,
>   Finding their Hearts to stand in need of Hands.
>
> (II. 1)

It seems an appropriate style for a poet whose stated aim is 'that we every circumstance may show,/The state of Things, and truly what they be' (I. 12), but it would be misleading to think of Drayton as concerned with 'pure' history. His poem is thoroughly artful and imaginatively sophisticated.

In a dedicatory poem, John Selden refers to Drayton's 'Epique straine', while in his address to the reader Drayton himself mentions Homer, Virgil, Statius, 'The Italians', and 'our first late great Reformer, Master Spenser'. As these references suggest, Drayton is concerned to write of the wars between Edward II and his barons as material of high significance, something which calls for an 'answering style'. So although Drayton's norm is lucid and direct, the lack of elaboration in some passages is not the same as colloquialism, and the poet is capable of heightening whenever he feels that this is appropriate:

> The Winds were hush'd (no little Breath doth blow)
> Which seems sat still, as though they list'ning stood,
> With trampling Crowds, the very Earth doth bow,
> And through the Smoake, the Sunne appear'd like Blood.
>
> (II. 32)

Throughout the poem Drayton uses variations of style, patterning his material to his rhetorical purposes, and often using extended similes to suggest the epic dimension:

> Like as a Heard of over-heated Deere,
> By hot-spur'd Hunters lab'red to be caught.

Or

> When, as from Snow-crown'd Skidow's loftie Cleeves,
> Some fleet-wing'd Haggard, tow'rds her preying howre,
> Amongst the Teyle and Moore-bred Mallard drives.
>
> (II. 53, VI. 65)

The Skiddaw simile, with teal and mallard, indicates something of Drayton's patriotism, and since epic references and features occur regularly it seems obvious that the poet is trying to project native material as of epic dimensions. But Drayton's patriotism goes beyond this, to become part of the theme itself. In a sense his departure point is the 'Noble Nation, furnished with Armes,/So full of spirit, as almost match'd by none' (I. 44), and his deepest concern is with how such a nation comes to be so divided that 'Englands Red Crosse upon both sides doth flye' (II. 34). And since Drayton has a·strong feeling for how the past may shape the present his involvement with the rebellion of the barons is not antiquarian but with the consequences of the shedding of 'that Bloud, which many an Age shall rew' (II. 20); and this is for him a matter of tragic significance:

> New sorts of Plagues were threat'ned to the Earth,
> The raging Ocean past his Bounds did rise,
> Strange Apparitions, and prodigious Birth,
> Unheard of Sicknesse, and Calamities.
>
> (IV. 41)

(This is also a good example of how Drayton uses an artistic heightening to stress an event's significance, rather than holding himself to literal truth.)

Drayton finds it difficult to apportion blame for the tragedy. He condemns the rebels, but also has hard words for Edward's favourites and for the King himself. At times, indeed, Drayton explicitly refrains from defining fault, either by evasion – 'Whether the Kings weake Councels causes are . . . Or that the Earle did of our state despayre . . . Ile not dispute, but leave it as a doubt' (IV. 6) – or by withdrawing into mysticism:

> For when just Heaven, to chastise us is bent,
> All things convert to our due punishment.
>
> (IV. 20)

The impression the poem as a whole gives is that Drayton is clear that division is such an evil that the fact of division overshadows the reasons for it, and while this emphasis means that *The Barons' Wars* lacks weight as political analysis, Drayton's steady account of 'the pity of it' can be very impressive.

Drayton's interest in history and in the contemporary significance of history is matched by his concern to find artistic ways of rendering that interest and significance. The result is something more carefully worked than chronicle, the basic narrative being significantly patterned along epic lines, although 'history' is not transformed, as in *The Iliad*, by a sense of Man's struggle in a world which the gods manipulate on a regular if erratic basis. Drayton's poem remains a specifically historical one and its significance national rather than perennial. In studying rebellion in a long poem, Drayton is taking part in the great Elizabethan and Jacobean discussion of power and obedience; while his inability to rest content with simple attri-

butions of blame, or to offer political alternatives to kingship, suggests
something of the handicap under which the Stuart crisis developed.

Although Drayton's poem gains much from his feeling for how the past
takes toll of the present, he rarely uses the present as explicit contrast, and
he does not suggest that awareness of the past justifies complacency about
the present or future. For him the past is a warning, albeit a somewhat
mysterious one once we move beyond the powerful emotional response.
Samuel Daniel, however, in his *The Civil Wars* (1609),[2] shows a strong
tendency to flatter Elizabeth I. He is even explicit about this:

> Here sacred Soueraigne, glorious Queene of Peace,
> The tumults of disordred times I sing,
> To glorifie thy Raigne, and to increase
> The wonder of those blessings thou doost bring
> Vpon thy Land.
> ('To Her Sacred Maiestie')

At the beginning of the poem proper, Daniel shows that he feels, as Dray-
ton does, the horrors of civil war, when 'people hautie, proud with forraine
spoils,/Vpon themselves turn-backe their conquering hand' (I. i), but after
he has invoked the 'fury' and 'madnes' which he associates with the end
of Richard's reign, he calls his own response into question:

> Yet now what reason have we to complaine?
> Since hereby came the calme we did injoy;
> The blisse of thee Eliza; happie gaine
> For all our losse.
> (I. 3)

Paradise lost leads to paradise regained, so mourning is pointless. But this
leaves Daniel free to respond to the pathos inherent in his material. His
Richard is the 'poore distressed Lord' of the second book, who typically

> To Flint, from thence, vnto a restless bed,
> That miserable night . . . comes conuayd;
> Poorely prouided, poorely followed,
> vncourted, vnrespected, vnobayd.
> (II. 52)

As the piling up of the language of pathos suggests, Daniel responds
strongly to the tragic romance of king and queen, the overall effect being
that the poem seems less an account of the national tragedy of civil war
than the description of one man and one relationship.

The fact that Daniel's style is plainer and less varied than Drayton's,
together with the scarcity of epic features, makes his poem not so much
a national epic as an extended romance spiced with adroit flattery. Only
the length of the poem suggests true epic. Also, while Drayton's strong
sense of the damage of civil war prevents him from offering glib solutions,

or even a politically coherent analysis, Daniel's desire to flatter Elizabeth leads him into an account which is hardly an analysis at all (even though his material prevents him from simplifying Bolingbroke too much or fully explaining him). Daniel can neither see fully what, at the political level, Bolingbroke's challenge represents nor share Drayton's instinct that the tensions in the material preclude slick dispersal of them. To that extent it is not unfair to suggest that Drayton has far greater awareness that civil war was not merely part of an evil past, something distanced by a blissful present, or to be accepted as having, in half-explained ways, made the present possible.

Towards epic: Fletchers, Davenant, and Cowley

Drayton spoke of Edmund Spenser as 'our first late great Reformer' (see above, p. 167) but his attempt to develop Spenser's example led him, in *The Baron's Wars*, to a more direct effort at patriotic epic than is *The Faerie Queen*. On the other hand, Giles and Phineas Fletcher, by combining Spenserian influence with that of Du Bartas and his English translator, Sylvester, produced something more exotic than Spenser's poem, let alone Drayton's.

At the beginning of his *The Purple Island* (1633) Phineas Fletcher presents the poet-figure as concerned to discover whether there is now any room left in which to operate:

> Tell me, ye Muses, what our father-ages
> Have left succeeding times to play upon:
> What now remains unthought on by those Sages,
> Where a new Muse may trie her pineon?
>   What lightning Heroes, like great Peleus heir, . . .
>   May stirre up gentle heat, and virtues wane repair?
>
> (I. 9)

Fletcher then gives an allusive list of the poets who crowd the scene, a list which makes it clear that he thinks of his own poem as in the epic tradition, or, at least, as aspiring to this, for Fletcher sees himself as trapped in an iron age where '(Hard daies) afford nor matter, nor reward!', and he cites Spenser as a fellow victim:

> . . . all his hopes were crost, all suits deni'd;
> Discourag'd, scorn'd, his writings vilifi'd:
> Poorely (poore man) he liv'd; poorely (poore man) he di'd.
>
> (*The Purple Island*, I. 17, 19)

To some extent this kind of lament is commonplace, and it does not prevent Fletcher attempting the most elaborate and ambitious of Jacobean epics, but it may help to explain the particular nature of the attempt.

Whereas both Drayton and Daniel write a basically plain style and depend a great deal upon narrative, Phineas Fletcher operates in a more self-consciously witty manner and his poem displays itself as artefact in a distinctly mannered way. Both aspects are evident in the antitheses and wordplay of the lines on Spenser and in a stanza like this:

> Heark then, ah heark, you gentle shepheard-crue;
> An Isle I fain would sing, an Island fair;
> A place too seldome view'd, yet still in view;
> Neare as our selves, yet farthest from our care;
>   Which we by leaving finde, by seeking lost;
>   A forrain home, a strange, though native coast;
> Most obvious to all, yet most unknown to most.
>
>   (I. 34)

The style is a distancing agent (which here takes on a riddling aspect) and this distancing is increased by the pastoral frame for each canto and by Fletcher's constant use of personification. The result is a strange mixture, an attempt to treat of the human body in epic terms and in a broadly Spenserian manner.

Fletcher, in fact, does not have a story. Instead he has an object, the human body, and he sees this in terms of its centrality to a view of creation. The decision to provide an account of the body in the context of 'history' makes *The Purple Island* epic in scale, but a very odd poem indeed, for – all else apart – the style is constantly transforming the basic anatomy into self-conscious art:

> Below, a cave rooft with an heav'n-like plaister,
> And under strew'd with purple tapestreie,
> Where Gustus dwells, the Isles and Princes Taster,
> Koilia's Steward, one of th' Pemptarchie.
>
>   (v. 54)

But although Fletcher is in a sense writing a poem about the human body (and a very detailed one it is) he is presenting the body as the central fact in human history. This microcosm is macrocosmic, the detailed working or unity of the body being possible only because of Christ's sacrifice for Man:

> Now was this Isle pull'd from that horrid main,
> Which bears the fearfull looks and name of death;
> And setled new with bloud, and dreadfull pain,
> By him who twice had giv'n (once forfeit) breath.
>
>   (II. 2)

Fletcher's constant moralizing interventions remind a reader of Man's sinfulness in a way which gives some tension to the poem, but the ground plan, with its insistence upon a comprehensive survey of the body, prevents the theme's significance from being steadily in view, and the poem works not as a shaped and shapely epic but as a Gothic construction, one with its own fascination, but not reminiscent of Homer or Virgil. Although a reader is aware of the importance of the theme, the act of reading is less one of response to that theme than of interest in Fletcher's style and resourcefulness, while the distancing produced by style and the pastoral device means that *The Purple Island* works as a hybrid, including elements of epic, together with pastoralism and medieval psychomachia, in a way which both makes it characteristic of Jacobean Spenserianism and clearly apart from the more directly 'realistic' preoccupations of Donne and Jonson.

For Giles Fletcher, Du Bartas and Spenser are 'two blessed Soules', and his epistle to the reader makes clear his wish to promote the cause of religious verse. As the titles of his four linked poems (1610) suggest,[3] he seeks to do this by treating the central Christian mystery, the sacrifice and triumph of Christ himself. This, of course, immediately suggests an anticipation of Milton, but whereas the latter was to work with a firm narrative base, Giles Fletcher has relatively little interest in narrative, something which immediately weakens the link between his work and the epic tradition. In place of story we are given style and argument, as the first stanza of *Christ's Victorie in Heaven* makes clear:

> The birth of him that no beginning knewe,
> Yet gives beginning to all that are borne,
> And how the Infinite farre greater grewe,
> By growing lesse, and how the rising Morne,
> That shot from heav'n, did backe to heaven retourne,
>   The obsequies of him that could not die,
>   And death of life, ende of eternitie,
> How worthily he died, that died unworthily.

As this stanza indicates, Fletcher likes paradox ('I looke for joy, but finde a sea of teares;/I looke that we should live, and finde him die;/I looke for Angels songs, and heare him crie'; *Christ's Triumph over Death*, st. 4). A feeling for paradox is invaluable for a religious poet, but the way in which Fletcher is drawn by this and by the attraction of witty effects leads to the material being dominated by the manner:

> It was but now they gathered blooming May,
> And of his armes disrob'd the branching tree,
> To strowe with boughs, and blossomes all thy way,
> And now, the branchless truncke a crosse for thee,
> And May, dismai'd, thy coronet must be.
>
> (*Christ's Triumph* . . ., st. 33)

Further, Giles Fletcher's seeming lack of interest in narrative is accompanied by a lack of feeling for dramatic effect, and this makes it virtually impossible for him to bring out – as, of course, Milton was to do – the epic potential of his material. Thus Fletcher's Christ is tempted by personifications, and he lacks the ability to give these the vitality found, say, in Langland. The result is that Christ's victory over temptation, and thus over Satan, is anticlimatic:

> Thus sought the dire Enchauntress in his minde
> The guilefull bayt to have embosomed,
> But he her charmes dispersed into winde,
> And her of insolence admonished,
> And all her optique glasses shattered.
>   So with her Syre to hell she tooke her flight,
>   (The starting ayre flew from the damned spright,)
>   Whear deeply both aggriev'd, plunged themselves in night.
>   (*Christ's Victorie on Earth*, st. 60)

The effect is rather like that of Marvell's 'Dialogue between the Soul and body', spiced with luxurious Spenserian writing:

> The roofe thicke cloudes did paint, from which three boyes
> Three gaping mermaides with their eawrs did feede,
> To Lions mouths, from whence it leapt with speede,
> And in the rosie laver seem'd to bleed.
>   (st. 48)

Giles Fletcher's writing often has considerable local colour and interest, but the final effect is hazy, partly because the dramatic potential of the material is understated. Epic, as normally defined, involves the sense that the issues it deals with are both vital and difficult, but Fletcher lacks this sense. He can decorate and speculate, but is without Drayton's feeling for the uncertainty of things, let alone Milton's deep doubts. This may be as much a matter of talent and temperament as of anything alse, but it is interesting to notice that the full realization of the epic possibilities in the Christ-story only occurs in the aftermath of the Civil War. Both of the Fletchers belong to a post-Spenser group which finds withdrawal from society attractive, but they show little sign of withdrawal as the result of any real pressure, either of the type so movingly represented in Lovelace's 'The Grasse-hopper' or of that seen in the Milton of the Restoration. It is too simple to see the pastoralism of Phineas Fletcher and William Browne as mere escapism and to regard the lack of tension in Giles Fletcher as evidence of complacency, but whereas Spenser found ways of using the pastoral and fantasy to make *The Faerie Queen* a commentary upon his own society, there is the feeling with these poets that they have largely withdrawn from any real engagement. Phineas Fletcher writes:

> But (ah!) let me under some Kentish hill
> Near rowling Medway 'mong my shepherd peers,

With fearlesse merrie-make, and piping still,
Securely passe my few and slow-pac'd yeares:
    While yet the great Augustus of our nation
    Shuts up old Janus in this long cessation,
    Strength'ning our pleasing ease, and gives us sure vacation.

(The Purple Island, i. 28)

The desire may well be genuine, but it is hard not to feel that it is ener-
vated, particularly given the abnegation of any part in the business of state.
With such wishes and attitudes, the Fletchers create pseudo-epic worlds in
which art is nearly all, with the result that the sense that epic deals with
vital issues is weakened. Epic may – in fact usually does – find its material
in stories apparently very far from contemporary, but it achieves signifi-
cance through the poet's feeling that the issues inherent in his material have
value for the contemporary. The Fletchers, however, seem interested
mainly in the decorative and rhetorical possibilities of their material. That
being so, true epic is beyond them.

As the instances so far discussed suggest, epic in seventeenth century
England is dominated by the Bible and by native history, but Sir William
Davenant's *Gondibert* (1651) is a curious attempt at inventing epic. David
F. Gladish, the Oxford editor of the poem, points to several moments
which seem designed to create a 'mask of historicity',[4] but the allusions are
obscure and the bulk of the poem seems to lack any source. Yet it is clear
that Davenant is aiming to break new ground. Rather than being concerned
to naturalize traditional features of classical or Italian epic, he aims to follow
the precedent of the five-act drama and to adapt this to non-dramatic pur-
poses.[5] Davenant is fully conscious of what he is doing, and, indeed, self-
consciousness is a striking feature of the whole enterprise.

Gondibert was begun during Davenant's exile in France in the late 1640s,
and the first three books were published in 1651. Although 'The seventh
and last Canto of the Third Book of Gondibert' was printed later (1685)
nothing of the projected fourth and fifth books survives, and, indeed, noth-
ing of these books may have been written, The self-consciousness of the
venture, however, may be seen in the fact that 'The Author's Preface to
his much honor'd friend, M. Hobbes', an elaborate and lengthy account
of his purposes, was published in advance of the incomplete text.

In the preface Davenant places his own poem by recalling the great
names of epic poetry (Homer, Virgil, Lucan, Statius, Tasso, and Spenser),
but then speaks of his work as 'this new Building', and goes on:

> I cannot discerne by any help from reading, or learned
> men . . . that any Nation hath in represention of great
> actions (either by Heroicks or Dramaticks) digested Story
> into so pleasant and instructive a method as the English
> by their Drama: and by that regular species . . . I have drawn
> the body of an Heroick Poem.

(ll. 491–7)

He explains his choice of form (ABAB stanzas – the so-called 'heroic stanza') and is also explicit about the function of heroic verse. It 'in a perfect glasse of Nature gives us a familiar and easy view of our selves', but this 'glasse' is not to be thought of as the mirror of naturalism. Instead it is the familiar renaissance glass which reflects what should be, or platonically is, and Davenant feels that Christianity will provide the appropriate material, 'because the Principles of our Religion conduce more to explicable vertue, to plaine demonstrative justice, and even to Honor . . . then any other Religion that e're assembl'd men to Divine Worship' (ll. 9–10, 257–262). Using the pattern of 'regular' English drama, Davenant aims to produce a poem which exemplifies the moral qualities in which he is interested.

Since almost half of *Gondibert* is missing it is obviously impossible to tell exactly how the story would have worked out, but few readers are likely to care very much, for one of the main weaknesses of the poem is its failure as narrative. Had Davenant been working with a known story, that in itself might have provided some narrative interest, even if Davenant himself had not been primarily interested in story. But his decision to invent means that he needs to interest a reader in his narrative or to provide some compensation for lack of narrative excitement. This might have come from the sheer quality of the story, or from the interest of argument, or from insight into character. Unfortunately, Davenant can provide none of these, and *Gondibert* is something of a disaster. Yet just why this is so has its interest in relation to English epic in the seventeenth century.

Much of the poem's weakness comes, I think, from the sense that it is located nowhere. The names of characters – Ulfin, Gondibert, Astragon and so on – provide a vaguely exotic feeling, and there are references to Lombardy, Brescia, and other places, but there is a crippling lack of detail and specificity. Drayton, who has some claim to be seen as a real historian, is knowledgeable about his country and its history, and is thus able to give his writing mass and weight. Spenser had shown what the imagination can do, the wandering wood in the first book of *The Faerie Queen* providing a good example of how allegory can, as with Langland earlier, have tangible presence. But Davenant's preface suggests that he is interested in the heroic qualities of his characters, and his writing suggests that he is less interested in anchoring this in fully realized places and situation. What he produces is too easily typical.

Then there is Davenant's inability to allow his material to make its own points, a weakness which seems connected with the lack of imaginative grasp. Not having imaginatively grasped or experienced his story, Davenant feels a constant need to explain. Spenser, of course, is also anxious to explain (which is one reason why it is misleading for Spenserians to stress the difficulty of his epic), but he usually does so having given his readers a fully realized incident. In *The Faerie Queen*, as in *Paradise Lost*, the material and the explanation interact, sometimes conflict, and the reader is thereby drawn into dialogue with the work, whereas in *Gondibert* explanation dominates to such an extent that dialogue is virtually impossible. From the beginning of the poem Davenant shows reluctance to trust either material or reader. The former must be made to exemplify the poet's moral antitheses, while the latter must be made to accept the placing of the characters not primarily because of what is done, but because of the poet's direct statements. Thus, when we are told that Hubert's 'Princely qualitie more frees/Him then the rest, from all command, unless/He finde it such as with his will agrees' (I. iii. 68), we are not being given a view which we can check against performance. All that happens is that performance will be made to enact what has already been asserted.

Such lack of elasticity and such rejection of the complexity of personality and experience are common in romance and in heroic writing, but authors of ability can work back from the simplicities of idealization to awareness of the difficulty of the actual, and it is the struggle between the ideal and the actual which creates complexity and the peculiar poignancy of great art. Davenant's lack of a sense of such struggle is crippling, especially since he is not a good enough poet to offer much compensation through style.

In fact the style of *Gondibert* is as unlocated as the poem's setting. It shows a tendency to heroic periphrasis. King Aribert's lack of a son is described as 'no male Pledg, to give a lasting name,/Sprung from his bed', while the desire to avoid the colloquial can lead Davenant into near-gibberish:

> And twice the Tierce of these consists of those
> Who for Prince Oswald's love of Empire bled.
>
> (I. i. 9; I. v. 56)

There is the feeling that poetic writing should be metaphoric, but little sense that Davenant sees metaphor as anything more than decorous ornament. His use of imagery may exemplify, but seldom illuminates:

> This gave cold Ulfinore in Love's long Night
> Some hope of Day; as Sea-men that are run
> Far Northward finde long Winters to be light,
> And in the Cynosure adore the Sun.
>
> (III. v. 73)

Unfortunately, too, the writing is often rhythmically flat or uncertain:

> We Rivals were in Laura, but though she
> My griefs derided, his with sighs approv'd;
> Yet I (in Love's exact integritie)
> Must take thy life for killing him She lov'd.

Or

> From thence breaks lov'ly forth, the World's first Maid;
> Her Breast, Love's Cradle, where Love quiet lies;
> Nought yet had seen so foule, to grow afraid,
> Nor gay, to make it cry with longing Eies.
>
> (I. iv. 26; II. vi. 63)

Revealingly, Davenant also has a number of awkward repetitions of sound, as here, within seven stanzas:

> Mildly as mourning Doves love's sorrow felt;
>   whose jealous shame
> Deny'd her Eyes the knowledge of her glass;
>
> But Oswald never knew love's ancient Laws,
> The awe that Beauty does in lovers breed.
>
> (I. i. 43, 44, 49)

It is difficult to avoid feeling that *Gondibert* is no more than an exercise, an extended literary whim showing no real understanding of the drama on which it is allegedly based and no genuine feeling for language either. Moreover, the lack of location commented on earlier suggests that Davenant does not have anything he really wants to write about, and this is the final indictment of the enterprise, because the material of the poem might have been used to some purpose.

Gladish, somewhat nervously seeking to protect the text he is presenting, says that 'under the mask of historicity the poem is a prodigious collection of literary, philosophical, and historical bits and pieces'. He goes on to suggest that 'among the most intriguing aspects of the poem, are many allusions, apparently, to contemporary history. *Gondibert* plays about the fringes of the *roman à clef*'[6]. Gladish then offers several illustrations of his claim, while being carefully diffident about the whole matter, yet nevertheless concluding that '*Gondibert* may well be a kind of veiled allegorical discussion of current vital issues'[7].

There is no space here to discuss this possibility, although it is obvious that the theme of a power struggle for the inheritance of Aldibert's throne, with the accompanying moral issues, is one which could have resonance in the 1640s. It is also interesting that in the second canto of the first book Davenant writes of the stag hunt with rather more verve than he can usually summon up, and the figure of the old stag being hunted, with the strong symbolic connections between stag and monarch, suggests Denham's treatment of the same motif in *Cooper's Hill*. Finally, there is, within the poem, an undercurrent of cynicism which might be associated with the disillusionment which is common enough among royalists in the mid-century. But what is striking is not the possibility that Davenant is alluding to contemporary history, but that he so rarely manages to convey any sense of real involvement with anything real. *Gondibert* is a dead poem, but it does suggest how difficult it was to make native epic. Abraham Cowley's efforts illustrate this point further.

As Allan Pritchard reminds us, Cowley says, in the preface to his *Poems* of 1656, that he had written three books of a poem on the Civil War, leaving it unfinished after the first Battle of Newbury. A version of the first book was published in 1679 as 'A Poem on the Late Civil War,' but it was only in the 1960s that the complete incomplete text came to light. Pritchard, who discovered one of the two manuscripts now known to exist and who has edited the text[8], takes the view 'that Cowley began *The Civil War* in the

summer or early autumn of 1643' and abandoned it at the time of First
Newbury. We shall return to the significance of the text's incompleteness
later. At this stage, however, two points should be made – that the text is
apparently not finalized, but unrevised as well as incomplete, and that it
represents an effort to write epic about events as they unfold. In choosing to
write of the Civil War as epic, Cowley is choosing a pattern for a segment of
history which was not complete as he wrote; and his choice of hero thus
involved prediction. The King must win, and Cowley's epic becomes vatic
and a statement of faith, rather than the account of history or myth.

Yet history and myth play important parts in *The Civil War*. Native
history is used throughout to judge the present, while classical allusion and
myth are employed, both in this way and to give the contemporary material
the dignity of epic. Cowley begins the poem by stressing the pain of internal
war:

> What rage does England from it selfe divide
> More then Seas doe from all the world beside?

and his first major rhetorical device is the formula 'It was not so . . .' which
is used to remind readers of aspects of a more glorious past, 'when Henryes
dreadfull name;/Not Sword, nor Cause, whole Nations overcame', or
'when in the happy East/Richard, our Mars, Venuses Isle possest' (I. 13–14,
21–2). This heroic past, by definition one of unity and conquest, is pre-
sented as a chronology which leads into the reign of Charles I, and that
reign is seen as one of peace, broken only by ingratitude on the part of the
King's subjects. Within the first 100 lines of the first book, Cowley's basic
thesis is plain enough: civil war is unnatural, and untypical of England's
history; and it has come about for reasons which have nothing to do with
any faults of King Charles.

But while Cowley is concerned to set the war in the context of native
history, he is also anxious that his poem should be seen as more than chron-
icle, and one aspect of this elevation is classical allusion. So Rupert and
Maurice, the King's nephews, are compared to Castor and Pollux, twin
sons of Leda and Jove (I. 189–90), while at the beginning of the second
book the use of classical myth to define the standing of the native conflict
is very clear, with the mention of 'dire Alecto, ris'en from Stygian strand'
and of Triptolemus acting as introduction to an account of the Battle of
Hopton Heath in March 1643. And although classical allusions are, per-
haps, less frequent than might be expected, they work with the careful and
sustained elevation of style and the use of such epic features as the extended
simile to make it clear that, to Cowley, the Civil War is an event on the
scale of the fall of Troy.

But the poem's style is also a witty one, marked by paradox and anti-
thesis. So brave rebels in book two are 'Damn'd, and infam'ed for fight-
ing ill soe well!' and Cowley clearly enjoys the witty paradoxes here:

> Some feele hot wounds shot through the dashing flood,
> They drinke in Water, and supply't with Blood.
>
> (*The Civil War*, II. 136, 325–6)

Such witty writing runs through the poem, and is conducive to an air of confident analysis, of knowing how the war has come to be and of which are heroes, which villains. So Charles's innocence and the sanctity of his cause are established by the conceit here:

> More then Hee them, the Bullets fear'd his head,
> And at his feete lay innocently dead.
>
> (I. 247–8)

Such a style works well in satirical writing, reinforcing the basic satiric device of seeing experience in terms of black and white, and it allows Cowley to create some forceful invective aimed at the rebels, but it is less satisfactory when related to the complexity of Cowley's material and to the need for tension in a poem of epic length. Cowley, in fact, does not offer any real analysis of the causes of the war. His opening catalogue is highly selective and his account of the reigns of the first Stuarts equally partial. Moreover, all he offers as explanation of how 'our Happinesse' (I. 92) passed away is a muddle of ingratitude and the Scots. There is no sense in Cowley of the accumulating uncertainties and distrusts which underlie the peace of Charles's reign up to the coming of the Civil War, and no understanding that these were, at least in part, the result of the King's limitations. This might matter less if Cowley had a feeling for the imaginative possibilities of the fundamental situation. Even if one reads Shakespeare's *Henry VI* plays as basically in support of a Tudor establishment line on kingship (which I do not) it is impossible not to respond to the sense of the pity of the disunity and bloodshed, but internecine tragedy is beyond Cowley's grasp. He has a feeling for the sadness, even pathos, of royalist deaths (especially that of Falkland at the end of book three) but is blank, or just jubilant, at the deaths of rebels. Cowley lacks Spenser's sense of the power of evil, Homer's balance of heroisms, Milton's feeling for the complexity of motives; and such lack of imaginative response is finally fatal, granted the material with which Cowley is working. True epic becomes impossible, and good-quality invective/propaganda the most Cowley can achieve.

This is not so just because Cowley's analysis is simple, but also because he makes a basic choice that renders epic impossible. When Dryden came to write *Absalom and Achitophel* he made Shaftesbury a figure of real ability and menace, thereby creating a threat to Charles/David which allowed the latter genuine heroic possibilities. But Cowley regards the rebels of his poem as both despicable and weak. Faced by the force and rightness of Rupert in book one, Cowley's rebels can only disperse with maximum ignominy:

> Soe swift the Rebells fly, as if each Feare,
> And Jealousie they fram'd, had met them there.
> They heard warrs Musicke and away they flew,
> The Trumpets fright worse then the Organs doe.
>
> (I. 265–8)

In the third book Cowley has a long account of those who joined to defend
London from the King, and the passage is quite a well-sustained piece of
invective, emphasizing the social and religious impoverishment of these
rebels, 'base Mechanicks', 'hot-brained Calvinists', Independents 'Who into
Rags the seamelesse Vesture rent' (iii. 41, 59, 83–4). The effect of all this,
however, is to make the opposition to Charles seem hopelessly ineffectual;
and, indeed, it seems that this opposition only keeps in the field at all be-
cause of satanic malice. So in book two there is a council in hell, as a result
of which 'Hast to their London prey the Furies made' (iii. 2). But this use
of the satanic only makes things more difficult for Cowley, for if the rebels
are backed by Satan, Cowley's Charles is as clearly endorsed and supported
by God:

> . . . tis heaven this swift assistance bringes;
> The same is Lord of Hosts, thats King of Kings.
> Had men forsooke him, Angells from above . . .
>
> Would all have muster'd in his righteous ayd,
> And thunder 'gainst your Canon would have playd.
>
> (i. 173–8)

There are two problems here, only one of which is caused by the fact
that the Civil War went wrong, from Cowley's point of view. Given his
loyalties and granted the way in which he has lined up heaven and hell
behind, respectively, King and rebels, there must either be a victory for
Charles or Cowley must find a way of seeing final victory emerging from
seeming defeat. Failing either of these he has no choice but to abandon his
poem or to enter deep waters of heresy. But, at a literary level, Cowley
would still have had problems even if the war had gone as he wished. Since
the rebels are a weak and despicable rabble, cowardly and socially below
contempt, Charles has nothing to beat at a human level; and this, of course,
reflects social views not solely Cowley's own, one of the contemporary
enigmas being how the traditional superiorities of King and gentry could
fail to defeat an opposition so often, if misleadingly, seen as socially in-
ferior. Given this view, Cowley clearly needs something like satanic sup-
port for the rebels if his poem is to have any tension. But although Cowley
writes quite powerfully about hell, he fails to keep the metaphysical di-
mension consistently in our minds, and the satanic propping up of his
miserable rebels seems little more than an excuse to explain how a sequence
of royalist victories fails to bring collapse of the rebellion. Homer, in his
Iliad, had shown how it is possible to blend supernatural interference in the
affairs of humankind with a feeling for heroism at the human level, but
Cowley cannot, it seems, learn from the Greek example.

The first Battle of Newbury brings Cowley to a pause, and although
that battle did not mean that the royalist cause was lost, it did provide a
check which was, it seems, too severe for the simplicity of Cowley's chosen
pattern. He himself, in his 1656 preface, says that the battle and 'succeeding
misfortunes of the party stopt the work; for it is so uncustomary, as to

become almost ridiculous, to make Lawrels for the Conquered'. Cowley, of course, had set out to make laurels for the conquerors, but events had gone awry. At the end of his third book there is a moving account of the death of Falkland; and the passage is moving because it registers that death as the ultimate blasphemy of the rebels and also because it implicitly records Cowley's recognition that he had cast events into a mould which they finally refused to take. This enforces the abandoning of the project, and suggests a contrast with Milton, who fought the issues through in his epics. But the themes of loyalty and distrust, which Milton and Cowley have in common, are ones which the latter takes to some sort of resolution in his other attempt at epic, the *Davideis*.

Cowley was fifty years old when the *Davideis* was published in 1668 and, although the poem may have been started much earlier, it is in a sense authorized late in its creator's career.[9] Technically, Cowley was well equipped to write a long poem, having a fluent and lucid style, a variety of manners, some structural ability, and considerable learning. *Davideis* is carefully written and presented, with summaries before each book and extensive annotation. The poem is conscious of itself as epic, and a reader is quickly aware, through invocation, extended simile and digression, that he/she is reading a serious effort at English heroic poetry. Moreover, the lucidity suggests from the start that the poem might work really well, since the verse moves fluently and points are clearly marked:

> The malice now of jealous Saul grew less,
> O'recome by constant Virtue, and Success;
> He grew at last more weary to command
> New dangers, than young David to withstand
> Or Conquer them; he fear'd his mastring Fate,
> And envy'd him a Kings unpowerful Hate.
> Well did he know how Palms by' oppression speed,
> Victorious, and the Victors sacred Meed!
>
> (Waller, p. 243)[10]

In choosing a Christian topic, Cowley is, of course, participating in the effort to write Christian epic which goes back to Renaissance Italy and which aims to show that biblical authors had produced material as worthy of epic treatment as had classical ones. Further, the Bible was living material in Cowley's time. People knew the text and widespread feeling for typology ensured that parallels between past and present were both expected and felt to be natural. The story of David was widely known and applied to contemporary circumstances. Although Dryden's *Absalom and Achitophel*, because of its quality, is sometimes seen as a virtuoso piece there is nothing unusual, by seventeenth century standards, in his having used the Bible to write about contemporary politics. And while the story of David's relationship with the jealous ruler, Saul, might not fit very obviously with the politics of mid-century England, the theme of loyalty could scarcely have been more relevant, and Cowley's use of Hebrew history allows the possibility of a complex examination of ideas of responsibility and rule. There seems no good reason why the *Davideis* should not be a success.

It was, however, suggested earlier that narrative is one of the basic expectations of epic; and it is obvious that a good story, told with a feeling for its shape and rhythms, will be a considerable asset to any long poem. Also, the pattern of a good story is often so clear and so archetypally moving that the points a writer wishes to stress are hardly in need of explication. Elaboration then becomes more a way of manipulating tension than of anything else, and epic set pieces can be seen to have a functional purpose. But Cowley seems, in the *Davideis*, to be interested in set pieces at the expense of his story and the poem is remarkably lacking in tension. There is, for instance, the attempt on David's life in the first book, when his wife uses a lie to save him. Her loyalty in face of peril and the fragility of her story to Saul's soldiers make for an effective scene, but Cowley deals with it briefly and does little to engage the reader's sympathy. Or, more strikingly, there is the treatment of David's meeting with Goliath in book three. This is a natural subject for dramatic treatment and Cowley spends a lot of time setting up the encounter, only to disperse tension by a flat, anticlimatic account of the fight itself:

> For now from Davids sling the stone is fled,
> And strikes with joyful noise the Monsters head.
> It strook his forehead, and pierc'ed deeply there;
> As swiftly as it pierc'ed before the Ayre.
>
> (Waller, p. 338)

In epic the hero proves himself in battle or duel, which, of course, is what David does here, but Cowley misses completely the opportunities offered by Goliath's physical superiority and David's humble circumstances.

This lack of dramatic sense is also found in the patterning of the poem as a whole. Epic encourages digression and allusion, these working, when properly controlled, to set the central action and its heroes in a wider context of heroic history. Cowley seems to want to use stretches of Jewish history to make David an exemplary figure and to establish continuity between the 'historical' location of his career and the subsequent history of the Jews, as well as indicating how the Old Testament prefigures the New. So he uses visions and a flexible time-sequence which should establish the central relationship between David and Saul as a matter of great significance. But since he fails to make the central action prominent or exciting, a reader is left feeling that the elaborate context dominates what it should serve, a problem made the more acute by Cowley's failures of characterization.

The problem here is simply that there is little real characterization in *Davideis*. David himself is uninteresting, being given no self-doubt and an essentially passive role. Saul is seen as torn between good and bad impulses, but the potential for a complex, even tragic, figure is wasted by the poem's anxiety not to be misunderstood, as a result of which we are constantly being told how to react and are left with little imaginative work to do.

Since we fail to be interested in the main figures of the poem, and since action in *Davideis* is intermittent and often flatly presented, there is little left except passages of lucid writing to admire.

It is not easy to see why Cowley's poem is so dead. Particular weaknesses are obvious enough, but the poet's basic competence leaves one wondering why no impulse gives life to the overall conception. *The Civil War* had been an attempt to apply epic to present circumstances, while the *Davideis* might have been an attempt to use biblical material to figure analysis of contemporary politics. There are moments of general reflection:

> a falling state
> Has always its own errours joyn'd with fate.

And

> . . . wo to Kingdoms that have Friends too strong!
>
> (Waller, pp. 297, 300)

But there is little sense in the poem as a whole that it is to be read as comment on the present, and little feeling that its material is fired by any committed response to the political issues inherent in that material. In fact, Cowley seems to be so anxious to write a proper epic that he has simply stifled his own creation. The *Davideis* is certainly a very respectable poem, tediously so, with the apparatus showing the poet's learning but resolutely failing to illuminate the text.

Cowley seems to lack loyalty. This is not so much a matter of public loyalty (although the record there is suspect[11]) but more of a deeper loyalty to self and his art. He was a prodigy and had success in a variety of manners, his fluency and wit making his work pleasantly accessible. But in the *Davideis* he seems content with displaying his learning, leaving the tensions in his material largely undisturbed. It is easier, it seems, to be stylish than to think.

Milton and epic

Since *Paradise Lost* (1667) is both a great and a controversial poem it has inevitably been much written about. Also, since the poem concerns God and Satan and the Fall, the criticism of the poem includes some highly charged and committed writing about the presentation of Satan (how far he is to be seen as heroic) and about the poet's conscious or unconscious attitude to his God, as well as about the view of the relationship of Adam and Eve, whether the Fall is fortunate or unfortunate and whether Milton's style is to be admired or deplored. The poem, too, can be studied from many different angles – as Christian epic, as seventeenth-century controversy; for its theology, its articulation of Milton's beliefs, its version of the Paradise myth, and so on.

Little of this, obviously, can be discussed here, and I aim to concentrate mainly on *Paradise Lost* as an epic of the seventeenth century which is very much a part of the religio–political controversies of its time. Professor Hearnshaw said in 1913 that '*Paradise Lost* is not only the epic of the Fall of Man, it is also the epic of the ruin of the cause of the Commonwealth . . . it could have been written . . . only at the precise moment when it was written',[12] but the working out of the implications of such a view has been mainly the work of another historian, Christopher Hill, and what I have to say is much indebted to him.[13] This does not, however, mean that other approaches to the poem are wrong or unprofitable, but Hill has made it clear that some of the main areas of controversy about *Paradise Lost* can be clarified by reference to the situation of the mid-seventeenth century.

Paradise Lost is essentially about power and autonomy. It is concerned with God's power over Satan and with his rights over Man, but also with Satan's rejection of God's power and effort to exercise dominion over his fellow fallen angels and over Adam and Eve, as well as with the issues of Adam's control of Eve and of her right to self-hood, and with the limits of their freedom of choice in relation to God's injunctions and Satan's temptations. Since these issues are set at the very beginnings of Man's history and are vital to understanding the situation of mankind through history, it follows that they are of perennial concern. This remains true even in a society which has largely rejected the *Genesis* myth as historical truth, while such concern will clearly be more acute so long as the story is seen as history. It should be added that the seventeenth-century belief in typology means that the events of which Milton writes can be seen as anticipating the redemption of Man by the sacrificial Christ and as prefiguring contemporary events as well.

It is vital, if *Paradise Lost* is to be a living poem, that Milton should avoid making it simply a chronicle, an account of events in the past. Obviously it is that, at one level, but the rebellion of Satan continues, and the Fall is re-enacted whenever a believer sins, just as Christ's redemption of mankind is repeated whenever a sinner repents. Moreover, since God is beyond time and space, all events happen simultaneously to him and all places coexist. It is clear that awareness of the need to keep a reader alert to all this is very much in Milton's mind. Milton does, of course, use narrative sequence, and can do so brilliantly, as notably with Satan's temptation of Eve, but the poem's narrative is constantly involved with anticipations and reminders. The perpetual re-enactment of the events of the poem is indicated in its very first line – 'Of Mans First Disobedience, and the Fruit': not 'Adam's' or 'Eve's', but 'Mans', while 'first' suggests that there are/have been others. These opening lines are, in fact, a microcosm of the whole work and contain its essential drama. The 'First Disobedience' 'Brought Death into the World, and all our woe' (I. 3), but this reason for despair is checked by the immediate reminder of the 'one greater Man' who redeems mankind. The importance of this is that it presents at once the poem's main dilemma, to keep a reader constantly aware that he/she deserves damnation but may achieve salvation: the drift to despair must always be checked by the recognition of perennial grounds for hope.

Simultaneity is therefore very important in Milton's poem. A good example of this comes in book three. The unfallen angels sing of creation and of the Son's contribution to Satan's defeat:

> . . . Thou that day
> Thy Fathers dreadful Thunder didst not spare,
> Nor stop thy flaming Chariot wheels, that shook
> Heav'ns everlasting Frame, while o'er the necks
> Thou drov'st of warring Angels disarrayd.
>
> (III. 392–6)

But the angels go on to sing of mankind's involvement in Satan's rebellion, of God's pity for mankind, and of the Son's self-sacrifice–'Second to thee, offered himself to die/For mans offence' (ll 419–10) – before concluding with rhapsody of such 'unexampl'd love' (ll. 410). Here again the whole epic is epitomized within a few lines. It is worth adding that this temporal summary is followed by a spatial contrast, between 'Heav'n, above the starry Sphear' (l. 416) and the 'firm opacous Globe/Of this round World' (ll. 418–19) where 'Satan alighted walks' (ll. 421). Morever, Milton plays tricks with perspective here: 'a Globe farr off/It seem'd, now seems a boundless Continent/Starless expos'd . . .' (ll. 422–3).

Such presentation of themes and places as simultaneous, with such shifts of perspective, do much to make *Paradise Lost* dynamic in a way in which no other English epic of the century is, this dynamism being also enacted through syntax and shifts of tense, all of these things working to impress the poem's urgency upon the reader. But it is also important to note that the very dynamism of *Paradise Lost* means that the kind of resolution of the issues the poem raises which many critics seem to want may be unattainable and irrelevant to the poem's function. We can see this in the case of Satan.

The story tells us that Satan fell because he rebelled against God and that he rebelled because of pride and ambition. Since the story also tells us that God is good and that mankind fell because of Satan's temptation of Eve, it is fundamental that Satan is to be seen as evil, is to be despised and rejected. All else apart, salvation is, so the story says, only possible if Satan *is* rejected. And Milton is concerned that we do not forget that Satan is pride, ambition, and rebellion personified, and that his revolt has imperilled mankind.

But the Satan of *Paradise Lost* is much more complex than this summary suggests. The impression of the first two books is not of a figure of sly and sordid treachery, but of a massive, worthy opponent of a God seen by Satan as a tyrant. What is striking is the quality of Satan's resistance and his ability to infuse his followers with this, symbolized by the building of Pandemonium and by the resolution to carry on the struggle. The story tells us that the resistance is hopeless and that it is vicious, as well as dangerous for Man, but the same story has put Satan into a position reminiscent of heroes who resist powers greater than they are and who refuse to surrender or cease to struggle. It may be wrong from any orthodox theological viewpoint to think of Philoctetes or of the end of *The Battle of Maldon*, but imaginatively that is just what we do. And it can be argued that the discomposure that results, whereby we find ourselves drawn to a figure we know to be basically destructive, is something which Milton encourages rather than seeks to avoid. Satan, like Face in Jonson's *The Alchemist*, is the most active force in the poem, and his activity, while fundamentally malicious, is also that of the traveller who takes great risks to attain his goal. Satan is a perverse pilgrim, his goal not the Heavenly City but the ruin of mankind and the thwarting of God. And even though we know that success for Satan is peril for mankind, Milton's evocation of chaos is sufficiently powerful to ensure that we identify with the Satan who challenges that chaos with such determination:

> So eagerly the Fiend
> O'er bog or steep, through strait, rough, dense or rare,
> With head, hands, wings or feet persues his way,
> And swims or sinks, or wades, or creeps, or flies:
> . . . thither he plies,
> Undaunted to meet there what ever Power
> Or Spirit of the nethermost Abyss
> Might in that noise reside . . .
>
> (*Paradise Lost*, II. 947–50, 954–7)

It is true, of course, that unmixed identification with Satan is dangerous and also true that Milton keeps us aware of the danger, but much of the tension of *Paradise Lost* depends upon the reader being drawn towards identification even while knowing of the danger, and this blend cannot be explained away by critics who want simple responses. Here Milton's use of perspective is again important, sending the reader from the massive Satan spread over the lake in the first book to the image of Satan as toad (IV. 800); from the triumph of Satan's return to his fellows in book ten to the transformation of the fallen angels into serpents (ll. 504–47). Satan, therefore, is both a hero struggling against the odds (and the more admirable in that those odds are impossible) and a vicious ingrate desperate for revenge.

If readers are drawn to divided responses in relation to Satan, the same is true of Milton's God, although in a rather different way. His God the Father is not a figure with whom it is possible to identify (and it would, arguably, be blasphemous if a reader did). By definition he is ineffable and ultimately inscrutable, his 'human' attributes embodied in his son. A reader knows that theologically God is right, but also that God cannot be comprehended by mankind. The primary struggle for the reader, at least while engaging imaginatively with the poem, is to accept God's goodness, even when it seems that mankind is being asked to do so against the evidence. The riddle of the relationship between free will and predestination can only, it would seem, be solved through faith; and faith is what *Paradise Lost* is, in important part, about. The proper difficulty of the poem lies precisely in the fact that as fallen people we share something with Satan and a lot with Adam and Eve. There is nothing wrong, I feel, with a reader sharing Eve's sense of constraint at the start of book nine and Adam's ache at the thought of losing her later in the same book. Since God is God there can be no equivalent identification with him, while the human development of the Son will only come fully in *Paradise Regained* (1671).

Yet, in the terms of *Paradise Lost*, a reader must not be seduced, for that would be the road to damnation (or to the rejection of the entire theology of the poem). Stanley Fish[14] has written very eloquently about what he sees as Milton's strategies in this situation; of the ways in which we are both seduced and saved through the creativity of the poem. But what Fish fails to take full account of is the pain of the struggle to avoid despair and retain faith, and it is here that Hill's work is particularly valuable.

Milton has not written a parliamentary version of Cowley's *The Civil War*, but he had identified himself with the rebellion against Charles I. To that extent he sides with Satan, and the aspect of *Paradise Lost* which responds to Satan's pride and ambition can be seen as a distressed recognition that the revolt against Charles had gone wrong. The rule of the Saints had not come into being; the second coming had not eventuated. This does not mean that *Paradise Lost* is an allegory of the Civil War and Commonwealth, but only that the poem's pattern and themes relate closely at some points to the period through which Milton had lived. As Hill points out, for instance, God's ways must have seemed very mysterious to Milton during the period of the poem's creation.[15] If allegory would require the identification of Satan and his followers with the parliamentary party, it would follow that Charles and his supporters would have to be identified with God and the loyal angels – and nothing in Milton's record would validate this. But the myth with which Milton is working is suggestive and it allows him to express such emotions as resentment of God's mysteriousness and bitterness at the betrayal of the revolution. But is also allows him, as we shall see, to examine ways in which faith can continue.

The outer crust, so to speak, of the poem is the knowledge of how its events will turn out. Such knowledge is fundamental to all Christians and Milton is at pains to keep readers aware of it throughout his poem, and also to stress continually that the pattern is one in which God is justified. Paradoxically, this foreknowledge is liberating, in that it allows exploration of motives and alternative possibilities. A reader knows what will happen (and has, in a sense, already happened), but reads as if other results are conceivable. This is again a matter of perspective: we are drawn to lose sight of the overall pattern as we experience the detail.

Satan's perverse pilgrimage is in search of mankind, and, although God does not journey to defend his latest creation, he does send messengers to advise and guard Adam and Eve. Therefore, although Satan attracts a lot of our attention, the poem's focus is upon its human beings. They inhabit Eden and their direct experience is limited to that experience, which is supplemented by what their visitors tell them. At the centre of their experience is the prohibition on eating from the tree which gives knowledge of good and evil. In so far as they believe the God who created them, they know what will happen if they disobey and this knowledge is parallel to a reader's knowledge of the story of which they are part. Adam and Eve

are free (at least by some accounts) to obey or disobey, while a reader of
the poem is free to choose which aspects of the whole to emphasize and
which to underplay. In the poem's terms we can be damned with Satan
or remain unfallen or repent with Adam.

Since, however, we are fallen people, it is natural that we respond to
that in Adam and Eve which matches our fallen curiosity, and so we are
inclined to sympathize with Eve's wish to garden apart from Adam, with
her vulnerability when faced with the Satan-serpent, and with Adam's de-
cision to be loyal to her. Theologically, we are wrong to make these identi-
fications, since they involve disloyalty to God, just as the wishes and
vulnerabilities themselves express the disloyalty of Adam and Eve. But in
a sense it is pointless to dwell on the issues which follow. Adam and Eve
could have stayed faithful if they had suppressed their desire for experience
(and if Adam had maintained his God-given authority over Eve) but that
in them which decides not to suppress that desire originates with God in
any case, and so the quicksands of free will and determinism call. What
matters, however, is that to a reader of *Paradise Lost* the events of the poem
are, in one way, historical: Man did fall and was expelled from Paradise.
What matters is understanding how these things came to be, so that the
pattern is not repeated unto damnation. Here, of course, the simultaneity
spoken of earlier is important, for that device provides the answer to po-
tential despair, in the reminder of salvation through Christ. Further, it is
important to recall that *Paradise Lost* itself does not end in despair. That fatal
state is not far away at the end of book nine, which finishes:

> Thus they in mutual accusation spent
> The fruitless hours, but neither self-condemning,
> And of their vain contest appear'd no end.

Adam is close to damnation when, in the following book,

> On the Ground
> Outstretcht he lay, on the cold ground, and oft
> Curs'd his Creation, Death as oft accus'd
> Of tardie execution . . .
>
> (x. 850–3)

But Adam and Eve work their way to repentance and the Son intercedes
for them to the Father. They are banished from Paradise, but are not aban-
doned, and the famous final lines of the poem catch beautifully the blend
of sorrow and opportunity:

> The World was all before them, where to choose
> Thir place of rest, and Providence their guide:
> They hand in hand with wandring steps and slow,
> Through Eden took their solitarie way.

Milton's 'great Argument', he had stated at the beginning of his epic, had been to 'assert Eternal Providence,/And justifie the wayes of God to men' (I. 24–6). Satan rebels against God's ways, as do Adam and Eve, and their rebellions are against absolute authority. Moreover, rebellion in such cases is blasphemous, not only in itself but also because it represents a lack of faith, the assertion that the rebel's wishes can be more important than obedience. Obviously, the issues involved here are theological and can be discussed in purely theological terms. But they are also issues which have urgency in the social and political life of the seventeenth century. James I had developed and argued for the divine right of kings, and Charles I was acutely sensitive to questionings of his right. Much seventeenth-century discussion of monarchy works within the view that there are limits to monarchic authority, but also accepts that monarchy is divinely appointed and has a sacred dimension which it is blasphemous to question.[16] The arguments, including those which lead up to the Civil War, are about the extent of monarchic authority, not about whether such a thing should exist.

Satan sees God as a tyrant, and some theoreticians argued that a tyrant could rightfully be opposed. But Satan is proud and ambitious, and orthodox theology denies God's tyranny. Adam and Eve come to believe, temporarily, that God's prohibition is unjust or arbitrary, while orthodox theology teaches that it is a fair test of the loyalty of his creation. What is clear is that God has the power, and that Satan, Adam, and Eve all suffer for questioning that power, although the first of these must pay eternally for his revolt, while the human pair have the possibility of redemption through God's grace.

Milton had been actively involved in the struggle against Charles, and by the time he came to write *Paradise Lost* had lived to see the deterioration of the Commonwealth. Remembering that his poem is not allegory, we can nevertheless see its suggestiveness. Does the hard case of Satan mean that resistance to Charles was wrong? Where will the assertiveness of Adam and Eve lead? If God's power is limitless, as by definition it is, how can we achieve and sustain faith in his inscrutable plan, while retaining self-respect? What is the lesson of Abdiel

> who single hast maintaind
> Against revolted multitudes the Cause
> Of Truth, in word mightier than they in Arms?
>
> (VI. 30–2)

Andrew Marvell, working on a smaller scale than Milton, had made much use of shifts of perspective to create disconcerting worlds, and Marvell has a rich sense of the possibilities in his material for radically different readings; hence the disagreements about where loyalty lies in 'An Horatian Ode' and the arguments about meaning in 'The Garden'. In *Paradise Lost* Milton has retold the fundamental Christian myth in a way which forces a reader to attend closely to the issues inherent in the myth. These are issues which bear powerfully on the seventeenth century, and Milton's treatment of them has such imaginative richness that the material comes to reveal a range of possibilities that links Milton and Marvell. As Milton reflects on the myth, he is aware of the chances missed, the pathos of failure, the heroism of resistance, the dignity of choice, the wonder of experience. It is thus appropriate, if inconvenient, that *Paradise Lost* finishes, not with the trite reduction of its material to the sort of single message some moralists and critics call for, but with a pregnant, tense range of possibilities.

In the myth this range is only possible because the Son of God sacrifices himself for mankind, thus co-operating with the will of the Godhead, of which he is part. Christ's preparation for his self-sacrifice is Milton's subject in *Paradise Regained*,[17] its pattern of temptation, rebellion, acceptance being one which recalls not only *Paradise Lost* but also 'Lycidas' and *Comus*.

Paradise Regained, however, has a new emphasis upon patient and persevering acceptance of the virtue of obedience. The stress is there from the beginning:

> I who erewhile the happy Garden sung,
> By one mans disobedience lost, now sing
> Recoverd Paradise to all mankind,
> By one mans firm obedience fully tri'd
> Through all temptation . . .

The 'one man' is, of course, Christ, and Milton emphasizes Christ's commitment to the will of God:

> . . . and now by som strong motion I am led
> Into this wilderness, to what intent
> I learn not yet, perhaps I need not know;
> For what concerns my knowledge God reveals.

> (*Paradise Regained*, I. 290–3)

And again:

> Who brought me hither
> Will bring me hence, no other Guide I seek.

> (I. 335–6)

But such constancy and confidence are not solely attributes of Milton's Christ. They are found in Mary (II. 105–8) and in Simon and Andrew, who, we are told, after the revelation of Christ as Messiah, 'Began to doubt, and doubted many days' (II. 11) but who recover to assert:

> Let us be glad of this, and all our fears
> Lay on his Providence; he will not fail
> Nor will withdraw him now, nor will recall,
> Mock us with his blest sight, then snatch him hence,
> Soon we shall see our hope, our joy return.

> (II. 53–6)

The references to Job, taken together with the examples given, create a pattern of obedient fortitude which is a specifically Christian version of the loyalty of epic, even though in *Paradise Regained* the physical tests of epic are replaced by psychological ones, while the inclusion of Simon and Andrew makes the point that the central loyalty of Christ can be repeated at the purely human level.

Christ is the object of temptation in *Paradise Regained*, as Adam and Eve had been in *Paradise Lost*, and the tempter is the same in both poems – Satan, who had been himself tempted and had fallen through pride and ambition. In *Paradise Lost* there is, for the reader, tension at the re-enactment of the Fall of mankind and it is vital to the poem's purpose that there be the sense that the Fall was avoidable. But in *Paradise Regained* there can be no such tension, not only because the known story is different, but because its central figure, Christ, is not fallible. Christ does not only not fall, but is not even brought to doubt, He deflects Satan's efforts with calm confidence:

> To whom thus Jesus patiently repli'd . . .
> (II. 432)

and

> To whom our Saviour answerd thus, unmov'd.
> (III. 386)

This assurance helps explain why it is that the Satan of *Paradise Regained* has so little of the power of his performance in *Paradise Lost*. But it is important to recognize that the faded and fading Satan of the later poem is functional. His failure to shake Christ's confidence marks the quality of the shield which there now is to protect mankind. Satan is now more aware of what he is up against and to that extent seems almost defeated before he begins to tempt the Son of God. Moreover, it is clear that Milton wants the reader to be making constant comparisons between the two parts of the Christian story. So Satan, tempting the fasting Christ in the second book, recalls Eve in Eden:

> What doubts the Son of God to sit and eat?
> These are not Fruits forbidden, no interdict
> Defends the touching of these viands pure.
> Their taste no knowledge works, at least of evil.
> (*Paradise Regained*, II. 368–71)

Similarly, Satan's original fall is reenacted (IV. 560) and as a result 'A fairer Paradise is founded now/For Adam and his chosen Sons' (IV. 613–4). And just before the second fall of Satan, he has been made to acknowledge his defeat in face of the loyalty and patience of Christ:

> . . . opportunity I here have had
> To try thee, sift thee, and confess have found thee
> Proof against all temptation as a rock
> Of Adamant, and as a Centre, firm.
>
> (IV. 531–4)

Satan in *Paradise Regained*, having turned down Belial's suggestion that sex be used as temptation, and having failed to shake Christ with a banquet in the desert, concentrates upon the temptation of power and glory, but fails in the face of Christ's patient reiteration that the glories of martial conquest and the support of the people ('A miscellaneous rabble, who extoll/Things vulgar, and well weighd, scarce worth the praise', III. 50–1) are not what he is about. Satan offers power over the kingdoms of this world and his emphasis upon such and the glory associated with it are reminders of the traditional material of epic. Christ's insistence upon the otherness of his goals both makes him an unorthodox epic hero and marks him out as unique. His concern is with 'all the flourishing works of peace' (III. 80) and he asks 'But why should man seek glory?' (III. 134). Also, in so far as he can see a virtue in glory, it is to be achieved

> By deeds of peace, by wisdom eminent,
> By patience, temperance.
>
> (III. 91–2)

Christ's question about man seeking glory recalls the passage about fame in 'Lycidas', but *Paradise Regained* lacks the tension of that poem. By the time that the later poem was written Milton had endured far more serious trials than the drowning of a Cambridge acquaintance. If 'Lycidas' is finally a poem about the psychological attainment of inner peace and the reassertion of faith, *Paradise Regained* strikes me as an effort to calm self by repeating the story of one who resisted temptation and confidently resided in the will of God, however mysterious that will might be. The figure of Christ being invited to betrayal by Satan could stand for anyone in the middle of the seventeenth century who had associated resistance to Charles I with the will of God; who had been drawn into doubt by the failure of the Commonwealth and towards despair by the restoration of the monarchy. And, of course, contemplation of Christ's victory over Satan could provide consolation, together with reaffirmation that purposeful life was still possible. But the way of Christ the redeemer is a severe one of dedication to the will of God, to the exclusion of everything else. One of the things which is rejected in *Paradise Regained* is the pleasure of the classics, and Christ is almost harsh in his reaction to Satan's invocation of them:

> . . . these are false, or little else but dreams,
> Conjectures, fancies, built on nothing firm.
>
> (IV. 291–3)

The passage seems disproportionately long in relation to Christ, but it makes good sense for Milton himself. His classical education and love of

the classical poets are matters of fact, and the temptation to turn to them
and away from the miseries of the Restoration may well have been strong.
The rejection of them here may thus be seen as a determined effort at re-
dedication of self to the will of God. But the example of Christ could not
be more than an inspiration to a puritan in the mid-century, an affirmation
that mankind was not alone, for Christ, however human the poet might
make him, remains the Son of God, participating in the Godhead as mortal
man cannot. Samson, however, is mortal man.[18]

The Samson of *Samson Agonistes* (1671) is, moreover, sinful man. Christ
is without sin and untainted by the Fall of Adam and Eve, but Samson is
post-lapsarian, and sin can be seen as rebellion against God. More specifi-
cally, Samson's sin is disloyalty, the betrayal of God's trust, and there is,
at the beginning of the poem, the danger that Samson will despair and thus
be damned. His marriages have been disasters, he has been blinded by his
captors, reduced to the status of slave, and drawn to wonder what point
there can be to his life:

> Why was my breeding orderd and prescrib'd
> As of a person separate to God,
> Design'd for great exploits, if I must die
> Betray'd, Captiv'd, and both my Eyes put out,
> Made of my Enemies the scorn and gaze,
> To grind in Brazen Fetters under task
> With this Heav'n-gifted strength?
>
> > (*Samson Agonistes*, ll. 30–6)

He knows the danger of such a line of thought –

> Yet stay, let me not rashly call in doubt
> Divine Prediction;

and

> But peace, I must not quarrel with the will
> Of highest dispensation . . .
>
> > (ll. 43–4, 60–1)

– but the questions go on:

> Why am I thus bereav'd thy prime decree?
>
> > (l. 85)

There has always been a tendency to suggest that there is identification
between Milton and Samson, blindness and failed marriages being the ob-
vious common factors, and certainly Milton's imagination works powerful-
ly when describing Samson's sense of the loss of sight and his bitter resent-
ment at Dalila's behaviour. But although these factors provide quite close
personal links, they are finally less interesting than the suggestive similarity

of the basic situations of the poet and his creation. Samson is oppressed by the sense of failure and by the apparent purposelessness of his being. He understands that he had been 'divinely called' to 'begin Israels Deliverance' (ll. 225–6)

> But I
> Gods counsel have not kept, his holy secret
> Presumptuously have publist, impiously,
> Weakly at least, and shamefully . . .
>
> (ll. 496–9)

He also knows that his fall is his own responsibility:

> Appoint not heav'nly disposition, Father,
> Nothing of all these evils hath befall'n me
> But justly; I myself have brought them on . . .
>
> (ll. 375–5)

But he still has to fight against inertia ('This only hope relieves me, that the strife/With mee hath end', ll. 460–1) and despair ('Nor am I in the list of them that hope;/Hopeless are all my evils . . .', ll. 647–8).

The chorus reminds Samson that

> Just are the ways of God,
> and justifiable to Men
>
> (ll. 293–4)

– and a reader is likely to remember the overt purpose of *Paradise Lost*, as well as the struggle in 'Lycidas' for the poet-figure to come to terms with the death of Lycidas and so avoid blasphemy. In *Samson Agonistes* the poet's task is to demonstrate God's justice while Samson himself has the task of accepting that justice which in a sense he knows of from the beginning. This task of Samson's is one which mirrors the situation of any supporter of Parliament against the King. More specifically, Samson defeated, captive, and humiliated among the Philistines can be seen as a type of the parliamentary supporter at the Restoration. And for such a supporter, in such a situation, there are urgent questions – How did I come to this? Does it mean that I was mistaken? Am I now abandoned? What does the situation tell me about God's plans for me and others like me?

But, in a sense, the point about such questions is that the questioner needs to learn that formulating them is part of the problem. Paradoxically, the answer lies not in finding answers but in the faith that goes beyond the questions to acceptance that God is just. This involves the giving up of self, with the egocentricity of questioning, and the exercise of patience, perseverance, and faith. Such exercise marks *Paradise Regained*, and if one accepts the traditional chronology it is striking what a distance there is between the patience of Christ and the resistance of Samson. Yet this distance is the mark of the difference between the divine and the human, even though, in *Paradise Regained*, the examples of Mary, Simon, and Andrew indicate that Christ-like patience is possible for mankind.

Samson's struggle is not so much one to learn anything as to accept what he already knows, to prepare himself to be ready for God's call, if and when it comes. Milton presents the journey to acceptance statically, in the sense that Samson does nothing 'on stage' except receive visits which prompt his examination of what he is and has been, as well as providing opportunities for him to define what is no longer appropriate for him. In the context of traditional epic, this process is one whereby the epic hero learns that epic roles are not for him. He is not to escape or be released, like Odysseus or the Red Cross Knight; he is not to fight 'The Giant Harapha of Gath' (l. 1068) as Hector fought Achilles; and he is not to be rewarded with the love of a good woman – there is no Una for Samson. Instead Samson slowly comes to a situation in which he responds to 'Som rouzing motions in me which dispose/To something extraordinary my thoughts' (ll. 1382–3), this being the point at which his ego fully gives way to God's prompting. This process has some similarity to that of 'Lycidas', in which the poet-figure needs to express, and thus expel, responses to the death of Lycidas which obstruct acceptance of the justice of God. Samson is, for the bulk of the poem, a long way short of being free of such obstructions. He resents his blindness and captivity (utterly understandably from a human point of view), has a bitterness against Dalila which is powerfully expressed though perhaps not expelled, longs to deal with the boasting Harapha by exercising his strength in the ways of his past, and proudly resists the messenger's summons to perform for the Philistines. What is missing until late in the poem is the ability to listen for the voice of God, and here again Samson's dilemma is one which suggests a parallel with the situation of a parliamentarian in the Restoration.

And, of course, Samson's great feat comes at the centre of his greatest humiliation. Prompted by 'rouzing motions' he obeys the messenger, performs for the Philistines, like one of those 'Gymnic Artists' of whom he is so contemptuous (l. 1324), and destroys them, together with himself. His victory thus comes at the moment of the most public display of his defeat. Samson had been strongly drawn to display himself in a duel with Harapha; God gives him the chance to slaughter the unrighteous in larger numbers.

There has been critical discussion about the tone of the closing episode of *Samson Agonistes*, and in particular about the 'suicide' of the hero. Milton presents the issue in what seems a deliberately quizzical way:

Manoah   by whom fell he,
What glorious hand gave Samson his deaths wound?
Mess.   Unwounded of his enemies he fell.
Man.   Wearied with slaughter then or how? explain.
Mess.   By his own hands. *Man.* Self-violence? what cause
Brought him so soon at variance with himself
Among his foes? *Mess.* Inevitable cause
At once both to destroy and be destroyd . . .

Manoah, Samson's father, has reason to be anxious about the manner of the death (suicide being the ultimate sin of despair), but the messenger's fuller account of the episode seems to leave Manoah in no doubt that Samson dies honourably:

> no time for lamentation now,
> Nor much more cause; Samson hath quit himself
> Like Samson, and heroicly hath finisht
> A life Heroic . . .
>   (ll. 1708–11)

and the Chorus, in the last speech, offers a stress which would fit ill with the idea that Samson has sinned again:

> All is best, though we oft doubt,
> What th'unsearchable dispose
> Of highest wisdom brings about,
> And ever best found in the close.
>   (ll. 1745–8)

In that final speech, the last notes are of acceptance and peace:

> His servants he with new acquist
> Of true experience from this great event
> With peace and consolation hath dismist,
> And calm of mind all passion spent.

It would be a perverse joke to see this 'calm of mind' as arising from an act which damned the doer, especially one 'With inward eyes illuminated' (l. 1689).

But the line between suicide and acceptance of God's will may be a fine one, and the fineness of the distinction gives to the conclusion of *Samson Agonistes* a proper tension, especially if we see the poem as bearing on the situation of the English Restoration. It seems likely that, for a believer in the Good Old Cause, the most urgent problem, as Hill suggests[19], was to keep faith and to be alert for God's prompting, in the full awareness that mistakes had occurred and might easily occur again. Correct judgement calls for alertness, and there is a tense difference between acceptance and apathy. Samson had been drawn at times to the latter in the early part of the poem, this alternating with resentment, but his end indicates that acceptance may be positive, or, in Manoah's terms, heroic. If the example of Christ in *Paradise Regained* had been a shield against despair, that of Samson may be seen as marking the possibility of active human intervention in mankind's destiny – but such intervention can only come when the individual responds to 'rouzing motions' rather than the prompting of the ego.

It is a weakness of English epic in the seventeenth century that it so often fails to achieve what was earlier called 'shaped scale'. As we look back from, say, 1671, it is clear that only Milton writes epics which fully justify themselves by this criterion. Drayton has a satisfying shape which is, however, not fully epic, while Davenant and Cowley both seem intimidated by the epic tradition. In *Paradise Lost* Milton produces the first English poem which unifies the length of epic both with epic significance of subject and proper control of it. This is partly a matter of focus. As in the *Iliad* Homer relates multiple subjects to his central theme, so Milton in *Paradise Lost* focuses variously on God the Father, Christ, Satan, Adam and Eve while keeping us always in mind of the central theme of mankind's first disobedience and its consequences. This achievement includes the mastering of renaissance and classical epic traditions and the application of these to the fundamental Christian myth of the Fall. But *Paradise Regained* is in its way as significant a triumph of shaped scale. In that poem there is a single dominant focus upon Christ and a much simpler topic: the demonstration of Christ's fitness for the task of salvation. Milton writes a poem stripped of epic length and complexity; and in doing this shows his confidence. But the important point is that the poem's austerity of manner is appropriate to the concentrated significance of the theme. If *Paradise Lost* is a triumph of the expectations we have of the epic, *Paradise Regained* is a triumph of Milton's self-confidence in that he turns away from the expected length to create the severe, compressed shape proper to his theme and material.

The publication of *Paradise Regained* and *Samson Agonistes* in 1671 does not end the story of English epic in the seventeenth century. Richard Blackmore, for example, wrote several (*Prince Arthur*, for instance, was published in 1695) and Samuel Garth's *The Dispensary* (1699) is an important part of the curious tradition of long poems about seemingly non-heroic topics which runs through the eighteenth century. But Milton's work provides the last truly important achievement in epic of the seventeenth century. As one looks at the work of Drayton and Daniel, Cowley, Davenant, and the Fletchers it is hard to disagree with Hearnshaw's view of Milton's achievement. The times and the man were right.

Notes

1. See B. Newdigate, *Michael Drayton and his Circle* (Oxford, 1941) *passim*. (*The Barons' Wars* is a rewriting of *Mortimeriades* (1596). It was first published in 1603 and Drayton revised it for the 1619 edition of his poems.)
2. *The Civil Wars*, edited by L. Michel (New Haven, 1958). See J. Rees, *Samuel Daniel* (Liverpool, 1964), especially pp. 122–46.
3. *Christ's Victorie in Heaven*; *Christ's Victorie on Earth*; *Christ's Triumph over Death*; *Christ's Triumph after Death*.

4. *Gondibert*, edited by David F. Gladish (Oxford, 1971), p. xiii. See A. Nethercot, *William Davenant* (Chicago, 1938), *passim*.

5. Davenant's Preface; Gladish, pp. 15f.

6. Ibid., p. xiii.

7. Ibid., p. xiv.

8. *The Civil War*, edited by A. Pritchard (Toronto, 1973).

9. See D. Trotter, *The Poetry of Abraham Cowley* (London, 1979), pp. 83–5.

10. *Poems*, edited by A. Waller (Cambridge, 1905).

11. See A. Nethercot, *Abraham Cowley* (Oxford, 1931) for a full account of Cowley's public record.

12. F. J. C. Hearnshaw, *English History in Contemporary Poetry*, no. iv Historical Association (reprinted 1969), p. 41.

13. C. Hill, *Milton and the English Revolution* (London, 1977). There is a mass of critical writing about *Paradise Lost*. Apart from the books by Hill and Fish (note 14) the following are among the more useful recent studies: D. H. Burden, *The Logical Epic* (London, (1967); C. Patrides (ed.) *Approaches to Paradise Lost* (London, 1968); S. Revard, *The War in Heaven* (Ithaca, 1980). See also Individual Authors – notes.

14. S. Fish, *Surprised by Sin* (Berkeley, 1971).

15. Hill, pp. 354–60.

16. There is a useful summary of these issues in Maurice Ashley, *The Glorious Revolution of 1688* (London, 1966), pp. 96–109.

17. On *Paradise Regained* see B. Lewalski, *Milton's Brief Epic* (London, 1966) and B. Weber, *Wedges and Wings* (Carbondale, 1975).

18. *Samson Agonistes* is, of course, not epic but closet drama. But it is so closely bound up with *Paradise Lost* and *Paradise Regained* in its themes that it would be unnatural to ignore it here. See G. Crump (ed.) *Twentieth Century Interpretations of Samson Agonistes* (New Jersey, 1968); W. Kirkconnell, *That Invincible Samson* (Toronto, 1964); A. Low, *The Blaze of Noon* (New York, 1974).

19. Hill, pp. 428–48.

Chronology

Note: Dates refer to first publication of works, except in the case of plays, where the given date is that of first performance.

DATE	WORKS OF POETRY	OTHER WORKS	HISTORICAL/CULTURAL EVENTS
1600	*England's Helicon* (anthology)	Shakespeare *Twelfth Night*	b. of future Charles II d. of Hooker Fortune theatre built
1601	Campion *A Booke of Ayres* Daniel *The Works . . . Newly Augmented*	Shakespeare *Hamlet* Jonson *Cynthia's Revels*	Rebellion, execution of Essex Parliament (–1603)
1602	*A Poetical Rhapsody* (anthology)	Shakespeare *Troilus and Cressida* Campion *Observations in the Art of English Poesie* Daniel *A Defence of Rhyme*	
1603	Drayton *The Barons' Wars*	Jonson *Sejanus* Florio (trans.) *Essays of . . . Montaigne* James I *Basilicon Doron*	d. of Elizabeth I Accession of James I Plague

DATE	WORKS OF POETRY	OTHER WORKS	HISTORICAL/CULTURAL EVENTS
1604		Marston *The Malcontent*	Parliament (−1610) Peace with Spain
		Shakespeare *Measure for Measure* *Othello*	Hampton Court Conference
		Revised Book of Common Prayer	
1605	Drayton *Poems*	Shakespeare *King Lear*	b. of Thomas Browne Gunpowder Plot
	Daniel *Certain Small Poems*	Jonson *Masque of Blackness*	
		Bacon *Advancement of Learning*	
1606	Drayton *Eclogues*	Jonson *Volpone*	b. of Waller b. of Davenant
		Shakespeare *Macbeth*	d. of Lyly Red Bull theatre built
		Tourneur (?) *Revenger's Tragedy*	b. of Corneille
		Middleton *A Mad World My Masters*	
1607		Shakespeare *Antony and Cleopatra*	
		Beaumont *Knight of the Burning Pestle*	
1608		Shakespeare *Coriolanus*	b. of Milton
		Dekker/Middleton *Roaring Girl*	
		Jonson *Masque of Beauty*	

DATE	WORKS OF POETRY	OTHER WORKS	HISTORICAL/CULTURAL EVENTS
1609	Shakespeare *Sonnets* Spenser *Faerie Queene* (folio) Daniel *Civil Wars* (2)	Beaumont/Fletcher *Philaster*	b. of Suckling Galileo's telescope
1610	G. Fletcher *Christ's Victorie, and* *Triumph ...*	Jonson *The Alchemist* Shakespeare *Winter's Tale* Chapman *Revenge of Bussy* Beaumont/Fletcher *The Maid's Tragedy* Galileo *Siderius Nuncius*	Assassination of Henri IV of France
1611	Spenser *Works* (folio) Chapman (trans.) *Iliad*	Authorized version of the Bible Shakespeare *The Tempest* Middleton *Chaste Maid in Cheapside*	
1612	Drayton *Poly-Olbion*	Webster *The White Devil*	b. of Butler b. of Crashaw d. of Prince Henry
1613	Wither *Abuses Stript and Whipt* Drummond *Teares on the Death of* *Moeliades* Campion *Two Bookes of Ayres* W. Browne *Britannia's Pastorals* (1)		b. of Cleveland m. of Elizabeth (dau. of James) to Ferdinand (Elector Palatine)

DATE	WORKS OF POETRY	OTHER WORKS	HISTORICAL/CULTURAL EVENTS
1614	Chapman (trans.) *Odyssey*	Webster *Duchess of Malfi* Jonson *Bartholomew Fair* Raleigh *History of the World*	Addled Parliament
1615	Wither *The Shepherd's Hunting*	Jonson *Golden Age Restor'd*	b. of Denham b. of Baxter Donne takes Holy Orders
1616	W. Browne *Britannia's Pastorals* (2)	Jonson *Works* (folio) James I *Works*	d. of Shakespeare d. of Francis Beaumont d. of Cervantes d. of Hakluyt
1617	Campion *Third and Fourth Booke of Ayres*		Bacon Lord Keeper Raleigh to Guyana d. of Isaac Oliver
1618			b. of Lovelace b. of Cowley Start of Thirty Years War Bacon Lord Chancellor Execution of Raleigh
1619	Drayton *Poems* (rev.)	Middleton *Inner Temple Masque*	d. of Daniel d. of Hilliard
1620		Bacon *Novum Organum*	d. of Campion b. of Evelyn
1621	Quarles *Hadassa*	Burton *Anatomy of Melancholy* Middleton *Women Beware Women* (?)	b. of Marvell Donne Dean of St Paul's Impeachment of Bacon Parliament

DATE	WORKS OF POETRY	OTHER WORKS	HISTORICAL/CULTURAL EVENTS
1622	Drayton *Poly-Olbion* (2) Wither *Fair Virtue*	Middleton/Rowley *The Changeling*	b. of Vaughan (?) b. of Molière
1623	Daniel *Whole Works*	Shakespeare first folio	d. of G. Fletcher b. of Pascal Amboyna 'massacre'
1624	Quarles *Sion's Elegies*	Middleton *A Game at Chess*	Parliament War with Spain
1625			d. of James I Accession of Charles I m. of Charles I and Henrietta Maria Parliament Plague
1626		Donne *Five Sermons*	d. of Bacon d. of Dowland Parliament War with France
1627			d. of Middleton
1628		Harvey *De Motu Cordis*	b. of Bunyan Parliament Petition of Right Assassination of Buckingham
1629			Dissolution of Parliament (–1640)
1630	Quarles *Divine Poems*		b. of Cotton b. of future Charles II Treaty of Madrid

DATE	WORKS OF POETRY	OTHER WORKS	HISTORICAL/CULTURAL EVENTS
1631	Wither *Psalms of David*	Ford '*Tis Pity She's a Whore* (?) *The Broken Heart* (?)	d. of Donne b. of Dryden d. of Drayton Famine
1632	Quarles *Divine Fancies*	Massinger *The City Madam* *A New Way to Pay Old Debts* (?) Donne *Death's Duel*	b. of Locke b. of Spinoza b. of Wren d. of Gustavus Van Dyke to England Rembrandt: *Lesson in Anatomy*
1633	Donne *Poems* G. Herbert *The Temple* P. Fletcher *The Purple Island* Cowley *Poetical Blossoms*		d. of G. Herbert b. of Pepys Laud Archbishop of Canterbury
1634	Habington *Castara* Wither *Emblems*	Milton *Comus*	d. of Chapman d. of Marston d. of Webster (?) b. of Etherege (?) Ship Money Rembrandt: *Old Woman*
1635	Quarles *Emblems*	Shirley *The Traitor*	
1636		Corneille *Le Cid*	Plague
1637	Milton *Lycidas*	Descartes *Discourse on Method*	d. of Jonson b. of Traherne (?) *Rex* v. *Hampden*

DATE	WORKS OF POETRY	OTHER WORKS	HISTORICAL/CULTURAL EVENTS
1638	Randolph *Poems*	Suckling *Aglaura*	
1639		Corneille *Cinna*	b. of Racine d. of Carew First Bishops' War
1640	Carew *Poems* Harvey *The Synagogue*	Jonson *Works* (2 vol. folio) Corneille *Polyeucte*	d. of Massinger d. of Burton d. of Ford (?) b. of Wycherley (?) Second Bishops' War Short Parliament Long Parliament (−1653) Impeachment of Laud
1641	Wither *Hallelujah* Denham *Cooper's Hill* (1)	Milton *Of Reformation* *Reason of Church* *Government*	d. of Dekker (?) d. of Suckling (?) d. of Van Dyke Plague Grand Remonstrance Execution of Strafford
1642		T. Browne *Religio Medici* Hobbes *De Cive*	d. of Galileo b. of Newton Civil War First Battle of Edgehill Rembrandt: *The Night Watch*
1643	Denham *Cooper's Hill* (2)	Milton *Of Divorce* *Areopagitica* *Of Education*	d. of W. Browne d. of Pym d. of Falkland First Battle of Newbury Solemn League and Covenant
1644		Descartes *Principles of Philosophy*	d. of Quarles Second Battle of Newbury Battle of Marston Moor

DATE	WORKS OF POETRY	OTHER WORKS	HISTORICAL/CULTURAL EVENTS
1645	Milton *Miscellaneous Poems* Waller *Poems*		New Model Army Self-Denying Ordinance Battle of Naseby Execution of Laud
1646	Suckling *Fragmentum Aurea* Crashaw *Steps to the Temple* Vaughan *Poems* Shirley *Poems*	T. Browne *Pseudodoxia* Clarendon *History of the Rebellion* begun (pub. 1702–4).	b. of Leibniz End of First Civil War
1647	Cowley *The Mistress* Stanley *Poems* Cleveland *Several Select Poems*	Beaumont/Fletcher First folio	b. of Rochester Heads of Proposals Declaration of the Army
1648	Herrick *Hesperides*		Second Civil War Battle of Preston Pride's Purge

1649	Lovelace
	Lucasta: Epodes
		Winstanley
		True Leveller's Standard
		
		Lilburne
		England's New Chains
		
		Gauden (?)
		Eikon Basilike
		
		Milton
		Eikonoklastes
			d. of Drummond
			d. of Crashaw
			Execution of Charles I
			Commonwealth
			  declared
			Abolition of the
			  monarchy and House
			  of Lords
			Cromwell in Ireland

1650	Vaughan *Silex Scintillans* (1)		d. of P. Fletcher d. of Descartes Battle of Dunbar

DATE	WORKS OF POETRY	OTHER WORKS	HISTORICAL/CULTURAL EVENTS
1651	Davenant *Gondibert* (1–3) Cleveland *Poems* Vaughan *Olor Iscanus*	Hobbes *Leviathan* Milton *Defensio pro Populo Anglicano*	Battle of Worcester
1652	Crashaw *Carmen Deo Nostro*		b. of Otway d. of Inigo Jones 'Pacification' of Ireland Dutch War (–1653)
1653		Walton *Compleat Angler*	b. of Oldham Rump dissolved Barebone's Parliament Cromwell Lord Protector
1654		Milton *Defensio Secunda*	First Protectorate Parliament (–1655)
1655	Denham *Cooper's Hill* (rev.) Vaughan *Silex Scintillans* (2)	Hobbes *De Corpore Politico*	War with Spain
1656	Cowley *Poems*	Harrington *Oceana* Davenant *Siege of Rhodes*	Second Protectorate Parliament Vermeer: *Woman and Soldier*
1657	King *Poems*		d. of Harvey Humble Petition and Advice Cromwell refuses crown

DATE	WORKS OF POETRY	OTHER WORKS	HISTORICAL/CULTURAL EVENTS
1658		T. Browne *Urn Burial* *Garden of Cyrus*	d. of Cleveland d. of Lovelace (?) d. of Cromwell Richard Cromwell Lord Protector
1659	Lovelace *Lucasta: Posthume Poems* Suckling *Last Remains*		Marvell MP (−1678) Resignation of R. Cromwell Recall of Rump b. of Purcell James (II) m. Anne Hyde
1660	Dryden *Astraea Redux*	Milton *The Ready and Easy Way* Pepys *Diary* (−1669)	b. of Defoe (?) d. of Velasquez Charles II lands in England and accedes to throne Royal Society founded
1661			Pension Parliament
1662	Rump poems	Molière *L'École des maris* *L'École des femmes*	Charles II m. Catherine of Braganza d. of Pascal
1663	Butler *Hudibras* (1)		
1664	Butler *Hudibras* (2) Waller *Poems*	Etherege *The Comical Revenge*	b. of Prior b. of Vanbrugh
1665			War with Holland (−1667) Great Plague

DATE	WORKS OF POETRY	OTHER WORKS	HISTORICAL/CULTURAL EVENTS
1666		Molière *Le Misanthrope* Bunyan *Grace Abounding*	Great Fire of London
1667	Milton *Paradise Lost* Katherine Philips *Poems* Dryden *Annus Mirabilis*	Racine *Andromaque* Molière *Tartuffe* Dryden *The Indian Emperor*	d. of Wither d. of Cowley b. of Swift
1668	Cowley *Davideis* Denham *Poems and Translations*	Dryden *Of Dramatic Poesy* Molière *L'Avare* La Fontaine *Fables*	Dryden Laureate d. of Davenant
1669		Racine *Britannicus* Pascal *Pensées*	d. of King d. of Denham d. of Rembrandt d. of Henrietta Maria
1670		Racine *Bérénice*	b. of Congreve
1671	Milton *Paradise Regained* *Samson Agonistes*	Molière *Le Bourgeois Gentil- homme*	d. of Anne Hyde
1672		Dryden *Marriage à la Mode* *Conquest of Granada*	b. of Addison b. of Steele

DATE	WORKS OF POETRY	OTHER WORKS	HISTORICAL/CULTURAL EVENTS
1673			d. of Molière Test Act James (II) m. Mary of Modena
1674			d. of Milton d. of Herrick d. of Traherne d. of Clarendon
1675		Wycherley *The Country Wife*	
1676		Etherege *The Man of Mode* Dryden *Aureng-Zebe* Wycherley *The Plain Dealer*	
1677		Dryden *All for Love* Behn *The Rover* Racine *Phèdre* Spinoza *Ethics*	d. of Cowley b. of Farquhar (?) d. of Spinoza Mary (dau. of James) m. William of Orange
1678	Vaughan *Thalia rediviva* Butler *Hudibras* (3)	Bunyan *Pilgrim's Progress* (1) Rymer *The Tragedies of the Last Age*	d. of Marvell Second Test Act Titus Oates and the Popish Plot
1679	Spenser *Works* (Second folio)	Hobbes *Behemoth*	d. of Hobbes Exclusion Bill

DATE	WORKS OF POETRY	OTHER WORKS	HISTORICAL/CULTURAL EVENTS
1680	Rochester *Poems*	Bunyan *Mr. Badman* Filmer *Patriarcha* Otway *The Orphan*	d. of Butler d. of Rochester
1681	Marvell *Miscellaneous Poems* Oldham *Satires upon the Jesuits* Dryden *Absalom and Achitophel*	Otway *Venice Preserved* Dryden *The Spanish Friar*	Exclusion Bill reintroduced
1682	Dryden *The Medal* *Religio Laici*	Bunyan *The Holy War* Behn *The City Heiress*	d. of T. Browne
1683	Oldham *Poems and Translations*		d. of Oldham d. of Walton d. of Shaftesbury Rye House Plot
1684	Norris *Poems and Discoveries*	Bunyan *Pilgrim's Progress* (2)	d. of Corneille
1685	Waller *Divine Poems*	Rochester *Valentinian*	d. of Otway b. of Gay d. of Charles II Accession of James II Monmouth Rebellion Bloody Assize Edict of Nantes revoked
1686	Anne Killigrew *Poems*		

DATE	WORKS OF POETRY	OTHER WORKS	HISTORICAL/CULTURAL EVENTS
1687	Dryden *The Hind and the Panther* Cleveland *Works*	Newton *Principia*	d. of Cotton d. of Waller First Declaration of Indulgence
1688			b. of Pope d. of Bunyan Second Declaration of Indulgence William lands at Torbay Flight of James II
1689	Cotton *Poems on Several* *Occasions* *Poems on Affairs of State*		b. of Richardson d. of Behn William and Mary monarchs Declaration of Right Convention Parliament War with France James II lands in Ireland Purcell: *Dido and Aeneas*
1690		Locke *Treatises of Government* *Essay Concerning Human* *Understanding*	Battle of the Boyne
1691		Racine *Athalie*	d. of Baxter
1692		Jonson *Works* (Second folio)	Glencoe massacre d. of Etherege
1693		Congreve *The Old Bachelor*	
1694		Congreve *The Double Dealer*	d. of Mary b. of Voltaire Bank of England founded

DATE	WORKS OF POETRY	OTHER WORKS	HISTORICAL/CULTURAL EVENTS
1695		Congreve *Love for Love*	d. of Vaughan d. of Purcell
1696	Suckling *Works*	Vanbrugh *The Relapse*	Jacobite rising
1697		Vanbrugh *Provoked Wife* Collier *Short View of the English Stage*	b. of Hogarth
1698			
1699			d. of Racine

General Bibliographies

Note: The place of publication is London, unless otherwise stated

(i) Seventeenth-century history and culture

There is a great deal of excellent writing on English seventeenth-century history. The list given below is a selection made with the interests of literary students in mind.

Ashley, M.　*The Glorious Revolution of 1688* (1966). (A clear account of events, issues, and personalities.)

Ashton, R.　*The English Civil War* (1978). (A lucid discussion of issues; particularly good on the conservative aspect of the rebellion.)

Haller, W.　*The Rise of Puritanism* (New York, 1938). (Very full account of its subject, with many valuable corrective insights.)

Hill, C.　*The Century of Revolution, 1603–1714* (1961). (Hill has redefined the seventeenth century: this volume is a good introduction to his approach.)

Hill, C. and Dell, E.　*The Good Old Cause* (1949). ('Extracts from Contemporary Sources'. Inevitably selective but still invaluable.)

Jones, J.　*Country and Court: England 1658–1714* (1978). (Good coverage of the second half of the century.)

Kenyon, J.　*The Stuarts* (1958). (Stimulating essays on individual monarchs.)

Lamont, W. and Oldfield, S. (eds)　*Politics, Religion and Literature in the Seventeenth Century* (1975). (Selections from seventeenth-century material, arranged by topic.)

Laslett, P.　*The World we have Lost* (1965). (Important pioneering social history.)

Manning, B.　*The English People and the English Revolution* (1976). (Long, detailed, and stimulating.)

Morrill, J.   *The Revolt of the Provinces* (1976). (Similar ground to Ashton, but briefer and includes documents.)

Plumb, J.   *The Growth of Political Stability in England 1675–1725* (The early part offers a persuasive 'Whig' account of the significance of the Restoration period.)

Russell, C.   *The Crisis of Parliaments: English History 1509–1660* (The relevant sections provide both information and interpretation.)

Stone, L.   *The Causes of the English Revolution, 1529–1642* (1972). (A useful account of the once vexed topic of the rise or fall of the gentry, with good bibliography.)

Wrightson, K.   *English Society 1580–1680* (1982). (A fine piece of social history.)

Readers interested in the non-literary arts in seventeenth-century Britain will find help in the following.

Girouard, M.   *Life in the English Country House* (New Haven, 1978). (Architecture and social history.)

Murdoch, J., Murrell, J., Noon, P. and Strong, R.   *The English Miniature* (New Haven, 1981). (Substantial seventeenth-century section, with reproductions.)

Piper, D.   *Painting in England 1500–1800* (Harmondsworth, 1960). (Brief introduction.)

Robertson, A. and Stevens, D. (eds)   *The Pelican History of Music*, Volume II (Harmondsworth, 1963). (Helpful introductory account.)

Summerson, J.   *Architecture in Britain 1530–1830* (Harmondsworth, 1953). (Relevant section is more technical than Girouard, but accessible to the layman.)

(ii) General accounts of the literature of the period

Bush, D.   *English Literature in the Earlier Seventeenth Century* (Oxford, 1962). (Clear, concise account of writers and trends.)

Ford, B. (ed.)   *The New Pelican Guide to English Literature*: Volume
III, *From Donne to Marvell* (Harmondsworth, 1982).
Volume IV, *From Dryden to Johnson*
(Harmondsworth, 1982).
(Revisions of the original *Pelican Guides*.)

Ricks, C. (ed.)   *Sphere History of Literature in the English Language*,
Vol. II (1970). (Contains a lot of useful information
and some good criticism.)

Sampson, G.   *Concise Cambridge History of English Literature*
(Cambridge, 1941).

Sutherland, J.   *English Literature in the Late Seventeenth Century*
(Oxford; 1969). (A good basic guide.)

(iii) Studies of aspects of seventeenth-century poetry. (See also Individual Authors – notes.)

Alvarez, A.   *The School of Donne* (1961). (Still the classic
account of its topic, although the case is
overstated.)

Farley Hills, D.   *The Benevolence of Laughter* (1974). (Useful but
rather pedestrian account of Restoration comic
poetry.)

Grundy, J.   *The Spenserian Poets* (1969). (A sympathetic
discussion of such poets as Browne and the
Fletchers.)

Lewalski, B.   *Protestant Poetics and the Seventeenth century Religious
Lyric* (New Jersey, 1979). (A good account of an
important topic.)

Love, H. (ed.)   *Restoration Literature: Critical Approaches* (1972).
(Some useful essays.)

Martz, L.   *The Poetry of Meditation* (New Haven, 1954).
(Standard work on meditative practice and
devotional verse.)

McClung, W.   *The Country House in English Renaissance Poetry*
(Berkeley, 1977). (A thorough discussion of poems
and context.)

Miner, E.   *The Meditative Mode from Donne to Cowley* (New Jersey, (1969); *The Cavalier Mode from Jonson to Cotton* (New Jersey (1971). (Exhaustive and very competent survey of mainly lyric verse.)

Rivers, I.   *The Poetry of Conservatism* (Cambridge, 1973). (Interesting study of the Horace/Jonson line.)

Selden, R.   *English Verse Satire 1590–1765* (1978). (The relevant section is useful if rather thin.)

Skelton, R.   *Cavalier Poets* (1960). (Still useful and shrewd.)

Turner, J.   *The Politics of Landscape* (1979). (A valuable attempt to relate poetry and social/political history.)

Wedgwood, C.   *Poetry and Politics under the Stuarts* (Michigan, 1964). (Interesting material; little critical sense.)

Wilson, J.   *The Court Wits of the Restoration* (1967). (Lively but critically weak.)

(iv) Anthologies

Cain, T. (ed.)   *Jacobean and Caroline Poetry* (1981). (Substantial and wide-ranging selection.)

Gardner, H. (ed.)   *The Metaphysical Poets* (Harmondsworth, 1957). (More restricted than Cain, but a good account of the so-called metaphysical school.)

Howarth, R. (ed.)   *Minor Poets of the Seventeenth Century* (1931, 1953). (Most of the poems of E. Herbert, Carew, Suckling, and Lovelace.)

Kerr, W. (ed.)   *Restoration Verse* (1930). (Good range, handicapped by censorship situation in 1930.)

Lord, G. (ed.)   *Anthology of Poems on Affairs of State* (New Haven, 1975). (Valuable selection of Augustan satirical verse – 'Augustan' beginning at 1660.)

Love, H. (ed.)   *The Penguin Book of Restoration Verse* (Harmondsworth, 1968). (Plenty of good, unfamiliar poems.)

Parfitt, G. (ed.)   *Silver Poets of the Seventeenth Century* (1974). (Full selections from Waller, Vaughan, Crashaw, Denham, and Cowley.)

Individual Authors

Notes on biography, major works and criticism

BROWNE, William (1591–1643) was born at Tavistock and educated at
Oxford and the Inner Temple. Later tutor to Robert Dormer, Browne was
a prolific, mainly pastoral poet, best remembered for *Britannia's Pastorals*
(1613, 1616).

> *Poems*, 2 vols, edited by G. Goodwin (1894).
> *Britannia's Pastorals* (facsimile; Menston, 1969).

> See: J. Grundy, *The Spenserian Poets* (1969).
> F. Moorman, *William Browne* (1897). (Still the standard account.)

BUTLER, Samuel (1612–1680). Butler was son of a Worcestershire farmer and
was educated at Worcester G.S. He became secretary to various people
(including the Countess of Kent and the Earl of Carbery, the latter
appointing him steward of Ludlow Castle). Butler died in Covent Garden
of consumption. He is famous almost solely for *Hudibras* (1663, 1664, 1678)
which brought him fame but not fortune. Charles II, for example, liked
the poem but only gave the poet a lump payment of £300.

> *Hudibras*, edited by J. Wilders (Oxford, 1967).
> *Satires and Miscellanies*, edited by R. Lamar (Cambridge, 1928).

> See: D. Farley Hills, *The Benevolence of Laughter* (1974). (A helpful,
> brief account.)
> E. Richards, *Hudibras in the Burlesque Tradition* (New York, 1972).
> J. Veldkamp, *Samuel Butler* (Hilversum, 1923). (Solid presentation
> of life and work.)

CAREW, Thomas (1595–1639) was born at West Wickham and educated at
Oxford (which he left without a degree) and at the Middle Temple. Carew
travelled in Holland, France, and Italy (1613–19) and was closely associated
with the court of Charles I. A follower of Jonson and Donne, his poems
(popular in his lifetime) were published at his death. Carew is not a
representative court poet, but his verse can be seen as exemplifying
Caroline culture at its best.

> *Poems*, edited by R. Dunlap (Oxford, 1949).
> in *Minor Poets of the Seventeenth Century*, edited by R. Howarth
> (1931, 1953).

> See: E. Miner, *The Cavalier Mode from Jonson to Cotton* (New Jersey,
> 1971). (mainly about Carew's lyrics.)
> E. Selig, *The Flourishing Wreath* (New Haven, 1958). (A decent
> attempt to revive Carew.)

CLEVELAND, John (1613–1658). Cleveland was born at Loughborough, the son of a clergyman, and educated at Cambridge (BA, 1631; Fellow of St John's 1634 – ejected in 1645, having opposed Cromwell's election as MP for Cambridge).An active and committed royalist, he was arrested at Norwich in 1655 but released by Cromwell. His poems (and poems attributed to him) were very popular in the second part of the century.

> Poems, edited by B. Morris and E. Withington (Oxford, 1967).

See: D. Farley Hill, The Benevolence of Laughter (1974).
C. Wedgewood, Poetry and Politics under the Stuarts, (Michigan, 1964). Despite these accounts, however, there is no adequate study of Cleveland.)

COTTON, Charles (1630–1687) was born in Staffordshire, son of a father who was a friend of such men as Jonson, Selden, and Donne. Cotton travelled on the Continent when young. A moderate royalist who married Colonel Hutchinson's half-sister, he seems to have led a peaceful life, mainly in Derbyshire. Cotton was a friend of Izaak Walton and contributed a treatise on fly-fishing to the fifth edition of the Compleat Angler (1676). He translated Montaigne's Essays (1685) and also published Scarronides (1664) and Planter's Manual (1675).

> Poems, edited by J. Beresford (1923).
> Selected Poems, edited by G. Grigson (Harmondsworth, 1973).
> Selected Poems, edited by K. Robinson (Manchester, 1983).

See: E. Miner, The Cavalier Mode from Jonson to Cotton (New Jersey, 1971). (A sympathetic account.)
C. Sembower, Life and Poetry of Charles Cotton (Pennslyvania, 1911). (A good study.)

COWLEY, Abraham (1618–1667). Cowley was the posthumous son of a London stationer and educated at Westminster School and Cambridge (ejected in 1644). He also spent two years at Oxford. A loyalist and a precocious poet, Cowley lived in exile in France between 1646 and 1654, and was arrested when he returned to England. Went back to France at Cromwell's death, returning to England at the Restoration. He died at Chertsey. In a long and varied literary career he produced poems, plays, and essays, achieving a very high contemporary reputation, which has since declined. Poetical Blossoms (1633), The Mistress (1647), Poems (1656), Davideis (1668).

> Poems, edited by A. Waller (Cambridge, 1905).
> Selection in Silver Poets of the Seventeenth Century, edited by G. Parfitt (1974).

See: S. Johnson, Life of Cowley (in Lives of the English Poets; still a fascinating response).
A. Nethercot, Abraham Cowley, The Muses' Hannibal (Oxford, 1931). (A thorough, positive study.)
D. Trotter, Abraham Cowley (1979). (A brave attempt to argue a case for the poet.)

CRASHAW, Richard (c. 1613–1649) was born in London, the son of a puritan poet and clergyman. He was educated at Charterhouse and Cambridge, becoming a Fellow of Peterhouse *c.* 1636. Crashaw lost his fellowship in 1644 for refusing to take the Covenant and was converted to Catholicism around 1645 in Paris. He was recommended to Rome by Henrietta Maria and made a subcanon at Loreto in 1649, but died soon after. Latin *Epigrammatum Sacrorum Liber* (1634); *Steps to the Temple* (1646), revised as *Carmen Deo Nostro* (Paris, 1652).

> *Poems*, edited by L. Martin (Oxford, 1927).
> Selection in *Silver Poets of the Seventeenth Century*, edited by G. Parfitt (1974).

See: L. Martz, *The Poetry of Meditation* (New Haven, 1954). (Useful on tradition.)
M. Praz, *The Flaming Heart* (New York, 1958). (Still helpful on the European context for Crashaw.)
R. Wallerstein, *Richard Crashaw* (Madison, 1959). (Sympathetic and persuasive, but not fully responsive to the problems of Crashaw.)
A. Warren, *Richard Crashaw* (1939). (An intelligent treatment of the problems.)

DANIEL, Samuel (1562–1619) was the son of a music-master and was born near Taunton. Daniel was educated at Oxford (1597) but left without a degree. He was at different times a tutor (to William Herbert and Anne Clifford), a groom of the Queen's privy chamber, a theatre manager in Bristol, and a farmer in Somerset. Prolific and popular as poet, dramatist, masque writer, and critic, Jonson said of him 'a good, honest man . . . but no poet'.

> *Poems and A Defence of Ryme*, edited by A. Sprague (Chicago, 1930). (Selections.)

See: J. Rees, *Samuel Daniel* (Liverpool, 1964). (A sound survey of a poet who deserves more attention that he gets.)

DAVENANT, William (1606–1668). Davenant was born the son of a tavern-keeper, in Oxford, but seems to have encouraged the idea that he was Shakespeare's illegitimate child. Davenant studied briefly at Oxford, spent time in the households of the Duchess of Richmond and Lord Brooke (Fulke Greville) and was writing for the stage by 1628 (*The Cruel Brother*, 1630; *The Wits*, 1636). Became Poet Laureate (1628) and was knighted by Charles at the siege of Gloucester (1643). *Gondibert* (1651) was partly the result of two years in the Tower. Davenant was involved with the introductions of opera and women actors to the English stage.

> *Gondibert*, edited by D. Gladish (Oxford, 1971).

See: A. Nethercot, *Sir William Davenant* (Chicago, 1938). (An interesting account of a poor poet.)

DENHAM, John (1615–1669). Denham was born in Dublin, son of a judge, and educated in London and at Oxford. He was High Sheriff of Surrey at the outbreak of the Civil War and a royalist. He was captured by Parliament at Farnham Castle and sent to London, but soon released to Oxford. Denham fled to the continent in 1648, having been discovered spying for Charles I. Surveyor-General of Works at the Restoration and knighted in 1661, Denham seems to have been insane for a time, perhaps

because his young wife favoured the Duke of York, and died in poverty.
A tragedy (*The Sophy*) was acted in 1641, but Denham is now mainly
remembered for 'Cooper's Hill' (originally 1641, but much revised).

> *Poetical Works*, edited by T. Banks (New Haven, 1928).
> *Expans'd Hieroglyphicks* ('Cooper's Hill'), edited by B. O Hehir
> (Berkeley, 1969).
> Selection in *Silver Poets of the Seventeenth Century*, edited by G.
> Parfitt (1974).

See: O Hehir, *Harmony from Discord* (Berkeley, 1968). (An authoritative
        narrative and assessment.)

DONNE, John (1572–1631) was born in London, son of an ironmonger and
related on his mother's side to Thomas More. He was educated at Oxford,
Cambridge, and Lincoln's Inn (1592). Donne took part in Essex's
expeditions to Cadiz in 1597 and the Azores in 1598, before becoming
secretary to Sir Thomas Egerton, Keeper of the Great Seal, in the latter
year. Already handicapped in relation to a secular career by being a Roman
Catholic, Donne ruined his chances completely by marrying Ann More,
the Keeper's niece, without permission, this leading to dismissal and
imprisonment. After years of poverty Donne achieved preferment after
conversion to Anglicanism in 1614, becoming Dean of St Paul's in 1621.
He wrote verse satire, lyrics, epistles, and elegies, as well as religious
poetry. Little of his verse was published in his lifetime but it circulated in
manuscript. Donne was famous in the later part of his life as a preacher,
and also wrote prose, including an attack on the Jesuits and a defence of
suicide. His reputation declined in the eighteenth and nineteenth centuries,
but a revival late in the nineteenth culminated in Grierson's edition of 1912
and he has been very influential in this century.

> *Poems*, edited by H. Grierson (Oxford, 1912).
> *Divine Poems*, edited by H. Gardner (Oxford, 1952).
> *Complete English Poems*, edited by A. Smith (Harmondsworth, 1971).

See: A. Alvarez, *The School of Donne* (1961). (Good account of influence
        and characteristics.)
        R. Bald, *John Donne: A Life* (Oxford, 1970). (The standard
        biography.)
        J. Carey, *John Donne, Life, Mind and Art* (1981). (A mix of
        perception and oddness.)
        D. Guss, *John Donne Petrarchist* (Detroit, 1966). (A stimulating study
        of context.)
        L. Martz, *The Poetry of Meditation* (New Haven, 1954). (Better on
        tradition than on what Donne does with it.)
        M. Rosten, *The Soul of Wit* (1974). (A useful critical study.)
        A. Smith (ed.), *John Donne: The Critical Heritage*. (The material from
        pre-twentieth-century sources is particularly interesting.)

DRAYTON, Michael (1565–1631). Little is known of Drayton's life except in
connection with his prolific writing. He was born at Hartshill in
Warwickshire and had established himself as a poet by the turn of the
century. Although he had connections with the stage (probably for
financial reasons) he is remembered mainly for his non-dramatic verse.
Drayton wrote in a variety of styles and was a constant reviser (so much

so that his revisions are often new compositions). Drayton was a fine professional writer and a perfectionist: the difficulties created by his revisions may help to explain the neglect of his work. He is buried at Westminster Abbey.

> *Works*, edited by J. Hebel, 5 vols (Oxford, 1931–41).
> *Poems*, edited by J. Buxton 2 vols (1953). (A large selection.)

See: J. Grundy, *The Spenserian Poets* (1969). (A sympathetic introduction.)
B. Newdigate, *Michael Drayton and his Circle* (Oxford, 1941). (Lots of information.)

DRUMMOND, William (1585–1649) was born at Hawthornden and studied at Edinburgh (MA, 1605), Bourges, and Paris. He became Laird of Hawthornden at his father's death in 1610. Married one Elizabeth Logan in 1632 and seems to have lived a quiet, cultured, somewhat isolated life, punctured by a famous visit made to Hawthornden by Ben Jonson in 1618–19 (from which Drummond's *Conversations* came). Drummond took the Covenant with reluctance and was basically a firm loyalist. He was a prolific writer ('Tears on the Death of Moeliades', 1613; *Poems: Amorous, Funerall, Divine*, 1616, and other volumes) and consistently old-fashioned.

> *Poetical Works*, edited by L. Kastner (Manchester, 1913).
> *Poems and Prose*, edited by R. MacDonald (Edinburgh, 1976). (Selections.)

See: R. Fogle, *A Critical Study of William Drummond* (New York, 1952). (A thorough account.)

DRYDEN, John (1631–1700). John Dryden was born at a Northamptonshire vicarage and educated at Westminster School and Cambridge. He went to London in 1657 and, being child of a family which supported Parliament in the Civil War, attached himself to Cromwell's chamberlain in hope of employment. Dryden wrote plays for the Restoration court from the early 1660s and married a daughter of the Earl of Berkshire. He was appointed Poet Laureate and Historiographer Royal in 1670. In the 1680s Dryden was involved, as a poet, in 'party' conflicts and was rewarded with a post in the Customs in 1683. Dryden converted to Rome in 1685. There has been debate about his religious convictions and intellectual background, but Dryden is clearly one of the great English professional writers – dramatist (comedy, tragedy, tragi-comedy, opera), poet (satire, lyric, panegyric), verse-translator and adapter of Virgil, Chaucer, Juvenal, and critic (the first Englishman to leave a substantial body of criticism). Although much of his work is now little read, his achievement is remarkably solid and various. 'Astraea Redux' (1660), *The Indian Queen* (1665), 'Annus Mirabilis' (1667), *The Conquest of Granada* (1672), *Aureng-Zebe* (1676), *All for Love* (1678), *Absalom and Achitophel* (1681), *The Medall* (1682), *MacFlecknoe* (1682), *Religio Laici* (1682), 'Threnodia Augustalis', (1685) 'To the Pious Memory Of . . . Mrs Anne Killigrew . . .' (1686), *The Hind and the Panter* (1687), *Fables Ancient and Modern* (1700).

> *Poems and Fables*, edited by J. Kinsley (Oxford, 1970).
> *Works*, 19 vols, edited by E. Hooker, H. Swedenberg, et al. (Berkeley, 1956–).

See: P. Harth, *Contexts of Dryden's Thought* (Chicago, 1968). (A helpful and informative book.)
J. H. Kinsley, *John Dryden: The Critical Heritage* (1971). (An interesting selection of comments from across the centuries.)
E. Miner, *Dryden's Poetry* (Bloomington, 1967). (A thorough and sensible account.)
W. Myers, *Dryden* (1973). (A good introduction.)
M. Van Doren, *John Dryden* (Bloomington, 1920). (Dated but perceptive and enthusiastic.)
C. Ward, *A Life* (Chapel Hill, 1961). (The standard biography.)
D. Wykes, *A Preface to Dryden* (1977). (A useful introduction.)

FLETCHER, Giles (1588–1623) was the brother of Phineas and cousin of John Fletcher, the dramatist. He was educated at Westminster School and Cambridge, and became rector of Alderton in Suffolk. One of a small group of poets who took Spenser and Du Bartas as their masters, his particular contribution is religious – the four long linked poems *Christ's Victorie in Heaven*, *Christ's Victorie on Earth*, *Christ's Triumph Over Death* and *Christ's Triumph After Death* (1610).

> *Giles and Phineas Fletcher: Poetical Works*, edited by F. Boas, 2 vols (Cambridge, 1909).

See: J. Grundy, *The Spenserian Poets* (1969). (A helpful and sensible account.)

FLETCHER, Phineas (1582–1650). Brother of Giles and cousin of John Fletcher, the dramatist. Educated at Eton and Cambridge. Rector of Hilgay in Norfolk. A follower, like his brother, of Spenser and Du Bartas, his *Purple Island* (1633) describes the human body in terms of the natural world.

> *Giles and Phineas Fletcher: Poetical Works*, edited by F. Boas, 2 vols (Cambridge, 1909).

See: J. Grundy, *The Spenserian Poets* (1969). (A helpful account.)

HERBERT, Edward (first Baron Cherbury; 1583–1648). The elder brother of George Herbert and son of Lady Magdalen Herbert, Edward Herbert was born at Eyton in Shropshire and educated at Oxford. He was a traveller, diplomat, and philosopher as well as a poet. Knighted at the accession of James I, he was raised to the Irish peerage in 1624 and the English in 1629. A half-hearted royalist at the start of the Civil War, he surrendered to Parliament in 1644. Apart from philosophy and verse (Latin and English) he wrote a life of Henry VIII (1649) and one of the first English autobiographies.

> *Poems*, edited by G. Moore Smith (Oxford, 1923).
> in *Minor Poets of the Seventeenth Century*, edited by R. Howarth (1931, 1953).

See: *The Life of Edward, First Lord Herbert of Cherbury*, edited by J. Shuttleworth (1976).

HERBERT, George (1593–1633). Brother of Edward and son of Lady Magdalen Herbert, was educated at Westminster School and Cambridge (Fellow of

Trinity, 1619). Took Anglican orders in 1630, having earlier, it seems, hankered after a secular career, and served as a parish priest at Bemerton in Wiltshire. His manual, *A Priest to the Temple* (*Remains*, 1652) is an attractive version of the moderate Anglicanism he exemplifies, while Walton's *Life* conveys the man's likeable personality. His reputation as a religious poet has remained high since *The Temple* (1633) although emphasis upon 'sweetness' and 'quaintness' has at times obscured his artistry. He is often linked with Donne, but this is not particularly helpful.

>*Works*, edited by F. Hutchinson (Oxford, 1941).
>*The English Poems*, edited by C. Patrides (1974).

See: A. Charles, *A Life of George Herbert* (Ithaca, 1977). (A good
         biography.)
       S. Fish, *The Living Temple* (Berkeley, 1978). (An interesting,
         ingenious account.)
       L. Martz, *The Poetry of Meditation* (New Haven, 1954).
       A. Stein, *George Herbert's Lyrics* (Baltimore, 1968). (A perceptive
         critical study.)
       J. Summers, *George Herbert* (1954). (A good, sympathetic reading.)
       R. Tuve, *A Reading of George Herbert* (Chicago, 1969). (Particularly
         good on tradition.)

HERRICK, Robert (1591–1674) was the son of a London goldsmith and
    educated at Cambridge (BA, 1617). He was a priest at Dean Prior, in
    Devon, from 1629 to 1647 – when he was deprived of his living as a
    royalist – and again from the Restoration until his death. *Hesperides* (1648)
    contains most of his verse, but his religious poems (*Noble Numbers*) were
    published separately in 1647. He is particularly famous as a classicist and
    especially as following in English the Latin erotic elegists Catullus and
    Propertius.

>*Complete Poetry*, edited by J. Patrick (New York, 1963).

See: K. McEuan, *Classical Influence on the Tribe of Ben* (Cedar Rapids,
         1939). (Thorough on the classical borrowings.)
       F. Moorman, *Robert Herrick* (1910). (Enthusiastic and erratic.)
       S. Musgrove, *The Universe of Robert Herrick* (Auckland, 1950).
         (Informative on the intellectual background.)

JONSON, Ben (1572–1637). Ben Jonson was born in Westminster and educated
    at Westminster School under William Camden. He claimed Scottish
    descent. Jonson seems to have worked for some time as a bricklayer (his
    stepfather's occupation) and to have served in the army fighting in the
    Netherlands, as well as acting and doing hack-work on play scripts for
    Henslowe, before *Every Man in His Humour* (1598) established him as a
    dramatist of individuality. Jonson led a turbulent life, killing an actor in a
    duel, getting into trouble for his writings, being marginally involved in the
    Gunpowder Plot (having become a Roman Catholic for a while), and
    being, it seems, a consistently heavy drinker. He dominated the London
    literary scene for a long while, as dramatist, poet, masque writer, and
    character – as, in fact, one of the greatest men of letters in our culture.
    Jonson's reputation has had its ups and downs, but recent years have seen
    renewed interest in his poetry and rather more productions of his plays.

Every Man in His Humour (1598), *Every Man out of His Humour* (1599), *Sejanus* (1603), 'Masque of Blackness' (1605), *Volpone* (1606), *Epicoene* (1609), *The Alchemist* (1610), *Bartholomew Fair* (1614), *The Devil is an Ass* (1616), *Works* (folio, 1616, includes *Epigrams, The Forest*), *The Staple of News* (1626), *Works* (2-vol folio, 1640, includes *Underwoods*).

> *Works*, edited by C. Herford, P. and E. Simpson, 11 vols (Oxford, 1925–51).
> *Poems*, edited by I. Donaldson (Oxford, 1975).
> *Poems*, edited by G. Parfitt (Harmondsworth, 1975).

See: R. Dutton, *Ben Jonson: to the First Folio* (Cambridge, 1983). (A good chapter on the poems.)
J. Gardiner, *Craftsmanship in Context* (The Hague, 1975). (Solid, detailed account of the poems.)
R. Peterson, *Imitation and Praise in the Poems of Ben Jonson* (New Haven, 1981). (Not an easy book, but a very stimulating one.)
W. Trimpi, *Ben Jonson's Poems* (California, 1962). (Good on aspects of context.)

KING, Henry (1591–1669). The son of John King (Vice-Chancellor of Oxford and Bishop of London), Henry King was educated at Westminster School and Oxford (BA, 1611). King took Anglican orders and became Bishop of Chichester in 1641. During the latter part of the Civil War and until the Restoration he lived in uncomfortable retirement, but returned to Chichester at the Restoration. Of his poems (1657) one, 'The Exequy', is justly very famous.

> *Poems*, edited by M. Crum (Oxford, 1965).

See: H. Berman, *Henry King and the Seventeenth Century* (1964). (An informative and solid account.)

LOVELACE, Richard (1618–? 1658). Probably born at Woolwich, the son of a Kentish knight, Lovelace was educated at Charterhouse and Oxford. He was a resolute royalist who went on the 1639 Scottish expedition, was twice imprisoned (1642, 1648) for his loyalty, and spent his fortune backing Charles I. Lovelace is, rather misleadingly, thought of as an epitome of 'Cavalier' and he wrote a tragedy and a comedy as well as his poems. *Lucasta: Epode* (1649), *Lucasta: Posthume Poems* (1659).

> *Poems*, edited by C. Wilkinson (Oxford, 1925)
> in *Minor Poets of the Seventeenth Century*, edited by R. Howarth (1931, 1953).

See: C. Hartmann, *The Cavalier Spirit and its Influence on the Life and Work of Richard Lovelace* (1925).
E. Miner, *The Cavalier Mode from Jonson to Cotton* (New Jersey, 1971). (A sound introduction.)

MARVELL, Andrew (1621–1678) was born in south Yorkshire and educated in Hull and at Cambridge. Marvell travelled on the Continent between 1642 and 1646, then acted as tutor to Lord Fairfax's daughter and to Cromwell's ward, William Dutton, before becoming Milton's assistant as Latin secretary in 1657. He accompanied Lord Carlisle's embassy to Muscovy, Sweden, and Denmark (1663–65) and was MP for Hull from 1659. A consistent supporter of Parliament, his moderate line and independence of mind have led to his being sometimes seen as crypto-royalist. Best remembered as a writer of lyrics, he also produced verse satire (in the latter part of his life) and controversial prose (*Rehearsal Transpros'd* 1672–73). His verse has been highly regarded this century and much written about.

> *Poems and Letters*, edited by H. Margoliouth (Oxford, 1927).
> *Poems*, edited by E. Donno (Harmondsworth, 1972).

See: W. Chernaik, *The Poet's Time* (Cambridge, 1983). (A good, lively book.)

R. Colie, '*My Ecchoing Song*' (New Jersey, 1970). (One of the better critical accounts.)

P. Legouis, *Andrew Marvell: Poet, Puritan, Patriot* (Oxford, 1865). (Dated but sound and informative.)

J. Leishman, *The Art of Marvell's Poetry* (1966). (Rather better on tradition than art.)

A. Patterson, *Marvell and the Civic Crown* (New Jersey, 1978). (Contains useful, stimulating information.)

J. Wallace, *Destiny His Choice* (1968). (Mainly about the political poems, but very good on these.)

MILTON, John (1608–1674). Milton was born in Cheapside, the son of a London scrivener who was also a composer. He was educated at St Paul's School and Cambridge. After Cambridge he spent six years in private study at Horton, *Comus* (1634) and 'Lycidas' (1637) being products of this period. Milton was in Italy between 1638 and 1639, where he was favourably received because of the reputation of his Latin poems. A firm supporter of Parliament and a prolific pamphleteer for the Good Old Cause (writing on such topics as episcopacy, censorship, divorce, and monarchy) he allowed his literary life to be dominated by the Cause and controversy for some twenty years. Milton became Latin Secretary in 1649, was blind from 1652, and married three times. From 1660 he again devoted himself to poetry, this being the period of *Paradise Lost, Paradise Regained,* and *Samson Agonistes* (although some have argued an earlier date for this last work). Milton's great reputation and influence have survived Samuel Johnson's reservations and the later attacks of T. S. Eliot (who recanted) and F. R. Leavis (who did not). *Comus* (1634), 'Lycidas' (1637), 'The Reason of Church Government' (1641/42), 'Of Education', 'Areopagitica', 'Tetrachordon' (1643/45), 'Eikonoklastes' (1649), 'The Ready and Easy Way ...' (1660), *Paradise Lost* (1667), *Paradise Regained*, (1671) *Samson Agonistes* (1671).

> *Poetical Works*, edited by D. Bush (1966).
> *Paradise Lost*, edited by A. Fowler (1968).

See: from the great mass of writing about Milton: D. Burden, *The Logical Epic* (1967). (*Paradise Lost*.)

G. Crump (ed.), *Twentieth Century. Interpretations of Samson Agonistes* (New Jersey, 1968.)

D. Daiches, *Milton* (1957). (A good introduction.)

W. Empson, *Milton's God* (1961). (A famous, provocative account of *Paradise Lost*.)

S. Fish, *Surprised by Sin* (California, 1971). (Much to argue with, but properly challenging.)

C. Hill, *Milton and the English Revolution* (1977). (Brilliantly places Milton in his socio-political context.)

W. Kirkconnell, *That Invincible Samson* (Toronto, 1964). (Sensible reading of *Samson Agonistes*.)

B. Lewalski, *Milton's Brief Epic* (1966). (A good book on *Paradise Regained*.)

A. Low, *The Blaze of Noon* (New York, 1974). (Intelligent account of *Samson Agonistes*.)

W. Parker, *Milton: A Life*, 2 vols (Oxford, 1968). (Exhaustive standard biography.)

C. Patrides (ed.), *Approaches to Paradise Lost* (1968).

S. Revald, *The War in Heaven* (Ithaca, 1980). (Has a lot of interesting information.)

J. Thorpe, *Milton Criticism* (1951). (Selections from four centuries.)

A. Waldock, *Paradise Lost and its Critics* (1947). (A very sensible account of the reputation and its implications.)

B. Weber, *Wedges and Wings* (Carbondale 1975). (On *Paradise Regained*.)

D. Wolfe, *Milton in the Puritan Revolution* (1941). (Partly supplanted by Hill, but still useful.)

OLDHAM, John (1653–1683) was born near Tetbury and educated at Oxford. Oldham was a strong Protestant and came from a firmly Protestant family, but he seems to have been lively at Oxford and was acquainted with Rochester. In his short life he held several teaching posts, initially at Croydon. Remembered mainly as a satirist.

> *Poems*, edited by B. Dobrée (1960).
> *Selected Poems*, edited by K. Robinson (Newcastle upon Tyne, 1980).

See: P. Hammond, *John Oldham and the Renewal of Classical Culture* (Cambridge, 1983).

QUARLES, Francis (1592–1644). Quarles was born near Romford and educated at Cambridge and Lincoln's Inn. He was variously cupbearer to Princess Elizabeth (1613), secretary to Archbishop Ussher (*c.* 1629), chronologer to the City of London (1639). A moderate royalist, he fathered eighteen children and was also prolific in verse (mainly religious) and prose. He is chiefly remembered for *Emblems* (1635).

> *Works*, edited by A. Grosart, 3 vols (reprinted New York, 1978).

See: K. Høltgen, *Francis Quarles* (Tubingen, 1978). (In German – a thorough and sympathetic account.)

RANDOLPH, Thomas (1605–1635) was born near Daventry and educated at Westminster School and Cambridge. Little is known of his short life, but he was a high liver and a friend of Ben Jonson. As well as poems he wrote six plays and is buried near Oundle.

> *The Poems and Amyntas*, edited by J. Parry (New Haven, 1917).

ROCHESTER, John Wilmot, Earl of (1647–1680). Rochester was born at Ditchley in Oxfordshire and educated at Burford and Oxford. He travelled in France and Italy, but lived his brief life mainly as a court wit and rake, although a more thoughtful, disturbed and self-conscious man than these terms might suggest. Stories of Rochester's wit and outrageous behaviour are legion, and some seem to be true. He seems to have died penitent. The Rochester legends and his reputation (justified) for obscenity have tended to distract attention from the quality of his best verse.

> *Complete Poems*, edited by D. Vieth (New Haven, 1968).
> *Poems*, edited by V. Pinto (1953).
> *Letters*, edited by J. Treglown (Oxford, 1980). (With a good account of the life.)

See: D. Farley Hills, *The Benevolence of Laughter* (1974).
D. Farley Hills (ed.) *The Critical Heritage* (1972). (An interesting collection of responses.)
G. Greene, *Lord Rochester's Monkey* (1974). (An intelligent popular biography.)
D. Griffin, *Satires against Man* (Berkeley, 1973). (A useful assessment.)
V. Pinto, *Rochester* (1935). (Enthusiastic if inaccurate.)
J. Wilson, *The Court Wits of the Restoration* (1967).

SEDLEY, Charles (1639–1701) was probably born in London. Sedley was a courtier, wit, rake, poet, and dramatist. An associate of Rochester his name is synonymous with Restoration debauchery. Also as with Rochester, the legends have tended to deflect attention from the quality of the verse.

> *The Poetical and Dramatic Works*, edited by V. Pinto, 2 vols (1928).

See: D. Farley Hills, *The Benevolence of Laughter* (1974).
V. Pinto, *Sir Charles Sedley* (1927). (Enthusiastic but inaccurate.)

SUCKLING, John (1608–1641). Suckling was born at Twickenham and educated at Cambridge and Gray's Inn (1627). He may have been on the 1627 expedition to the Isle of Rhé and he served in the Netherlands as well as being part of an embassy to Gustavus Adolphus in 1631. Suckling was an inveterate gambler and in financial difficulties throughout his life. He took part in both Bishops' Wars (1639, 1640 and was briefly MP for Bramber (1640). His play *Aglaura* was produced at Blackfriars in 1637. He fled to France in 1641, having been involved in a plot to help Charles I, and was found guilty of treason *in absentia*. Suckling seems to have killed himself, probably with poison, in Paris in 1641.

> *The Works . . . Non-Dramatic*, edited by T. Clayton (Oxford, 1971). in *Minor Poets of the Seventeenth Century*, edited by R. Howarth (1931, 1953).

See: E. Miner, *The Cavalier Mode from Jonson to Cotton* (New Jersey, 1971).

VAUGHAN, Henry (1622–1695) was born in Breconshire and was the brother of Thomas Vaughan, the hermetic writer. Henry Vaughan was educated at Oxford and practised medicine and litigation for most of his adult life in the Brecon area. He wrote prose meditations and did translations, as well as writing the religious poems for which he is remembered (*Olor Iscanus*, 1651; *Silex Scintillans*, 1650, 1655).

Works, edited by L. Martin (Oxford, 1914).
in *Silver Poets of the Seventeenth Century*, edited by G. Parfitt (1974).

See: R. Garner, *Henry Vaughan* (Chicago, 1959). (A solid account.)
F. Hutchinson, *Henry Vaughan* (Oxford, 1947). (Full, standard
biography.)
L. Martz, *The Poetry of Meditation* (New Haven, 1954.)
E. Miner, *The Metaphysical Mode from Donne to Cowley* (New Jersey,
1969). (A decent introduction.)
E. Pettet, *Of Paradise and Light* (Cambridge, 1960.) (Perhaps the best
of the critical books on Vaughan.)

WALLER, Edmund (1606–1687). Born near Amersham and educated at Eton
and Cambridge. Waller was MP for various constituencies from around
1621. In 1643 he was involved in a plot against Parliament ('Waller's Plot')
and was arrested, expelled from the House, fined, and banished. Waller
lived abroad, mainly in France, until his banishment was revoked in 1651.
His courtship of Lady Dorothy Sidney in the late 1630s is reflected in his
'Sacharissa' lyrics, but there has been disagreement as to how serious the
courtship was. Waller had a very high contemporary reputation which has
gradually declined.

Poems, edited by G. Thorn Drury, 2 vols (no date).
Selection in *Silver Poets of the Seventeenth Century*, edited by G.
Parfitt (1974).

See: A. Alison, *Towards an Augustan Poetic* (Kentucky, 1962).
(Stimulating treatment.)
W. Chernaik, *The Poetry of Limitation* (New Haven, 1968). (An
intelligent case for Waller.)

WITHER, George (1588–1667) was born at Bentworth in Hampshire and
educated at Oxford and Lincoln's Inn. Wither was imprisoned in 1613 for
his satiric *Abuses Stript and Whipt*. A Puritan, he was made Master of the
Statute Office by Cromwell but was imprisoned again in 1661. The prolific
nature of Wither's output in verse and prose has obscured his real, if
minor, talent.

Poems, edited by H. Morley´ (1891).
Poetry of George Wither, edited by F. Sidgwick, 2 vols (1902).

Index